PEN

A SHORT RESIDENCE IN SWEDEN,

and

..RS OF THE AUTHOR OF THE RIGHTS OF
WOMAN

Wollstonecraft (1759–97) was an educationalist and feminist writer.
. founded a school at Newington Green with her great friend Fanny
Blood, travelled to Portugal, and worked as a governess in Ireland for Lord
Kingsborough. In 1788 she settled in London as a literary journalist and
translator for the publisher Joseph Johnson, becoming part of the radical
set that included Paine, Blake, Godwin and the painter Fuseli. Her great
work, *A Vindication of the Rights of Woman*, was published in 1792. She lived
in Paris during the French Revolution, and had a child by the American
Gilbert Imlay. In 1795 she travelled through Scandinavia, and later tried to
commit suicide. She conceived a second daughter, the future Mary Shelley,
by William Godwin, whom she married in 1797. Mary Wollstonecraft died
in childbirth at Somers Town, London, aged thirty-eight.

William Godwin (1756–1836) was a philosopher and novelist. Born in East
Anglia, he was educated at Hoxton Academy for the Presbyterian ministry.
He became an atheist and leading radical writer, well-known in the circle
including Priestley, Paine, Thelwall and Fuseli. He defended his friend
Thomas Holcroft during the Treason Trials of 1794. His major work of
rational anarchism, *An Enquiry Concerning Political Justice* (1793), was
followed by the novels *Caleb Williams* (1794), *Fleetwood* (1805), and
Mandeville (1817), and various discursive writings including a life of
Chaucer. He married Mary Wollstonecraft in 1797 and subsequently Mrs
Mary Jane Clairmont, with whom he ran a children's publishing business.
His philosophy influenced the young Romantic writers, especially his son-
in-law, the poet Shelley.

Richard Holmes was born in 1945 and educated at Downside School and
Churchill College, Cambridge. In 1974 he published his first book, *Shelley:
the Pursuit* which won the Somerset Maugham Award. He lived in Paris for
two years, translated Théophile Gautier's supernatural stories, *My Fantoms*,
and scripted a radio-drama about Gérard de Nerval. He has edited an
anthology of Shelley's prose and written a study of *Coleridge* for the Oxford
Pastmasters. His autobiography of a Romantic biographer, *Footsteps*, is
published in Penguin. He is a Fellow of the Royal Society of Literature.

MARY WOLLSTONECRAFT

A Short Residence in Sweden, Norway and Denmark

AND

WILLIAM GODWIN

Memoirs of the Author of The Rights of Woman

*Edited with an Introduction and Notes
by Richard Holmes*

PENGUIN BOOKS

Penguin Books Ltd, Harmondsworth, Middlesex, England
Viking Penguin Inc., 40 West 23rd Street, New York, New York 10010, U.S.A.
Penguin Books Australia Ltd, Ringwood, Victoria, Australia
Penguin Books Canada Limited, 2801 John Street, Markham, Ontario, Canada L3R 1B4
Penguin Books (N.Z.) Ltd, 182–190 Wairau Road, Auckland 10, New Zealand

A Short Residence in Sweden, Norway and Denmark first published 1796
Memoirs of the Author of The Rights of Woman first published 1798
This combined edition first published 1987

Introduction and Notes copyright © Richard Holmes, 1987
All rights reserved

Made and printed in Great Britain by
Richard Clay Ltd, Bungay, Suffolk
Filmset in Monophoto 10/12 Ehrhardt

FOR TESSA

Contents

Introduction

1

This book brings together two forgotten classics of English eighteenth-century non-fiction. They are also human documents of the most moving kind, whose appeal will last as long as men and women struggle to live happily – or shall I say, to live less unhappily – together.

The first is a travel book, which tells of a solitary journey, undertaken in mysterious circumstances, through Scandinavia. The second is a life-history of the extraordinary woman who made that journey (and many others), as seen by the man who subsequently became her lover, and then her husband. They were written within a few months of each other, in the closing years of the 1790s, that great decade of revolution in human affairs throughout Europe, when the possibilities of happiness and justice seemed for a moment infinitely extendible; and then in another moment, infinitely remote.

Both works are short, factual, readable and, in different ways, intensely passionate. Both are oddly untypical of their authors, or at least of the stereotypes by which they are known to history: the Feminist and the Philosopher. Yet, as literature, these are arguably the best books that either wrote. In re-publishing them together, as I have long wished, I hope to do their authors honour and to give the causes they believed in and fought for, a more complex and vivid life in the mind of the modern readers they have always deserved.

Mary Wollstonecraft and William Godwin first met at a publisher's dinner-party in London on 13 November 1791. It was given in honour of Tom Paine, the best-selling author of *The Rights of Man*, to celebrate his imminent departure for Paris. He was going to take up his seat as the delegate for the Pas de Calais in the French Revolutionary Convention. Their host was Joseph Johnson, the leading radical publisher of the day (his list would include Paine, Priestley, Coleridge, Wordsworth and Blake). The atmosphere was heady with the talk of rights, revolution and reform, and the Golden Age of Liberty which had dawned across the Channel.

Wollstonecraft and Godwin were the junior members of the party. She was thirty-two and he was thirty-five, and neither had yet published the works that were to make them famous: *The Rights of Woman* (1792) and *Political Justice* (1793). Both were known as reviewers and essayists for Johnson's magazine, the *Analytical Review* (a sort of *New Statesman* of its time), and had reputations for advanced political views within the small circle of North London radicalism. But neither were national figures like Paine, and by normal standards of behaviour they should have taken a back seat in the evening's proceedings, listening politely as the master expounded the cause of Liberty.

However, normal behaviour – by eighteenth-century standards – was never to be their *forte*. Instead, they promptly dominated the dinner-table with a series of noisy and increasingly angry arguments, which seem to have ended by practically reducing Paine and Johnson to silence. Whatever else it suggests (and to my mind it suggests a great deal), this incident shows that nothing so ordinary as love at first sight could ever be expected of these two remarkable authors.

Godwin presents this memorable evening with almost disconcerting candour seven years later in Chapter 6 of the *Memoirs*. He makes no sentimental attempt to disguise the clash of characters that occurred. He lists the subjects discussed, the grounds of disagreement, and his own growing irritation: 'as the conversation proceeded, I became dissatisfied with the tone of my share in it. We touched upon all topics, without treating forcibly and connectedly upon any . . .' He notes ironically that he heard Mary 'very frequently when I wished to hear Paine'; and that Paine himself was reduced to throwing in 'occasionally some shrewd and striking remarks'.

He indicates clearly their sharp differences in temperament: Wollstonecraft forceful, 'gloomy' and polemic; himself restrained, dogmatic, but too inclined to lavish indiscriminate praise. In fact he draws from this single incident a most convincing picture of their two contrasted personalities, their unusual combination of fire and ice. Godwin concludes with grave, yet faintly mocking, impartiality: 'The interview was not fortunate. Mary and myself parted, mutually displeased with each other ... We met two or three times in the course of the following year, but made a very small degree of progress towards a cordial relationship.' The whole scene serves to suggest the lack of conventionality, and the passion for sincere feeling, which was to be the hallmark of their lives. They were both clever, difficult, highly original people, and this is partly what gives their writings such lasting fascination and intellectual bite.

They were not to meet again for another four years, until the spring of 1796. A great deal had happened to them, and to the world, in the intervening period. They had matured, but they had also seen their political hopes darken.

After the publication of her great work on women's rights and education, Mary Wollstonecraft had herself gone to Paris for over two years, and witnessed the trial and execution of the French king and the coming of the Terror. She had seen many of her close friends among the Girondists, including Manon Roland, guillotined; and Tom Paine imprisoned under sentence of death and reduced to alcoholism. She had had a love-affair with an American adventurer, Gilbert Imlay, conceived and borne his illegitimate child, and returned to London only to find their relationship slowly and agonizingly collapse, amidst her recriminations and his betrayal of her with another woman. She had subsequently travelled in Scandinavia, twice tried to commit suicide, and somehow managed to write the account of her experiences that is here reprinted. She had become famous and, as is the way of the world, she had suffered deeply for it. Everything she believed in, and above all her vision of woman's independence and equality, had been tested to breaking point.

William Godwin's career had run a smoother but no less demanding course. *Political Justice*, his millennial work attacking oppressive government and advocating an anarchist society based on absolute reason and sincerity, had brought him to what Hazlitt later called 'the very zenith of a sultry and unwholesome popularity'. His novel *Caleb Williams* (1794), dramatizing the same issues in the form of a political thriller, had broadened his reputation. But his brave intervention before the Treason Trials of the same year, in favour of his friends, the defendants Thomas Holcroft and Horne Tooke, had made him a marked man for the gathering forces of political reaction.

He lived an isolated, scholarly bachelor's life in Somers Town, North London, varied only by dining out and theatre-going. While he flirted ineffectually with the blue-stocking ladies of his narrow circle (Mary Hays, Mrs Inchbald, Amelia Alderson), his fame only brought him increasing loneliness and anxiety, and a strange lack of emotional commitment. He took pupils, kept a meticulous diary, and sometimes wore racy yellow waistcoats. But he felt himself to be an unlovable man: childless, stiff in company, and strangely dependent on his old mother, who still lived far away in Norwich. It was only when Mary Wollstonecraft returned to England and published *A Short Residence* in January 1796 that a new light seems slowly to have risen over his cool, rational, philosophical horizon.

Godwin vividly describes his reaction to the work in Chapter 8 of the *Memoirs*, making perhaps the best of all introductions to it.

> The narrative of [her] voyage is before the world, and perhaps a book of travels that so irresistably seizes on the heart, never, in any other instance, found its way from the press. The occasional harshness and ruggedness of character that diversify her *Vindication of the Rights of Woman*, here totally disappear. If ever there was a book calculated to make a man in love with its author, this appears to me to be the book. She speaks of her sorrows, in a way that fills us with melancholy, and dissolves us in tenderness, at the same time that she displays a genius which commands all our admiration.

It was, characteristically, Mary Wollstonecraft who now took the decisive step to renew their acquaintance, by calling uninvited and unchaperoned (another breach of eighteenth-century proprieties) at Godwin's house in Chalton Street, near the present site of St Pancras railway station and the New British Library, on 14 April 1796.

Godwin found himself gazing on a mature woman of thirty-six, her face fuller and softer than he had remembered, but with the same large brown eyes and striking mass of auburn hair worn short, unpowdered, and falling carelessly over her left brow. Wollstonecraft found a stocky, energetic, balding man whose eyes sparkled behind round gold spectacles, and whose manner had grown patient, humorous and surprisingly tender. They now instantly accepted each other as fellow authors and intellectual colleagues. A lively and familiar correspondence sprang up between them during the early summer. Godwin was sensitive to her sufferings and violent swings of mood; while Mary Wollstonecraft instinctively understood his fear of emotions that might get out of hand and compromise him. They complemented each other, and they reassured each other, until they found, quite simply, that they were well matched.

In Chapter 9 of the *Memoirs* Goodwin tenderly describes the growth of their intimacy, though scorning any idea of a conventional courtship. 'It grew with equal advances in the mind of each . . . One sex did not take the priority which long-established custom has awarded it, nor the other overstep that delicacy which is so severely imposed.' Instead, in a passage of remarkable sensuousness, he tells how they secretly became lovers.

> It was friendship melting into love. Previously to our mutual declaration, each felt half-assured, yet each felt a certain trembling anxiety to have assurance complete . . . Mary rested her head upon the shoulder of her lover, hoping to find a heart with which she might safely treasure her world of affection – fearing to commit a mistake, yet, in spite of her melancholy experience, fraught with that generous confidence, which, in a great soul, is never extinguished. I had never loved till now; or, at least, had never nourished a passion to the same growth, or met with an object so consummately worthy. We did not marry.

It is a most striking paragraph for the chilly philosopher of absolute reason to have written. In fact it indicates a revolution far deeper than politics; and in the end, far more influential.

Godwin's diary shows that they were lovers by August 1796. But both held strong views on practical independence, and Mary Wollstonecraft took a separate flat for herself and her child (little Fanny Imlay, now two years old) at 16 Judd Place, near West Chalton Street, so that both could continue their literary work. They met in the evenings, and Fanny would anxiously ask after 'Man', as she called Godwin, who quickly became fond of her. In the winter Mary Wollstonecraft became pregnant, and after much discussion, the two anti-matrimonialists were finally married at Old St Pancras Church on 29

March 1797. They moved into 29 The Polygon, Chalton Street, but continued to work and often dine out independently, determined to avoid what they saw as the evils of 'cohabitation'. The open marriage caused gossip among their radical circle, much of it malicious, and several friends hypocritically refused to recognize the couple socially, as Godwin painfully recalls in the *Memoirs*. *The Times* noted jocosely in its Court and Social column that 'Mr Godwin, author of a pamphlet against matrimony' had clandestinely wedded 'the famous Mrs Wollstonecraft, who wrote in support of the Rights of Woman'. But the letters that continued to flit between the two addresses show how happy and supportive of each other they were.

The dénouement was tragically brief. Their love-child, the future Mary Shelley, was born five months later on 30 August. Mary Wollstonecraft contracted septicaemia after the delivery, and eleven days later, after much suffering, she died, on 10 September 1797. William Godwin, the unemotional philosopher, quietly wrote, 'It is impossible to represent in words the total revolution this event made in my existence. It was as if in a single moment "sun and moon were in the flat sea sunk".' Struggling to control his grief, he moved his study into Mary Wollstonecraft's own room at the Polygon, and immersed himself in her papers, and began to re-read all her books.

In October he began to write like a man possessed, and ten weeks later the entire *Memoirs* was drafted. He consulted with his old friend Joseph Johnson, and the work was finally published – together with a small four-volume edition of *The Posthumous Works* – in January 1798. It was the same year that marked the appearance of the *Lyrical Ballads*.

2

If the history of human affections can be said to have its landmarks, like those of politics or literature, the death of Mary Wollstonecraft is surely one of the most significant. Her brief life – she was only thirty-eight when she died – was regarded as a portent by her contemporaries, the moment they looked back on it. Nor was this only among radicals, or those sympathetic to feminism.

Mary Hay's obituary notice in the *Monthly Magazine*, praising her 'ardent, ingenuous, and unconquerable spirit', and seeing her as a victim to the 'vices and prejudices of mankind' (by which she meant 'unkind men') is representative of one body of opinion. But just as significant was the anonymous assessment published in the October 1797 issue of the *Gentleman's Magazine*, a periodical with solid, right-of-centre views, a strong patriotic tendency and a wide circulation. Here she is described as

> a woman of uncommon talents and considerable knowledge, and well-known throughout Europe by her literary works, under her original name of Wollstonecraft, and particularly by her *Vindication of the Rights of Woman* ... Her manners were gentle, easy, and elegant; her conversation intelligent and amusing, without the least trait of literary pride, or the apparent consciousness of powers above the level of her sex; and for the soundness of her understanding, and sensibility of heart, she was, perhaps, never equalled ... This tribute we readily pay to her character, however adverse we may be to the system she supported in politics and morals, both by her writings and practice.

Furthermore the liaison between Wollstonecraft and Godwin was understood as something symbolic. To the forces of reaction, as represented by the *Anti-Jacobin Magazine*, and now strongly in the ascendant, it was of course an unholy alliance – atheism, anarchism, feminism, French Revolutionary politics and free love, all brought together in one unseemly bed, and now swiftly and properly punished by Divine Providence. But to the small group of beleaguered radicals, to the larger body of liberal opinion, and to many of the younger writers of the day, it was a kind of culmination: a consecration of that New Sensibility in which the rational hopes of the Enlightenment were catalysed by that element of imagination and personal rebellion which we now know as Romanticism.

Godwin and Wollstonecraft were seen to bring together, through their books, their complementary views, their experiment in living, two most powerful strands in the tradition of progressive reform. They were seen as transitional figures, pointing towards a freer life and a more just society, and the new 'empire of feeling'. Coleridge, with his genius for identifying the abstract principle embodied in human affairs, put his finger on this in one of his brilliant, conversational asides recorded by the young William Hazlitt as they walked together in the West Country in 1797. 'He asked me,' recalls Hazlitt, 'if I had ever seen Mary Wollstonecraft, and I said I had once for a few moments, and that she seemed to me to turn off Godwin's objections to something she advanced with quite a playful, easy air. He replied, that "this was only one instance of the ascendancy which people of imagination exercised over those of mere intellect".'* Coleridge would alter his views on Godwin's 'mere' intellect; but the point was well made. Here was a significant new marriage between Imagination and Reason.

Both Wollstonecraft's *A Short Residence* and Godwin's *Memoirs* are, in my view, crucial documents of this historic moment of transition and the Romantic renewal of hope and feeling; and their literary quality has never been properly recognized. They are also records of the intense disruption it caused. They are full of pain, discontent and frustrated happiness. Though adopting different literary forms – the travel book and the biography – they are both essentially confessional. They are most intimately linked by the fact that they both give us portraits of Mary Wollstonecraft, but seen from the two distinct and opposite poles of life-writing: the autobiography and the biography, self-revelation and the objective character-study. These correspond wonderfully to the natural gifts of their authors. Yet both are alike in the urgency of their testament, swiftly composed at times of grief, when many of the barriers of reticence were down.

The result seems to me to be nothing less than a revolution in literary genres. Originally cast within certain well-accepted eighteenth-century conventions – the topographical travelogue and the pious family memoir – they explode these at a number of significant points through sheer intensity of feeling and sincerity of emotion. Wollstonecraft does this through a new wildness and richness of emotional rhetoric; Godwin through a new frankness and understatement. Both – paradoxically – are characteristic of Romanticism.

Readers may like to part company with me at this point and go

---

* William Hazlitt, 'My First Acquaintance with Poets', in *The Liberal*, No. 3, 1823.

directly to the texts to judge for themselves. The sections that follow contain a more detailed literary analysis, which can always be returned to later on. But for the student of literature – and we are all in some sense that – I would first put my claim for these beloved and unjustly neglected works even more precisely. Mary Wollstonecraft's is the most imaginative English travel book since Sterne's *A Sentimental Journey* (1768). Godwin's is the most significant and revolutionary short biography since Johnson's *Life of Richard Savage* (1744). Both mark the shift, as well as anything can, from an eighteenth- to a nineteenth-century world of feeling. Both bring the inner life of a human being significantly closer to our own experience of it.

3

From the first, *A Short Residence* must have seemed a highly unusual book. Not only was its narrator an unaccompanied woman, travelling with her child and a maid, and later entirely on her own. But stranger than this, she was travelling not to Europe, but to Scandinavia – a largely unknown region, almost indeed a boreal wilderness. The poet Robert Southey wrote excitedly to his publisher friend Joseph Cottle: 'Have you met with Mary Wollstonecraft's [travel book]? She has made me in love with a cold climate, and frost and snow, with a northern moonlight.'

Even the most mundane details of Scandinavian life – the feather-filled duvets, the wood-burning stoves, the salty fish and meats of the smorgasbord, the huge pine forests, the steep meadows with their bell-hung cattle, the wild cataracts and the glassy fjords – struck the reader as something 'rich and strange'. The novelty of this in cultural terms cannot be overestimated. Hitherto the English literary traveller (for the great part male, well-heeled and accompanied by guides, valets or tutors) had adhered to a well-defined circuit through Europe and the Levant that over three centuries had become known as the Grand Tour. 'The grand object of travel,' pronounced Dr Johnson, 'is to visit the shores of the Mediterranean' – though he himself got no further than Paris.

Sterne, Smollett, Gray, Walpole had all limited their itineraries to

France and Italy, or those parts of Germany and Switzerland reached by the river Rhine. The essential attraction was towards the cities and civilizations of the south. To go north and east – beyond say the international port of Hamburg and the old walled and turreted medieval city of Lübeck, was to journey beyond the pale of Western culture. The shores of the distant Baltic, and the half-legendary lands of the midnight sun beyond, were *terra incognita* for all but a few hardy sailors, merchants, diplomats, and the new race of commercial travellers. The latter were a significant class of whom Wollstonecraft had a great deal to say.

Her own itinerary was therefore remarkable in itself, and should be glanced at on the map. From Gothenburg in Sweden she travelled north across the Norwegian border as far as Halden. She crossed the Skaggerak to the wild, rocky shores beyond Larvik. She remained for several weeks at Tønsberg, and sailed west as far as Risør. Next she returned via Oslo (then Christiania) and travelled south again, crossing the Kattegat into Denmark, where she stayed in Copenhagen. Finally she crossed the straits to Schleswig, and so to Hamburg, where she took a regular ship home to Dover. The whole journey lasted three and a half months, from late June to early October 1795, at a time when the rest of Europe was at war with France, and all travel was generally hazardous.

The little that was then known about Scandinavian society, its arts, languages, social customs, laws and forms of government, is skilfully sketched in by Wollstonecraft during the course of her narrative, and brought alive by her sharp eye for detail and – even more – by her willingness to ask pertinent questions. She is characteristically pleased when her first host in Sweden, a naval district pilot and custom's officer, remarks bluntly at supper 'that I was a woman of observation, for I asked him *men's questions*'.

We learn from her of the political domination of Denmark over its neighbour Norway, and to a lesser extent Sweden; and the commanding influence of the great Danish statesman Count A. P. Bernstorff, who had put the whole of Scandinavia on a footing of 'armed neutrality' towards the conflicting powers in Europe. The dramatic assassination of the Swedish King Gustav III in 1792; and the amorous intrigues of Princess Matilda at the Danish court with the royal physician Struensee, both subjects of popular interest in England, also draw Wollstonecraft's attention.

But equally we feel we are entering a beautiful, unexplored world of Nature, which serves above all as a backdrop – sometimes poetically intense – for Wollstonecraft's own reflections and memories. Almost the only previous topographical work on the subject was William Coxe's *Voyages and Travels* (1784), which provided little more than a series of geographical and economic notes. The main link between Britain and Scandinavia remained the trade in raw materials and naval stores – timber, rope and certain minerals. Culturally it was a primitive world, on which the ideas of the Enlightenment, and the possibilities of political liberty touched off by the French Revolution were only just beginning to impinge. The northernmost state, Norway, with which Mary Wollstonecraft fell in love, was free only by the fact of its remoteness from Copenhagen. It had no proper constitution until 1814; no university until that founded at Christiania in 1811; and did not gain full political independence until more than a century later in 1905. It was on the other hand the first state in northern Europe to grant women the vote, in 1907.

The immediate question that arises, therefore, is the motive for Wollstonecraft's travels. What was she doing in Scandinavia at all, and why did she follow the curious, looping itinerary to the tiny ports of western Norway? This mystery is deepened by the sense of weariness and reluctance which strikes the opening chord of the book – not at all the light-hearted eagerness of the conventional, picturesque traveller. The tone grows steadily more thoughtful and melancholy as the journey progresses.

Part of the answer is provided by Godwin's *Memoirs*. The idea for the voyage was Gilbert Imlay's. After Wollstonecraft's return from France in the spring of 1795, and her first attempt at suicide in London, he was anxious to distract her and give her the chance to reflect on their situation. The shipping business he had embarked on when they were together the previous year at Le Havre had run into difficulties, and he suggested that she go as his agent to sort out the problems with his business partner Elias Backman, who was based in Gothenburg. This arrangement explains the immediate form of *A Short Residence*, which is written as a series of twenty-five letters to an unnamed correspondent in London, who, it becomes clear, has been the narrator's lover. The whole book is, in effect, addressed to Gilbert Imlay and makes frequent half-veiled references to their previous life together in France. This provides the essential confessional thread of the work.

It had long been thought that this curious business venture was largely a cynical manoeuvre of Imlay's to put Mary Wollstonecraft at a safe distance from himself. Yet this leaves out of the account several other factors. Having been brought up in various parts of England by her shiftless father, Wollstonecraft in adulthood was naturally restless. She was a born traveller and an instinctive seeker after new horizons and new societies. She could never rest very long in one place; she was always half-consciously looking for an ideal form of existence, a Golden Age.

In the previous ten years she had been not only in France (living in both Paris and Normandy), but also in Ireland and Portugal. This was exceptional, especially for a woman of that time. She had always longed to go to America, and had she lived, I suspect she would have persuaded Godwin to make a new life there. In all this she expresses that yearning spirit of Romanticism, half practical pioneering and half visionary Utopia, which becomes so explicit in the writers who followed her: Southey and Coleridge's dream of Pantisocracy on the banks of the Susquehanna; Lord Byron's excursions into Greece; Shelley's lifelong search for some ideal commune in Switzerland or Italy. These are all direct reflections of the same voyaging, un-appeased spirit.

Wollstonecraft added Norway to the list of enchanted destinations which fascinated the Romantics. Writing to Imlay from Christiania, in a characteristic passage, she conjures up one of those enduring images of the ideal life that is always just out of reach. Here the bitterness of her past experiences trembles in the balance with her unquenched hopes. It is a vivid piece of self-portraiture, the kind of thing with which Godwin (rather than Imlay) fell in love; and it is difficult to believe that it was written by a woman for whom travel was not a deep reflex, a profound need of intellect and heart.

She describes how autumn has come to Christiania, and the gath-ering clouds urge her to depart southwards. Yet despite the 'calls of business and affection', she feels a strange urge to press onwards into yet remoter regions. She continues:

> You will ask perhaps, why I wished to go further northward. Why? not only because the country, from all I can gather, is most romantic, abounding in forests and lakes, and the air pure, but I have heard much of the intelligence of the inhabitants, substantial farmers, who have none of that cunning to contaminate their simplicity, which displeased me so much in the conduct of the people on the sea coast ... The description I received of them carried me back to the fables of the golden age: independence and virtue; affluence without vice; cultivation of mind, without depravity of heart; with 'ever smiling liberty', the nymph of the mountain. – I want faith! My imagination hurries me forward to seek an asylum in such a retreat from all the disappointments I am threatened with; but reason drags me back, whispering that the world is still the world, and man the same compound of weakness and folly, who must occasionally excite love and disgust, admiration and contempt. (Letter 14)

This was not written by a woman who could be sent away on a fool's errand. It was written by one of nature's pilgrims, who would always seek, hoping against hope to find. If she quotes from the old Republican poet Milton, the spirit in which she admonishes and then encourages herself is not far from Bunyan.

4

Yet there is other evidence, of a different kind, that her journey was also a genuine business matter, and that Imlay had expressed remarkable confidence in her talents by putting it into her hands. Wollstonecraft was indeed a serious commercial traveller. Modern research has slowly revealed that she was responsible for the legal recovery of a very large sum of money: in fact nothing less than a treasure ship. As this extraordinary story is never revealed in her book, despite her long polemic passages on the commercial spirit and the destructive effect of the mercantile outlook (passages all aimed directly at Imlay), it is worth investigating it in some detail. It gives us a striking new perspective on Mary Wollstonecraft's exceptional abilities, and goes a long way to explaining both the itinerary she travelled and the daring nature of what she undertook.

Wollstonecraft's first modern editor, William Clark Durant, discovered in the Abinger Papers a remarkable legal document drawn up by Imlay, in which she is appointed his legal representative and given power of attorney throughout Scandinavia. It states:

> Know all men by these presents, that I, Gilbert Imlay, citizen of the United States of America, at present residing in London, do appoint Mary Imlay, my best friend and wife, to take the sole management of my affairs and business which I had placed in the hands of Mr Elias Backman, negotiant, Gottenburg, or those of Messers Myburg and Co. Copenhagen . . . For which this letter shall be a sufficient power, enabling her to receive all the money that may be recovered from Peter Ellyson, whatever the issue of the trial now carrying on, instituted by Mr Elias Backman, as my agent, for the violation of trust which I had reposed in his integrity . . .*

The exact implications of this document have for long remained obscure. Backman – a shrewd commercial fixer who subsequently became the first American Consul in Sweden – was known as Imlay's agent in a semi-legal trading business, shipping much-needed raw materials from Gothenburg to Le Havre, and running the British blockade round the neutral Baltic ports into wartime France. This was a business undertaken by British and American sympathizers with France, and connived at by firms like Myburg, but which was strictly speaking a 'traiterous correspondence' with the enemy. Nevertheless excise records show that similar businesses – in gold coin, tobacco, and spirits – were illegally maintained throughout the war from almost all the ports of southern England. Operations through Hamburg, Copenhagen, Gothenburg or Arendal were considerably more respectable, though not necessarily safer.

But the identity of 'Peter Ellyson', the reason for his 'trial', and the exact nature of his 'violation of trust' have not been known to modern

---

* William Clark Durant, ed., *Memoirs of Mary Wollstonecraft*, 1927, p. 295. Lord Abinger's great collection of manuscripts relating to the Godwin-Shelley circle is now housed in the Bodleian Library, Oxford.

biographers. They have therefore tended to discount Imlay's document, and to give little credence to its concluding statement. 'Thus, confiding in the talent, zeal, and earnestness of my dearly beloved friend and companion, I submit the management of these affairs entirely and implicitly to her discretion.'

Yet zeal and discretion were most certainly demanded of Mary Wollstonecraft. To what degree has been revealed, only recently, by a modern governor of Gothenburg, Mr Per Nyström. In the late 1970s Nyström began to interest himself in the early shipping records of his city. The result of his researches appeared in a little pamphlet published by the Royal Society of Arts and Sciences of Gothenburg in 1980.* What he shows is that Mary Wollstonecraft was in pursuit of a stolen treasure ship, packed with silver and Bourbon plate. The ship had been spirited away by its Norwegian captain from Imlay's trading company, which owned the vessel and its cargo. It represented the greater part of Imlay's assets. In fact, Wollstonecraft was on a treasure-hunt in Scandinavia.

The extraordinary story, as unfolded by Nyström, is briefly this. In June 1794, registration documents show that Gilbert Imlay purchased a cargo ship called *La Liberté* from a group of French merchants at the Normandy port of Le Havre. Imlay had already had some success with his blockade-running business, probably with cargoes shipped from Hamburg on Danish ships, and he now decided to set up on his own account as a clandestine importer of alum and naval construction materials from the Baltic. He was in an optimistic mood and full of schemes. He had recently rented a house for Mary Wollstonecraft in Le Havre, and the month before their daughter Fanny had been safely born. He felt expansive.

The ship was ideal for the task – fast, slim and highly manoeuvrable – and only required false papers to disguise her mission. To this purpose, he re-named her *Maria and Margaretha* (perhaps there was a private joke here, using the Italian version of his wife's name, Mary, and her maid's, Marguerite). He then hired a twenty-five-year-old Norwegian sailor to be her captain. The sailor's name was Peder Ellefsen, the son of a well-known merchant family from

* Per Nyström, *Mary Wollstonecraft's Scandinavian Journey*, RSAS Gothenburg, *Humaniora* No. 17, 1980 (see Bibliography).

Risør, the small port between Larvik and Arendal on the Skagerrak.

Imlay was now able to apply through Ellefsen to the Danish Consul in Le Havre (who dealt with all Scandinavian shipping), and re-register the ship as a neutral vessel. According to these new papers the *Maria and Margaretha* was a Norwegian cargo ship, based in Kristiansand, owned by Ellefsen himself, and carrying ballast back to Copenhagen. The flag of convenience was complete. Imlay now secretly loaded up his ship with its real cargo, intended as the convertible currency with which he would purchase the stores at Gothenburg, under Elias Backman's supervision. Nyström is able to show what this cargo was, from subsequent documents connected with the 'trial' of Peder Ellefsen. It consisted of thirty-two bars of silver, and thirty-six pieces of plate, some of it rumoured to carry the royal Bourbon coat of arms. The total value was £3,500; an enormous sum, equivalent to perhaps half a million pounds in modern currency.

How Imlay ever obtained such valuables remains a mystery. Perhaps it was through his connections in Paris, perhaps it was confiscated or even stolen aristocratic property, perhaps it was through some Franco-American syndicate involving his old friend Thomas Christie. At all events it was a capital investment far beyond his private means, and to lose it would have meant ruin. There can be no doubt that Mary Wollstonecraft, at the time she was acting as his agent in 1795, must have been fully briefed on all these details.

The ensuring events can be traced. The ship was dispatched under Ellefsen's command in August 1794 to run the British blockade through the North Sea. Norwegian shipping records show that she reached the shores of the Skagerrak safely on 20 August, and put in at one of the small ports near Arendal. But she never reached her destination port of Gothenburg, down the coast in Sweden. In reply to his urgent requests for information, Backman was first told that the treasure ship had sunk. But further inquiries during the autumn confirmed that Peder Ellefsen was in fact safely back in his home port of Risør. There were independent reports that the treasure had been taken off in a small boat by the captain, and that the first mate (who was English) had been given the ship as the price of his silence. Whatever the exact details, by the winter of

1794–5 when he had returned to London, Gilbert Imlay was aware that his venture had disastrously miscarried. The *Maria and Margaretha* had disappeared, the silver and plate had been misappropriated, and Peder Ellefsen had 'violated his trust'. It was, one may think, a case of poacher poached.

Legally speaking, of course, the situation was extremely delicate. It throws new light on all those mysterious business worries for which Wollstonecraft was continually reproaching Imlay, and which cast their shadow over *A Short Residence* in the tirades against the profit motive, and the obsession with trade, in Letters 23 and 24, from Hamburg. French law had no jurisdiction in the case; British law would have regarded both parties as criminal. Imlay's only recourse was to the Danish courts, and he instructed Backman to apply to Copenhagen, in an attempt to bring some kind of pressure to bear on the merchant community in Norway. To his great surprise, and perhaps through the influence of American traders with A. P. Bernstorff, the motions at least of legal redress were forthcoming.

Nyström's evidence is less clear-cut from this point onwards, but it appears that a preliminary Board of Inquiry was appointed, according to the Danish protocol in dealing with Norwegian matters. This consisted of three local judges or commissioners drawn from leading members of the Norwegian business community. The great significance of Nyström's researches on this point is his identification of the Scandinavian towns in which they lived. Christoffer Nordberg and A. J. Unger came from Strömstad, north of Gothenburg, on the Swedish-Norwegian border. Jacob Wulfsberg came from Tønsberg, on the southern Norwegian coast. If we add to these Peder Ellefsen's home port of Risør, we have at last the complete outline of Mary Wollstonecraft's Scandinavian itinerary in the summer of 1795.

It is now clear that, after an indecisive preliminary investigation by the Board of Inquiry in the spring of that year, Imlay had confided to 'his best friend and wife' the task of trying to reach some legal settlement through personal intervention. She was to discover the fate of the treasure ship, the attitude of all parties concerned, and to reach if possible some financial agreement, probably on an 'out of court' basis. It was by any standards an onerous undertaking, involving a foreign legal system, a series of delicate interviews, a six-hundred-mile round trip from Gothenburg and the prospect of an extremely difficult meeting with Peder Ellefsen himself on his home ground at Risør. Only someone as daring and determined as Mary Wollstonecraft would have attempted it.

5

For the literary purposes of *A Short Residence*, no explicit reference is made to this saga of the treasure ship. But Nyström's discoveries allow us to plot the stages of Wollstonecraft's northern journey with new understanding. They also help us to appreciate better than before the extraordinary skill with which she transformed a prosaic business venture into a poetic revelation of her character and philosophy.

The range of Wollstonecraft's practical interests is both delightful and formidable. She has strong views on everything from gardening to prison reform. She may spend her time visiting a salt works, discussing farmers' land rights, going sea-bathing, studying divorce laws, chatting to domestic servants, or simply climbing a cliff at sunset to blow a hunting horn and listen to its echoes swelling and fading among the distant, shadowy promontories. All these things tell us as much about her as about Scandinavia, and the reader will find I have fully explored them in my editorial notes at the back of the book.

But Wollstonecraft also uses certain intense, often solitary, moments of her travels almost like Wordsworthian 'spots of time' to establish the confessional themes, the hopes and fears, that give the book its inward and Romantic quality. Often these are achieved by the way in which, with perfect naturalness, she places herself within a landscape, or minutely observes it.

In Letters 5 and 6 she describes how she sets out alone in a small open boat to cross the Christiania sound for Larvik. She adopts the dauntless tone that vividly caught the imagination of her readers.

> The wind had changed in the night, and my boat was ready. A
> dish of coffee, and fresh linen, recruited my spirits; and I directly

set out again for Norway; proposing to land much higher up the coast. Wrapping my great coat around me, I lay down on some sails at the bottom of the boat, its motion rocking me to rest, till a discourteous wave interrupted my slumbers, and obliged me to rise and feel a solitariness which was not so soothing as that of the past night ... The sea was boisterous; but, as I had an experienced pilot, I did not apprehend any danger. Sometimes, I was told, boats are driven far out and lost. However, I seldom calculate chances so nicely – sufficient for the day is the obvious evil! We had to steer amongst islands and huge rocks, rarely losing sight of the shore, though it now and then appeared only a mist that bordered the water's edge. (Letters 5 and 6)

In this description of the solitary voyager, sailing through dangerous waters towards an unknown, misty shoreline, Mary Wollstonecraft's whole life seems for a moment to be symbolized. But more than that, something of the Romantic predicament itself is prophesied. How many other boats would be driven 'far out and lost'!

At the old merchant town of Tønsberg her business with Judge Wulfsberg detained her for three weeks. She settled into an inn overlooking the sea, walked daily over the rocks, rowed in the bay, and began to write her travel book (Letters 6 to 9). For the first time she sounds cheerful – 'I have recovered my activity, even whilst attaining a little *embonpoint*' – and her quick eye and inquiring spirit rove with marvellous freedom through these chapters. She notices everything: the sea captains who sing Republican songs but still venerate the Danish prince; the women who dress so charmingly but are ill-paid as domestic servants; the criminal who was branded on his third conviction, but who praised Judge Wulfsberg for providing him with financial relief afterwards (she sends him some money herself). But the most revealing of all is the way she shifts with startling ease from an abstract, sententious, philosophic reflection in the eighteenth-century manner, to a minute and poetically detailed observation of nature. It reminds us of nothing so much as the *Notebooks* of Coleridge or the *Journals* of Dorothy Wordsworth.

While drifting out on the bay in her rowing-boat, she suddenly reflects on her intense sensation of inner, unquenchable life. 'It appears to me impossible that I should cease to exist, or that this active, restless spirit, equally alive to joy and sorrow, should be only organized dust – ready to fly abroad the moment the spring snaps, or the spark goes out, which kept it together. Surely something resides in this heart that is not perishable – and life is more than a dream.'

Then immediately, in the next paragraph, she leans upon her oar and looks down into the water, and sees that external life again, but now in the humble yet surprisingly beautiful shapes of the jellyfish.

> They look like thickened water, with a white edge; and four purple circles, of different forms, were in the middle, over an incredible number of fibres, or white lines. Touching them, the cloudy substance would turn or close, first on one side, then on the other, very gracefully; but when I took one of them up in the ladle with which I heaved the water out of the boat, it appeared only a colourless jelly. (Letter 8)

It is in the close combination of these two kinds of observation that her Romantic genius is so well displayed.

At Peder Ellefsen's home port of Risør, hidden away among wild rocky headlands some 150 miles out from Christiania, she is overcome by fears. They are vividly expressed in her description of the claustrophobic, primitive and backward place, where a 'contraband trade makes the basis of their profit'. They seem too, to have revived memories of the old regime in France, and the terrors of imprisonment, the deepest nightmare, perhaps, of her spirit.

> We were a considerable time entering amongst the islands, before we saw about two hundred houses crowded together, under a very high rock – still higher appearing above. Talk not of bastilles! To be born here, was to be bastilled by nature – shut out from all that opens the understanding, or enlarges the heart. Huddled one behind another, not more than a quarter of the dwellings even had a prospect of the sea . . . The ocean, and these tremendous bulwarks, enclosed me on every side. I felt the confinement, and wished for wings to reach still loftier cliffs . . . I felt my breath oppressed, though nothing could be clearer than the atmosphere. (Letter 11)

Of the business finally transacted here, she says little, except that she was 'prevailed upon to dine with the English vice-consul'. One is amazed to learn such a person existed in such a place. For the rest she notes only her utter relief on departing after several days – 'it seemed to me a sort of emancipation'.

Returning to Christiania (Letters 13 and 14) she was notably well entertained by the family of Bernhard Anker, an anglophile and one of the leading merchants in Norway. Anker was a Fellow of the Royal Society, and besides owning the best private library in Norway and a fine collection of scientific instruments, he was also proprietor of a hundred of the 136 licensed saw mills in the district. No doubt she was still trying to get support and advice over the Ellefsen affair. But she also had time to tour the city (quarrelling with William Coxe's description in his *Voyages and Travels*), and to be taken out to the younger Anker's country estate, with its famous English-style gardens.

Here occurs one of those touching details which suddenly bring a sort of intimacy to our knowledge of the past. Four years later, in the summer of 1799, another young English traveller, Edward Daniel Clarke, also came to the Anker's country estate. Wandering out of the house, he came upon an unexpected sight, which he must be allowed to tell in his own words. 'In the gardens we were shown an old Norwegian dwelling, preserved as a specimen of what the Norwegian houses were two centuries before, with all its furniture and other appurtenances, as it then stood. Upon the walls of this building we observed the names of many travellers who had visited the spot, and, among others, that of the late Mrs Godwin, thus inscribed, with a pencil, near the door – "Mary Wollstonecraft".'*

It is difficult to say which is the more memorable aspect of this sudden, homely detail: that she wrote her name like any other English traveller (though modestly, in pencil, 'near the door'). Or that she signed herself not 'Imlay', but her real name, her writing name, 'Wollstonecraft'. It must have been worth the glimpse of a dozen 'Byrons' scrawled over the monuments of Europe.

Almost her last sight in Norway was the dramatic cascades near Frederikstad, which she approached through a devastated pine forest leading down to a dark, narrow valley booming with the sound of roaring water. This place seems to have hypnotized her, with its white crashing waters bursting out against the black rocks and

* Edward Daniel Clarke, *Travels in Various Countries*, 1824. Vol. 10, p. 389.

overhanging trees, an elemental force both thrilling and disturbing.
'My soul was hurried by the falls into a new train of reflections'
(Letter 15). The ideas of death – suicide perhaps – but also rebirth
and immortality, filled her mind. It is a passage that I think may
particularly have struck Coleridge when he read it the following year
at Nether Stowey, and we shall return to it.

But her observations on the pinewoods themselves, those living
symbols of wild nature throughout Scandinavia, have remarkable
particularity and philosophic power. Beginning with almost botanical
precision, and curiously foreshadowing the Darwinian notion of
the 'struggle for existence', they move characteristically towards a
poetic vision of death as a kind of regeneration of the spirit, of
'something getting free'. The organic society of the woods, Wollstonecraft seems to suggest, reflects the evolutionary possibilities of
the human spirit. This was to become a major theme, a commanding
vision, for later Romantic poets; and one can glimpse, perhaps, the
shadowy outline of some future ode by Shelley.

> . . . the spiral tops of the pines are loaded with ripening seed, and
> the sun gives a glow to their light green tinge, which is changing
> into purple, one tree more or less advanced, contrasting with an-
> other. The profusion with which nature has decked them, with
> pendant honours, prevents all surprise at seeing, in every crevice,
> some sapling struggling for existence. Vast masses of stone are thus
> encircled; and roots, torn up by the storms, become a shelter for a
> young generation . . . The grey cobweb-like appearance of the aged
> pines is a much finer image of decay; the fibres whitening as they
> lose their moisture, imprisoned life seems to be stealing away. I
> cannot tell why – but death, under every form, appears to me like
> something getting free – to expand in I know not what element;
> nay I feel that this conscious being must be as unfettered, have the
> wings of thought, before it can be happy. (Letter 15)

At Copenhagen she seems to have obtained an audience with Count
Bernstorff himself on the Ellefsen affair. But she describes the city
at length – it had recently been gutted by fire – with detailed reflections on the Danish government (Letters 18 to 21). The story of
Princess Mathilda and Struensee obviously touched her deeply – she
suggests their error was in attempting to push through liberal reforms

too quickly. She criticizes many aspects of Danish life, from the heavy drinking to the public execution of criminals. She looks 'in vain for the sprightly gait of the Norwegians' and their sense of liberty – and was repelled both by the 'promiscuous amours of the men of the middling class with their female servants' and the 'gross debaucheries' of the lower orders. 'Love here seems to corrupt the morals, without polishing the manners, by banishing confidence and truth, the charm as well as the cement of domestic life.' She particularly criticizes the 'cunning and wantonness' of the Danish women, and the illiberal and tyrannical behaviour of Danish husbands (Letter 19).

This letter is her most explicitly feminist chapter, and in a revealing aside she quickly meets the sarcastic objections that she feels sure Imlay, and perhaps other readers, will raise. 'Still harping on the same subject, you will exclaim – How can I avoid it, when most of the struggles of an eventful life have been occasioned by the oppressed state of my sex: we reason deeply, when we forcibly feel.' It is a remark that rings out with heartfelt conviction, and makes any idea that Mary Wollstonecraft had trimmed her views in later life not only absurd, but impertinent.

Yet the more tender side of her beliefs is also evident in the pleasure with which she describes the sexual freedom of the young people in Scandinavia (a subject to become notorious in Victorian England), and the 'kind of interregnum between the reign of the father and the husband' which the young women enjoyed in courtship.

> Young people, who are attached to each other, with the consent of their friends, exchange rings, and are permitted to enjoy a degree of liberty together, which I have never noticed in any other country. The days of courtship are therefore prolonged, till it be perfectly convenient to marry: the intimacy often becomes very tender: and if the lover obtain the privilege of a husband, it can only be termed half by stealth, because the family is wilfully blind. It happens very rarely that these honorary engagements are dissolved or disregarded . . . (Letter 19).

This liberal praise of premarital sexual understanding is typical of Wollstonecraft's lack of hypocrisy in such matters, and her fearlessness in saying exactly what she means. It is a fearlessness matched by Godwin, when he makes it clear in the *Memoirs* that it was just such a relationship that he and Mary shared in 1796.

Much at Copenhagen reminds her of her previous sojourn in France, of the fate of the émigrés, and the pretensions of rulers. At the Rosenburg Palace she reflects on the 'cabinets full of baubles and gems and swords' which once symbolized royal power in Denmark. 'It is a pity,' she remarks mischievously, 'they do not lend them to the actors, instead of allowing them to perish ingloriously.' Yet with a very modern reflex, she also sees the historical interest of the building. 'Every object carried me back to past times, and impressed the manners of the age forcibly on my mind. In this point of view the preservation of old palaces, and their tarnished furniture, is useful; for they may be considered as historical documents.' She does not seem entirely immune, either, to the wayward charm of the 'large silver lions' mounted at the entrance to the banqueting-rooms.

Several times she remarks that had she travelled in such primitive, or at least under-developed, societies before going to France, she would have taken a very different view of the French, and especially of the 'common people' and their behaviour during the Revolution. The concept of the 'Noble Savage' seems more than ever meaningless to her. What was achieved in France depended very greatly on the degree of sophistication which society in general had already reached. The 'virtues of a nation', she is more than ever convinced, 'bear an exact proportion to their scientific improvements'.

This reflection leads her to a view of travel which strikingly rejects the old eighteenth-century idea of the Grand Tour as an extension of classical education and the reverential study of the masterpieces of antiquity. Travel should be, she argues, a kind of sociological inquiry, which brings us a much more critical and comparative idea of how societies develop and progress. We should be interested in the primitive for the light it throws on the 'more polished'. We should be more forward looking, and more conscious of social evolution. We should travel more intelligently and more self-critically. 'If travelling, as the completion of a liberal education, were to be adopted on rational grounds, the northern states ought to be visited before the more polished parts of Europe, to serve as the elements even of the knowledge of manners, only to be acquired by tracing the various shades in different countries.' This attitude foreshadows much of the more strictly anthropological travelling of the nineteenth century, with its emphasis on comparative studies of particular societies and climates (Letter 19).

But this tone of philosophic detachment is hardly sustained through the final stages of the journey, which caused Wollstonecraft's increasing frustration and exhaustion. The maid Marguerite, with her amusing Parisian chatter about German fashions and 'the arch, agreeable vanity peculiar to the French' with which she retold her adventures at Gothenburg, had 'a *gaité du coeur* worth all my philosophy', thought Wollstonecraft with a sigh. Her own ennui and depression returned with her approach to Hamburg. She could no longer avoid the realization that Gilbert Imlay had no change of heart about meeting her, despite all her efforts in the Ellefsen affair. Her open appeals to Imlay dominate the last letters of the book, describing her arrival in the German city and her restless stay in the nearby suburb of Altona, determined to 'sail with the first fair wind for England'. She speaks of the 'cruelest of disappointments, last spring' – a barely veiled reference to her return to London from Paris, and the first suicide attempt – and describes herself as 'playing the child' and weeping at the recollection (Letter 22).

Her tirades against the commercial spirit here reach their climax. She sees Hamburg as – 'an ill, close-built, swarming' city, and as a symbol of everything that has corrupted Imlay and come between them. She bitterly attacks the profit motive, and 'the mushroom fortunes' that have started up during the war. She excoriates a race of traders and dealers who are insolent, vulgar and 'seem of the species of the fungus' themselves. These are among her most savage passages. She describes these 'sordid accumulators of *cent per cent*' as the most degraded form of masculine ambition, brutishly opposed to everything that is finest and most progressive in the spirit of the age. They 'term all virtue of an heroic cast, romantic attempts at something above our nature; and anxiety about the welfare of others, a search after misery, in which we have no concern' (Letter 23).

Mary Wollstonecraft is caught here in a terrible paradox, of course. For her own journey in search of the treasure ship had been undertaken partly for commercial reasons and to help Imlay in the recovery of a 'mushroom fortune' of war. Not only must she have felt betrayed by Imlay, but to some extent self-betrayed. It is this surely, that gives such despair to her final accusation, a passage which threatens to overturn the entire form of *A Short Residence*, transforming the voice of the literary traveller into that of the abandoned lover. Many previous passages in the book press towards this final act of self-exposure, giving what I have called the confessional tension to the entire work. But here it is most explicit, and most moving:

> You will say that I am growing bitter, perhaps, personal. Ah! shall I whisper to you – that you – yourself, are strangely altered, since you have entered deeply into commerce – more than you are aware of – never allowing yourself to reflect, and keeping your mind, or rather passions, in a continual state of agitation. – Nature has given you talents, which lie dormant, or are wasted in ignoble pursuits – You will rouse yourself, and shake off the vile dust that obscures you, or my understanding, as well as my heart, deceives me, egregiously – only tell me, when? (Letter 23).

The distance between this, and the most passionate of the private letters, is less than 'the thickness of a piece of paper'.

The strangely desultory and gloomy note on which the book ends – passing in a single anxious paragraph from Hamburg to Dover – makes the reader more than ever curious to know what was the practical outcome of Mary Wollstonecraft's journey. What was the upshot of the Ellefsen affair? The way the book breaks off, suggests that negotiations were broken off too. We know tantalizingly little. Nyström was never able to establish if the crucial interview with Peder Ellefsen in Risør actually took place; or if the sympathetic Judge Wulfsberg of Tønsberg was able to arrange an out-of-court settlement. It appears that the inquiry dragged on for many months afterwards. Yet there is one piece of evidence which might suggest that Wollstonecraft's efforts were by no means in vain. For the treasure ship itself was mysteriously recovered that autumn.

Swedish shipping records show that on 6 October 1795 a light cargo boat called the *Maria and Margaretha* was re-registered at Gothenburg as the property of Imlay's partner, Elias Backman. Its tonnage was slightly increased from that registered at Le Havre, which might perhaps mean that she had been refitted and re-rigged. It is not impossible that this could have been done at Ellefsen's expense, and thus represented some form of settlement and *quid pro quo*. The proximity of the re-registration date to that of Wollstone-craft's departure from Hamburg on the 27 September 1795 suggests that the two events were at least connected. The record is of course inconclusive, and the affair ends as mysteriously as it began. No authority knows what happened to the Bourbon plate. Yet the possi-bility that Mary Wollstonecraft had pulled off a most delicate piece of business negotiation, in a twilight world of wartime illegality, remains provokingly open. It seems quite within the scope of her extraordinary talents. One would certainly like to believe it.

The affair of the treasure ship is also important for the peculiar tension and atmosphere it lends her book. Though never once referred to explicitly in the text, it exerts its unseen pressure on the narrative of *A Short Residence*. It gives Wollstonecraft's travels their secret urgency, their sense of a mysterious, almost nightmare pursuit. It adds immeasurably to the feeling of inexplicable anxiety, of gloomy foreboding, which so marks Wollstonecraft's reflections on men and affairs and drives her continually to seek Romantic solace in the wilderness of the Scandinavian landscape, hoping to escape into a sublime vision of grand, impartial Nature: its magnificent forests, waterfalls, and seashores, so remote from the petty concerns of man.

It also, if I am not mistaken, subtly alters our perception of Gilbert Imlay, her unnamed correspondent. Mary Wollstonecraft's un-requited love for him, increasingly desperate and bitter, already casts him in the role of Romantic villain, withholding his affections and cruel in his absence. (How just or unjust this picture was, in bio-graphical terms, is a subject more fully explored in Godwin's *Mem-oirs*.) But the additional knowledge of his business interest in Wollstonecraft's expedition, adds – however unfairly – to our sense that he is exploiting her. In the context of the book, he becomes an almost demonic figure, driving her on to the limits of her physical, emotional and intellectual resources. I have already suggested that, in real life, I do not think this entirely reflected Imlay's attitude to his 'best friend and wife'. But in purely literary terms, the portrait she draws of him (always anonymously) is both haunting and convincing.

It is a brilliant piece of emotional projection. Imlay is slowly transformed into her demon-lover, and his shadow comes to brood over the Scandinavian countryside like something out of the Icelandic sagas or the enchanted folk music of Edvard Grieg. He tempts her over dizzy gulfs or the edge of precipitous waterfalls; he tortures her with the delusive promises of love and treasure and happiness. I do not wish to over-emphasize this aspect; it is nothing more than a mist that occasionally thickens round the largely factual and inquiring style of the narrative. But I think it is there; and that the later Romantic poets – especially Coleridge and Shelley – deeply and instinctively responded to it in their own work.

6

Letters Written during a Short Residence in Sweden, Norway, and Denmark was published by Joseph Johnson in January 1796. It was the most popular book Wollstonecraft ever wrote, and she must have been delighted with its reception. After the miseries and desperation of the previous year, the suicide attempts and the end of her relationship with Imlay, it represented a personal triumph over her circumstances. The professional writer had regained her self-respect, and also found a new readership. The reviews were widespread and favourable. The book was swiftly translated into German, Dutch, Swedish, and Portuguese. An American edition appeared in Wilmington, Delaware, through the good offices of her friend, the Irish revolutionary, Archibald Hamilton Rowan. A second edition was published by Johnson in 1802. The younger generation of writers were fascinated with it, and admiring references appear in the journals, poems, or correspondence of Coleridge, Southey, Wordsworth and Hazlitt. Though only one further nineteenth-century edition was published (by Cassell's Library, 1886), its underground reputation remained secure. Shelley and Mary took a copy with them when they eloped to France in 1814; and I have recently discovered that Robert Louis Stevenson had a copy of the first edition when he went to Samoa in 1890, which still exists in a private collection, sporting his Vailima bookplate.

The book was particularly admired in Godwin's circle, among those who knew the full circumstances surrounding its writing. Anna Seward and Mary Hays praised it, and the young Amelia Alderson, then an unknown and aspiring writer, wrote a fan letter which expressed the feelings of many of her younger contemporaries. 'I remember the time when my desire of seeing you was repressed by fear – but as soon as I read your letters from Norway, the cold awe which the philosopher has excited, was lost in the tender sympathy called forth by the woman. I saw nothing but the interesting creature of feeling and imagination.'

Some indeed felt that the feminist philosopher had sacrificed too much to 'feeling and imagination', and indulged rather shockingly in the modish melancholy and emotional self-revelations of the New Sensibility. (Though Godwin was to turn this point to her literary advantage, by describing her in the *Memoirs* as a sort of 'female Werther'.) The acid and amusing French traveller-writer, Bernard de la Tocnaye, made several criticisms of her observations in his *Promenade en Suède*, and added that she had caused great offence to the ladies of Gothenburg. But his greatest mockery was reserved for her highly emotional style in the description of landscape (failing to note that this is usually balanced by her minute and accurate observations of natural phenomena). He summarizes in the following passage, which I have translated from his sprightly and sarcastic French:

> In her book [Mary Wollstonecraft] often makes use of that special new vocabulary which is deemed *sentimental*, the grotesque linguistic garb adapted from Lawrence Sterne, and the new-fangled 'moonlight and apparitions' style of writing. So we meet with nothing but cowbells a-tinkling on the hillsides – the waves murmuring their melodies – the spirits of peace wandering o'er the hills – eternity in every moment – the sylphs dancing in the air – the dews gently falling – the crescent moon in the ethereal vault – and everything inviting her to turn aside her steps and wander afar, etc., etc., etc. In short, it's all modish nonsense.*

Well, there are no sylphs in Mary Wollstonecraft (though there are nymphs and one satyr). But it is true that her book was consciously literary in many aspects. This is partly what so excited her

* Bernard de la Tocnaye, *Une Promenade en Suède*, 1801, vol. 1, pp. 25–9.

readers. She understood a great deal about the traditional genre of travel-writing, and had perceptively reviewed and criticized the shortcomings of earlier works for Johnson's *Analytical*. These included the picturesque outpourings of Gilpin's *Tours*; Jean-Pierre Brissot's dry, topographical account of North America; and J. G. Forster's wild visions of the stars and icebergs of the southern seas (which fascinated Coleridge). Her private letters also show how fond she was of Sterne's *Sentimental Journey* and Rousseau's *Promenades*, and the image of her as a 'solitary walker' became a kind of private joke between her and Godwin. Throughout the text of *A Short Residence* she quotes freely from a small group of favourite eighteenth-century authors of an introspective kind – especially Thomas Gray, William Cowper and Edward Young of the *Night Thoughts*. She shows a marked tendency to identify with Shakespeare's Hamlet – that Danish Prince of melancholy. Many of her more empurpled landscape descriptions are direct extensions of Edmund Burke's doctrine of the sublime in nature, which so influenced the Romantic poets, reaching towards the fusion of the human spirit with some half-perceived and animating world-soul.

From the cliffs above Tønsberg she wrote:

> The fishermen were calmly casting their nets; whilst the seagulls hovered over the unruffled deep. Everything seemed to harmonize into tranquillity – even the mournful call of the bittern was in cadence with the tinkling bells on the necks of the cows, that, pacing slowly one after the other, along an inviting path in the vale below, were repairing to the cottages to be milked. With what ineffable pleasure have I not gazed – and gazed again, losing my breath through my eyes – my very soul diffused itself in the scene – and, seeming to become all senses, glided in the scarcely-agitated waves, melted in the freshening breeze . . . imperceptibly recalling the reveries of childhood, I bowed before the awful throne of my Creator. (Letter 8)

One may have sympathy with de la Tocnaye's impatient 'etc., etc., etc.', reading such passages as these. Yet if we compare them with the kind of verse landscape description soon to be written by Wordsworth and, especially, Coleridge, one can appreciate the kind of impact they had. A masterly poem like 'This Lime Tree Bower My Prison', composed by Coleridge at Stowey in 1797, seems to show an almost direct influence in places:

> ... *So my friend*
> *Struck with deep joy may stand, as I have stood,*
> *Silent with swimming sense; yea, gazing round*
> *On the wide landscape, gaze till all doth seem*
> *Less gross than bodily; and of such hues*
> *As veil the Almighty Spirit, when yet he makes*
> *Spirits perceive his presence.*

The emotional drama of the book – the solitary, outcast woman dreaming of her faithless lover – also had its literary effect. There is some evidence to suggest that Wordsworth's narrative poem 'Ruth', written in Germany in 1799, drew on the story of Imlay and Wollstonecraft, as well as on his own abandonment of Annette Vallon. Ruth's lover is a 'youth from Georgia's shore', who eventually deserts her to return to his old, wild life 'with roving bands of Indians in the West'. Ruth ends her life as Wollstonecraft might have done, had it not been for Godwin. She lives in solitude, half maddened by her memories, 'An innocent life, yet far astray'.

But the strangest, and most intriguing, of these influences may have been on the composition of Coleridge's mysterious poem 'Kubla Khan' in the autumn of 1797. There is probably no other short poem in the English language which has been credited, not to say over-endowed, with so many possible literary sources – from Plato, Purchas and Milton onwards. To add one more may seem like an unfriendly act. Yet the great bibliographic scholar, John Livingston Lowes, has already remarked on several explicit verbal echoes between the two works in his study, *The Road to Xanadu* (1927). Wollstonecraft's description of the falls and cataracts at Frederikstad in Letter 15, and those at Trollhättan in Letter 17, show close similarities to Coleridge's hypnotic description of the sacred river in Xanadu:

> *And from this chasm, with ceaseless turmoil seething,*
> *As if this earth in fast thick pants were breathing,*
> *A mighty fountain momently was forced:*
> *Amid whose swift half-intermitted burst*
> *Huge fragments vaulted like rebounding hail ...*

Where Wollstonecraft writes of 'the impetuous dashing of the rebounding torrent from the dark cavities' (p. 152), and later of 'the various cataracts, rushing from different falls, struggling with the huge masses of rock, and rebounding from the profound cavities ... [so] that fancy might easily imagine a vast fountain, throwing up its waters from the very centre of the earth' (p. 159), it is hard not to believe that the great echo-chamber of Coleridge's mind did not half-hear those Scandinavian waters amidst so many others.

But there is also a broader, emotional resemblance between this central part of the poem and Mary Wollstonecraft's particular situation in Scandinavia which has not previously been noticed. The misery she feels in being separated from Imlay presses hard upon the narrative during the return journey from Risør to Gothenburg, and is never far from the surface of her thoughts. In Letter 13, for example, she suddenly breaks off a formal discussion of dishonesty and stealing among the Norwegians, to exclaim passionately, 'These are, perhaps, the vapourings of a heart ill at ease – the effusions of a sensibility wounded almost to madness. But enough of this – we will discuss the subject in another state of existence – where truth and justice will reign. How cruel are the injuries which make us quarrel with human nature! – At present black melancholy hovers round my footsteps; and sorrow sheds a mildew over all the future prospects, which hope no longer gilds.'

This impression of 'a sensibility wounded almost to madness' by Imlay's cruelties, is felt nowhere more strongly than in her meditations on the terrible but beautiful waterfalls at Frederikstad and Trollhättan. Gazing down into the rushing waters, she seems hypnotically drawn in, and her thoughts flit round the dark possibilities of suicide. 'The impetuous dashing of the rebounding torrent from the dark cavities which mocked the exploring eye, produced an equal activity in my mind: my thoughts darted from earth to heaven, and I asked myself why I was chained to life and its misery?' These reflections gain a grim authenticity from her subsequent attempt at watery suicide by throwing herself into the Thames from Putney Bridge in October 1795.

Coleridge was deeply touched by this picture of the solitary woman lamenting her lost lover in such a wild and distant place. It is an image which has something of the archetypal force of the old Border ballads which so fascinated him. (He records in his *Notebooks* that he intended to write to her about the need for 'religion'.) This must surely lead us to speculate whether the 'deep romantic chasm' of Kubla Khan was not imaginatively located, at least in part, in that far north country of Scandinavia; and whether Coleridge did not – at some level of poetic correspondence – have Mary Wollstonecraft in mind when he wrote those inspired and thrilling lines:

> *A savage place! as holy and enchanted*
> *As e'er beneath a waning moon was haunted*
> *By woman wailing for her demon-lover!*

There is of course no certainty in such matters; no certainty above all in a poem which was itself composed in a dream. But the ripples spread out intriguingly into the mainstream of nineteenth-century poetry.

A Short Residence may be said to have entered into the literary mythology of Romanticism within a single generation. Its combination of progressive social views – Wollstonecraft's 'favourite subject of contemplation, the future improvement of the world' – with melancholy self-revelation and heart-searching, came to have an almost symbolic force within that extraordinary circle of poets, travellers, philosophers and autobiographers. Mary Wollstonecraft projected herself through the book as a model of the literary woman: audacious, intelligent, independent and free-thinking; and yet, equally, one who suffers endlessly and inevitably in a society which is not yet honest and just enough to accept her for what she is. The model, and the book, were to be largely forgotten in Victorian England, and to disappear for over a hundred years, except where fleetingly recalled by such rare women traveller-writers as Isabella Bird and Mary Kingsley. But the seed was sown, and like Shelley's 'Ashes and sparks, my words among mankind', they waited to burn up bright again in a different, freer world.

How far, and how strangely, that seed was sometimes scattered may be seen in one last and wholly unexpected literary tribute. In 1816 the Professor of Moral Philosophy at Edinburgh University published a poem entitled *The Wanderer in Norway*. Dr Thomas Brown was not a scholar to whom the principles of feminism would normally have appealed, yet he was captivated by the figure of Mary Wollstonecraft on her travels, and the whole work is inspired by her example. In the Preface to his poem, he movingly describes *A Short Residence*:

> It is a volume which cannot be read without interest – in some degree a picture of the country through which she passed, and of the manners of its inhabitants; – but still more as a picture of her who beheld what she describes, with feelings of which no traveller before her has left a record, and which few, if it is to be trusted, are again to have the sad fortune of recording. Mary was more than a *sentimental* traveller; she was truly an *impassioned* traveller – a traveller suffering deeply, and seeing Nature in those wildly contrasted views, with which Misery looks on it, in the moments of its greatest anguish, and in those strange gleams of hope, which sometimes fling a brightness more than natural on every object, – even when Misery herself is the gazer.*

Here it is clear that Mary Wollstonecraft has already been almost completely transformed into a Romantic heroine, even of the Byronic type. This is fully amplified in the course of Dr Brown's verses, which picture her arriving off the coast of Norway in a midnight storm, standing 'dim on the prow . . . with bosom bare', her 'loose tresses' flying in the wind, and her 'vacant eye' conscious only of the gusts of passion raging within her wounded heart.

> *As though with passion's fiercer swell opprest,*
> *She sought the tempest to her burning breast.*

Brown had responded to her work, like so many others, in terms of its confessional value; but he saw her whole life as a moral *exemplum*, with a purely tragic significance. For him, the great experiment of Romanticism was essentially a noble failure; and Mary Wollstonecraft, with her 'sad fortune', was one of its most tragic victims whose time had not yet come.

How far William Godwin was himself responsible for this view, and how far his biography managed to establish a more realistic and

* Thomas Brown, MD, *The Wanderer in Norway and Other Poems*, 1816, pp. 21–2.

complex interpretation, is the final and deeply interesting question to which I now turn.

7

It is fair to say that most readers were appalled by the *Memoirs of the Author of a Vindication of the Rights of Woman*. There was no precedent for biography of this kind. Godwin's candour and plain-speaking about his own wife filled them with horrid fascination. The *Historical Magazine* called the *Memoirs* 'the most hurtful book' of 1798. Robert Southey accused Godwin of 'a want of all feeling in stripping his dead wife naked'. The *European Magazine* described the work as 'the history of a philosophical wanton', and was sure that it would be read 'with detestation by everyone attached to the interests of religion and morality; and with indignation by any one who might feel any regard for the unhappy woman, whose frailties should have been buried in oblivion'.

For a start, the book belied its title. It was not a pious family memorial, or a work of feminist hagiography. It was a complete biography in miniature, intimate in detail and often critical of Wollstonecraft's behaviour, though always understanding and passionately committed to her genius. It covered every phase of her career: the restless and unhappy childhood, dominated by her father (Chapter 1); the 'fervent' friendship with Fanny Blood, which eventually took her on her first remarkable voyage to Portugal (Chapters 2 and 3); her experiences as a governess, teacher and educational writer, which also took her to Ireland (Chapter 4); her early work as a freelance writer in London, and friendship with Joseph Johnson (Chapter 5); her writing of the *Rights of Woman* and the ill-judged affair with the painter Henry Fuseli (Chapter 6); her expedition to revolutionary France, her falling in love with Gilbert Imlay, and the birth of their child, Fanny (Chapter 7); her journey to Scandinavia and two attempts at suicide (Chapter 8); her liaison and marriage with Godwin himself (Chapter 9); and finally, at great length and in almost gynaecological detail, her death after bearing her second daughter, Mary (Chapter 10).

It was Godwin's frankness over Mary Wollstonecraft's love-affairs and suicide attempts that seemed to cause the most immediate offence. Yet it would be impossible to understand anything of her remarkable temperament, that mixture of extroverted courage and introverted melancholy which made her such an original writer, without the fullest knowledge of these. The *Monthly Review*, previously her supporter, now wrote with hypocritical disapproval in May 1798: 'blushes would suffuse the cheeks of most husbands if they were *forced* to relate those anecdotes of their wives which Mr Godwin voluntarily proclaims to the world. The extreme eccentricity of Mr Godwin's sentiments will account for this conduct. Virtue and vice are weighed by him in a balance of his own. He neither looks to marriage with respect, nor to suicide with horror.'

It was hypocritical, because Godwin in fact takes great care to explain what he and Wollstonecraft sought in a true marriage of real trust; and analyses at length the motives for suicide, and why they are almost invariably mistaken. But his objectivity as a biographer, and his willingness to examine the violence of Wollstonecraft's emotions and her frequent depressions (which had good cause), merely shocked. This itself is an interesting point of literary history. The biographer had not yet gained his independent status; he was seen simply as an unfeeling husband who betrayed family secrets. (How far this has changed may be judged by the reception of a comparable modern work, Nigel Nicolson's *Portrait of a Marriage*, 1973.)

Godwin's frankness and sincerity were of course nothing less than revolutionary at the time. They arise directly from the anarchist principles of sincerity and plain-speaking which he enshrined in *Political Justice*. In literary terms his biography was as courageous an act as his earlier intervention, with a brilliant pamphlet, on behalf of his friend Thomas Holcroft, before the Treason Trials. Both sprang from the same set of convictions, that a writer's duty was to carry honest feeling from private into public life. But even his friends thought he was naïve, and many thought he was completely inhuman. The lawyer William Roscoe, friend of Fuseli and one of Wollstonecraft's greatest admirers and warmest correspondents, wrote the following bitter quatrain in his copy of the *Memoirs*:

Hard was thy fate in all the scenes of life
As daughter, sister, mother, friend and wife;
But harder still, thy fate in death we own,
Thus mourn'd by Godwin with a heart of stone.

Godwin's enemies naturally had a field day. They saw that the revelations of the *Memoirs* could be used to attack, and finally (as they thought) put to flight the whole monstrous regiment of feminists, freethinkers and radical reformers. The *Anti-Jacobin* delivered a general onslaught on the immorality of everything Mary Wollstonecraft was supposed to represent, from independent sexual behaviour and the formal education of young women, to disrespect for parental authority and non-payment of creditors. It implied that the case was even worse than Godwin made out – 'the biographer does not mention many of her amours' – and indexed the book under 'Prostitution: see Mary Wollstonecraft'. It concluded on a note of high sententiousness. 'Intended by [Mr Godwin] for a beacon, it serves for a buoy; if it does not show what it is wise to pursue, it manifests what it is wise to avoid.'

The *Anti-Jacobin* and other magazines kept up these attacks for months, and indeed years, descending to increasing scurrility and causing Godwin endless private anguish. One example, from a poem published in 1801, 'The Vision of Liberty', will suffice:

William hath penn'd a waggon-load of stuff
And Mary's life at last he needs must write,
Thinking her whoredoms were not known enough,
Till fairly printed off in black and white.
With wondrous glee and pride, this simple wight
Her brothel feats of wantonness sets down;
Being her spouse, he tells, with huge delight,
How oft she cuckolded the silly clown,
And lent, O lovely piece!, herself to half the town.

But perhaps the most damaging, and certainly the saddest, reaction came from those women writers who were essentially sympathetic to Wollstonecraft's cause, but who were dismayed to see it personalized in the actual details of her life. The facts of Wollstonecraft's sufferings, and the truths of her difficult personality, frightened them.

They felt Godwin had written too much about her emotional life and too little about her intellectual achievement. They thought that the very form of the biography betrayed the ideology of feminism. It made Mary Wollstonecraft seem too romantic and too dangerous a figure.

Mary Hays, quoted anonymously in the *Analytical*, regretted the intimate details of Wollstonecraft's life and criticized what she saw as Godwin's failure to explain the reasons behind her feminist principles. When, five years later, she compiled her five-volume *Dictionary of Female Biography* (1803), though she gave extensive entries on Manon Roland, Catherine Macauley, and Mary Astell, she completely omitted Wollstonecraft. The same astonishing omission occurs in Matilda Bentham's *Dictionary of Celebrated Women* (1804). Wollstonecraft's young admirer, Amelia Alderson, now married to John Opie, who had painted the celebrated last portrait of Wollstonecraft which always hung in Godwin's study, radically revised her views. Using Wollstonecraft's story, she produced a fictional account of a disastrous saga of unmarried love in *Adeline Mowbray* (1805). (It was this novel that the young Harriet Westbrook sent meaningfully to Shelley before their elopement to Scotland in 1811.) Maria Edgeworth wrote a comic attack on the Wollstonecraft type in the person of Harriet Freke, who appears in *Belinda* (1801). The whole position was soberly summed up by Harriet Martineau, who observed that 'women of the Wollstonecraft order . . . do infinite mischief, and for my part, I do not wish to have any thing to do with them', adding that she was neither 'a safe example, nor a successful champion of Woman and her Rights'.

This hostility to Godwin's revealing portrait still frequently occurs in modern biographers, who draw freely on all its details, but remain uneasy about its placing of feminism within the particular context of Wollstonecraft's personality. The cause, they believe, must always be greater than the woman who champions it. Even Claire Tomalin, Wollstonecraft's best modern defender, tends to take this line.

> In their own way, even the *Memoirs* had diminished and distorted Mary's real importance: by minimizing her claim to be taken seriously for her ideas, and presenting her instead as the female

Werther, a romantic and tragic heroine, [Godwin] may have been giving the truth as he wanted to see it, but he was very far from serving the cause she had believed in. He made no attempt to discuss her intellectual development, and he was unwilling to consider the validity of her feminist ideas in any detail.*

In fact the first six of Godwin's chapters concentrate almost exclusively on Wollstonecraft's intellectual development, through the particular influence of the radical Unitarian Dr Richard Price, through her experience of teaching at Newington Green, through her journeys to Lisbon and Dublin, through her reading of Burke and Rousseau and translating for the *Analytical*, and through the 'vehement concussion' produced by the general ideas of the French Revolution. It is true that he does not analyse her feminism in any detail, but he makes it clear at every point that he regarded the *Rights of Woman* as her major work and the one that she was 'destined' to write. He regards it as her 'most celebrated production' and her outstanding contribution to 'the public welfare and improvement'. He saw it as the focus of her career, and the passion of her life:

> Never did any author enter into a cause, with a more ardent desire to be found ... an effectual champion. She considered herself as standing forth in defence of one half of the human species, labouring under a yoke which, through all the records of time, had degraded them from the station of rational beings ... She regarded her sex, in the language of Calista, as 'in every state of life the slaves of man': the rich as alternately under the despotism of a father, a brother, and a husband; and the middling and poorer classes shut out from the acquisition of bread with independence ...

Though he justly criticizes the literary style and intellectual structure of the *Rights of Woman*, observing that it was written at white heat in 'no more than six weeks', he is more forthright on its historic importance than any other male writer before John Stuart Mill:

> But when we consider the importance of its doctrines, and the eminence of genius it displays, it seems not very improbable that it will be read as long as the English language endures. The publi-

* Claire Tomalin, *The Life and Death of Mary Wollstonecraft*, 1974, p. 238.

cation of this book forms an epocha in the subject to which it belongs; and Mary Wollstonecraft will perhaps here-after be found to have performed more substantial service for the cause of her sex, than all the other writers, male or female, that ever felt themselves animated by the contemplation of their oppressed and injured state. (Chapter 6, second edition wording)

It is difficult to see how Godwin could have nailed her colours (and his) more firmly to the mast.

Nevertheless, the symphony of outrage that the *Memoirs* caused in almost every quarter gave him a profound shock. In no other subsequent work – either philosophical or fictional – did he write again with such daring against the conventions of the age. The veiled and softened portraits that he draws of his wife in the novels *St Leon* (1799) and *Fleetwood* (1805) are milky and sentimental by comparison; though in the Preface to the former he freely acknowledges her influence on his thinking.

After anxious discussions with Joseph Johnson, Godwin decided to issue an amended second edition of the *Memoirs*, which swiftly appeared at the end of 1798. He made many small, discreet changes of phrase, and deleted some personal references (such as that to the powerful Wedgwood family in Chapter 3) which had caused offence. He also sensibly changed phrases that were taken (to his pain and surprise) as sexually ambiguous, such as the 'particular gratification' Wollstonecraft found in her friendship with A. H. Rowan during the dark days in Paris (at the end of Chapter 7). But the second edition is very far from being a biographical retreat or betrayal, as has frequently been suggested. In fact Godwin added many new, crisply analytical paragraphs (all of which can be identified in the present edition), which add to our understanding of Wollstonecraft's character, and show the sensitivity with which Godwin pursued his task and responsibility as a biographer. Indeed some of these additions, such as his reflection on the bitter irony of Wollstonecraft's suicide attempt at Putney Bridge (in Chapter 8) suggest that new levels of feeling and eloquence had been released in him. It remains greatly to his courage as a biographer that, despite all protests, he removed nothing of real significance from Wollstonecraft's story, and made no attempt to modify his account of her social or political beliefs. (The two passages quoted above, for example, appear in both editions.)

Of the three short passages (they total less than four pages) which he substantially rewrote, the first concerns her friendship with Henry Fuseli (in Chapter 6); the second describes his own view of marriage (Chapter 9); and the third consists of a final summary of Wollstonecraft's 'intellectual character' (in Chapter 10). These revisions are either printed in the footnotes, or given in the Appendix after the text, and can be fully assessed by the reader. They are also discussed in my editorial notes. Their basic effect was to replace Godwin's usual bold, clear-cut handling of issues with a more tentative, obfuscating style of explanation. But they are understandable, given the antagonisms he had aroused; and except in one place, they are hardly crucial to his interpretation.

In the Fuseli passage (pp. 234–5), the first edition had allowed the casual or hostile reader to suppose that Wollstonecraft had a sexual relationship with the painter: she 'conceived a personal and ardent affection for him', and she 'made light' of the circumstance that he was already married. This was not only untrue, but it weakened Godwin's marvellously perceptive account, in Chapter 7, of how she later became infatuated with Gilbert Imlay. In the second edition Godwin clarifies the sexual situation, and adds a long explanation of Wollstonecraft's scornful attitude to the social proprieties. But the revision is rambling and retreats to generalities, and one is left with the impression that Godwin himself was slightly at a loss to explain the exact nature of their friendship.

In the matrimonial passage (pp. 258–9), Godwin was largely concerned to palliate his own, evidently naïve early views on the desirability of avoiding wedlock. He also wished to distinguish them from Wollstonecraft's much more searching critique of contemporary marriage as an institute of social oppression. Nevertheless, he also deleted several fine sentences about the early, premarital stage of their love-affair; and it is evident that he had given way to the well-meaning, but cautious advice of his friends. For once he seems to have found a private truth that it was prudent to disguise from the public gaze. Yet the account of their unorthodox love-affair – 'we did not immediately marry' – still stands, daring and provocative.

The third passage that Godwin rewrote occurs at the very end of the *Memoirs* (pp. 272–3). In fact both versions are strangely unsatisfactory, and they for once clearly reflect Godwin's emotional state at the time he wrote. To 'summarize' Mary Wollstonecraft's mind in the way he attempted was a curious reflex of the philosopher, and we shall return to it in a moment.

No changes or explanations, however, could make the biography more popular or more acceptable to contemporary opinion. It remained a work of astonishing outspokenness, revolutionary in its implications. As such, it was inevitably condemned to obscurity. Though translations appeared in Germany (1799) and France (1802), no new English edition was published for over a hundred years. Even in America, beyond two small editions in 1799 and 1804, there was silence. Not until William Clark Durant's scholarly reprint and supplement, a labour of love, appeared in New York in 1927, was there the slightest recognition of what Godwin had achieved.

8

The modern reader is immediately struck by two outstanding qualities of the *Memoirs*: their coolness of tone and their authority of judgement. Though composed at a time of passionate grief, the portrait is lucid and thoughtful at every point. Here is a detached biographer, who has meditated deeply on his subject, and who is quietly intent on showing how such a remarkable character and mind was formed. His view of Wollstonecraft's psychology is complex, without lacking a moral discrimination which is sometimes Johnsonian in its weight. In common with a modern biographer, Godwin sees Mary Wollstonecraft's strengths as inextricably involved with her weaknesses of character, the one growing out of the other, as he makes explicit in a sentence from Chapter 9 of the second edition. 'She had errors; but her errors, which were not those of a sordid mind, were connected and interwoven with qualities most characteristic of her disposition and genius.' The slight shock of surprise with which we register the use of that dispassionate phrase, 'sordid mind', and then its utter rejection, is typical of the effect of Godwin's bold and unflinching style. It keeps us continuously alert and engaged.

Godwin's very modern interest in the psychology of Wollstone-craft's personality is evident throughout. In Chapter 1 he observes the troubled relationship between her parents – the bullying father and over-submissive mother – and finds in it the source of her later outlook on life, divided between disabling depressions and driving idealism.

> She experienced in the first period of her existence, but few of those indulgences and marks of affection, which are principally calculated to sooth the subjection and sorrows of our early years. She was not the favourite either of her father or mother. Her father was a man of a quick, impetuous disposition, subject to alternate fits of kindness and cruelty. In his family he was a despot, and his wife appears to have been the first, and most submissive of his subjects.

From this early experience of sexual warfare, she emerged a natural fighter: 'Mary was what Dr Johnson would have called, "a very good hater"' (Chapter 1).

Godwin sees the formative significance of her intensely emotional friendship with Fanny Blood, and the way the balance of the relationship slowly altered, with Wollstonecraft emerging as the dominant partner. 'Whatever Mary undertook, she perhaps in all instances accomplished; and, to her lofty spirit, scarcely anything she desired, appeared hard to perform. Fanny, on the contrary, was a woman of a timid and irresolute nature, accustomed to yield to difficulties, and probably priding herself in this morbid softness of temper' (Chapter 3).

This tenacity of purpose and 'firmness of mind' emerges as one of Wollstonecraft's greatest virtues as a woman. Godwin identifies it in many telling instances: dealing successfully with the difficult employer Mrs Dawson, in Bath, when she was still only nineteen; persuading the captain of a British ship to change his mind, off Lisbon; disciplining the hitherto ungovernable Kingsborough children in Dublin; exclaiming against the savagery of the guillotinings in Paris so as to endanger her own life; and completing the journey through Scandinavia at a period when she was almost disabled by suicidal thoughts.

At the same time he gives a penetrating and tender account of her emotional vulnerability, most especially in the affairs with Fuseli and Imlay. The masterpiece of his analysis occurs in a long passage in Chapter 7, going right back again to her childhood, and then retracing her emotional development in terms of her relations with her father, with Fanny Blood, with Fuseli, and finally with Imlay himself (pp. 241–2). This is indeed a 'romantic' interpretation – he calls her, in the famous phrase, 'a female Werter' – yet to my mind it carries extraordinary conviction. It ends with a celebration of her full sexual awakening, in beautiful pre-Freudian imagery:

> ... her whole character seemed to change with a change of fortune. Her sorrows, the depression of her spirits, were forgotten, and she assumed all the simplicity and the vivacity of a youthful mind. She was like a serpent upon a rock, that casts its slough, and appears again with the brilliancy, the sleekness, and the elastic activity of its happiest age. She was playful, full of confidence, kindness and sympathy. Her eyes assumed new lustre, and her cheeks new colour and smoothness. Her voice became chearful; her temper overflowing with universal kindness; and that smile of bewitching tenderness from day to day illuminated her countenance, which all who knew her will so well recollect, and which won, both heart and soul, the affection of almost everyone that beheld it. (Chapter 7)

Many things could be said of this passage, not least Godwin's generosity as the biographer-husband in writing it. But it is perhaps enough to note that its snake imagery was taken up almost word for word, in Shelley's triumphant chorus from *Hellas*, which carries forward Mary Wollstonecraft's hopes for happiness in a better world, like a flame passed from hand to hand:

> *The world's great age begins anew,*
> *The golden years return,*
> *The earth does like a snake renew*
> *Her winter weeds outworn . . .*

Godwin's powers of moral analysis as a biographer are matched – particularly in the second half of the *Memoirs* – by a considerable narrative gift. This is in a sense unexpected, until we recall that the philosopher was also a novelist. He recounts with great effect the rapid and fatal development of the love-affair with Imlay in Paris (Chapter 7); the suicide attempt from Putney Bridge (Chapter 8); and above all the agonizingly detailed account of Wollstonecraft's death, which occupies almost an entire chapter (Chapter 10). This last scene is itself a revolution in the biographer's art, depleted of all the traditional religious and literary comforts, but harrowing in its medical details and Godwin's supreme use of understatement to express unspoken emotion. It was perhaps this chapter which most shocked his intimate friends, and the modern reader may still find it strangely disturbing. He was much criticized for making no formal reference to Wollstonecraft's religious feelings at this time (though they are fully discussed in Chapter 3) – 'her religion was almost entirely of her own creating'. Yet Godwin's overwhelming grief – which we know from his later letters – seems to gain tremendous force from his effort to contain it. A single laconic sentence – 'She did not die on Thursday night' – carries a world of pain.

Yet for all this, Godwin does have certain important limitations as a biographer which must be briefly acknowledged. First, he lacked several sources. He had full access to Wollstonecraft's professional papers, and had private information from many of her closest friends: Joseph Johnson, Hugh Skeys, Mary Hays, Mrs Christie, and several others. But Wollstonecraft's family refused to cooperate with him, and her sister Everina Wollstonecraft withheld all correspondence. Equally, Henry Fuseli angrily refused to let Godwin even glance over Wollstonecraft's letters of 1791. Most significant of all, perhaps, Gilbert Imlay's side of the correspondence with Wollstonecraft in Paris, London and Scandinavia was never recovered. This is a lacuna which has probably affected all subsequent accounts of their affair. In general it meant that Godwin was always interpreting these emotional events through Mary Wollstonecraft's own account of them (in her own letters, and in her private talks with Godwin when they first fell in love). If there is any 'romanticizing' its cause lies here – in the kind of literary projection that we see in *A Short Residence* – rather than in Godwin's deliberate attempt to present an acceptable heroine to the age.

In the second place, Godwin's literary style as a biographer lacks a strong visual sense. (This was something first noted by Hazlitt, the painter turned critic, in his fine essay on Godwin in *The Spirit of the Age*.) This means that we are given very little awareness of Mary Wollstonecraft's physical presence, which must have been so striking: how she looked, the famous auburn hair, how she dressed, how she moved and talked in company. But more than that, and so crucial for a traveller like her, we have no impression of all those formative places that she visited – Lisbon, Dublin, Paris, Gothenburg, Christiania, Hamburg. In Godwin's mind, she always moves and lives in something of an abstract void. We cannot even easily imagine her little apartment in Store Street, with the cat; or her parlour in the Polygon with little Fanny. Her own manner in *A Short Residence* is so much the opposite of this abstraction, that the stylistic contrast between the two works – the biographic and the autobiographic vision – itself says more than anything else about the contrasting temperaments of their authors.

Finally, for all his astonishing detachment and sense of objective judgement, Godwin was far more influenced by Mary Wollstonecraft's intellect than he realized. One has the sense that he could see round her character far better than he could see round her mind. When he wrote the *Memoirs* he was still trying to digest the full implication of her ideas; and even his professional philosophic work was never to be the same again. This becomes most evident in his unavailing attempts to write a summary of 'the leading intellectual traits of her character' at the end of his book. He tried it twice, in the first and the second edition, and both are deeply unsatisfactory. In fact they tell us much less than he had already managed to show in the body of his narrative. His biographic explorations are far more convincing than his philosophic conclusions.

What he tries to do is enforce an arbitrary distinction between their two 'kinds' of intellect. In the first edition, he puts it like this: 'We had cultivated our powers (if I may venture to use this sort of language) in different directions; I chiefly an attempt at logical and metaphysical distinction, she a taste for the picturesque' (Chapter 10).

This strikes one as so ludicrously inadequate – and so far below what he had already brilliantly shown of her developing 'powers' –

that one loses confidence in a way that happens nowhere else in the book. Godwin himself seems to have been vaguely aware of something going wrong when he makes the apologetic parenthesis about using 'this sort of language'. One is hardly surprised to find a little later the absurd statement that 'in the strict sense of the term, she reasoned little'. We seem to have collapsed into an inferior mode of discourse.

In the second edition, he attempts the distinction again, with even more disastrous results. This time we are told that he and Wollstonecraft 'carried farther than to its common extent the characteristic of the sexes to which we belonged' – that the man reasoned, and the woman merely felt. Godwin has here so far declined into the conventions of eighteenth-century thinking (and even of modern cliché), that one cannot really take him seriously.

Yet it is his only major lapse as a biographer; and on reflection it is an instructive and even a touching one. Reading through both versions, I think one can see what has happened. In the first place he was really trying to describe the way in which Wollstonecraft had 'improved' the inadequacies of *his own* intellectual make-up, as he was now beginning to see them. It was her feeling, her imagination, her intuition, that he most valued. It was not that she merely felt, but that he merely reasoned – until he met her. (This was the very point made by Coleridge.) 'What I wanted in this respect, Mary possessed in a degree superior to any other person I ever knew . . . my oscillation and scepticism were fixed by her boldness.' For once, and once only, he was speaking with overwhelming subjectivity.

In the second place, Godwin was indeed reverting to another, and more conventional mode of literary discourse. For one crucial and revealing moment he was turning his back on the revolutionary vision and style he had forged as a biographer. He was reverting to the grand, dusty philosophic commonplaces of the previous age: the age which they had both so courageously stormed and subverted. He was attempting to generalize like a *philosophe* of the Enlightenment, on an experience they had lived out together with the passionate particularity of Romantic poets and lovers.

But from all one learns, I imagine Mary Wollstonecraft would have forgiven William Godwin, and the Feminist would have made peace with the Philosopher.

MARY WOLLSTONECRAFT

A Short Residence in Sweden, Norway, and Denmark

NOTE ON THE TEXT OF 'A SHORT RESIDENCE'

The text reprinted here is that of the first English edition of *Letters Written during a Short Residence in Sweden, Norway, and Denmark*, published by Joseph Johnson in 1796. The spelling of Scandinavian place-names has been standardized to conform with modern English usage and a few spellings, which might cause difficulty, have been modernized. Mary Wollstonecraft's journey can be followed on the accompanying map.

The full title of the book has been previously abbreviated in various odd ways, partly because of its awkwardness. Godwin called it, indiscriminately, *Travels in Norway* or *Travels in Scandinavia*; Wardle used the accurate, but clumsy, *Letters Written . . . in Sweden*. I have preferred a genuine, but more convenient, abbreviation: *A Short Residence*. This has the advantage of distinguishing it from Wollstonecraft's actual letters (which have been published); it also has a melancholy overtone which is not inappropriate to her restless travelling over the earth.

All the footnotes are Wollstonecraft's own, from the 1796 edition. The small numbers in the body of the text indicate that further information or commentary is available in my editorial notes at the back of the book. While avoiding a miniature history of Scandinavia, I have sketched in the background to people and events of interest; identified Wollstonecraft's quotations (which vividly suggest the range of her reading, especially poetry); drawn attention to her literary technique as a travel-writer; and tried to show how richly her intellectual concerns and imaginative themes flow into the mainstream of English Romanticism. I have been greatly helped by the previous scholarship of Carol Poston, Professor Ralph Wardle and Per Nyström.

LETTERS

WRITTEN

DURING A SHORT RESIDENCE

IN

SWEDEN, NORWAY, AND DENMARK.

BY *MARY WOLLSTONECRAFT.*

LONDON:

PRINTED FOR J. JOHNSON, ST. PAUL'S CHURCH-YARD.

....

1796.

Facsimile of the title-page
of the first edition

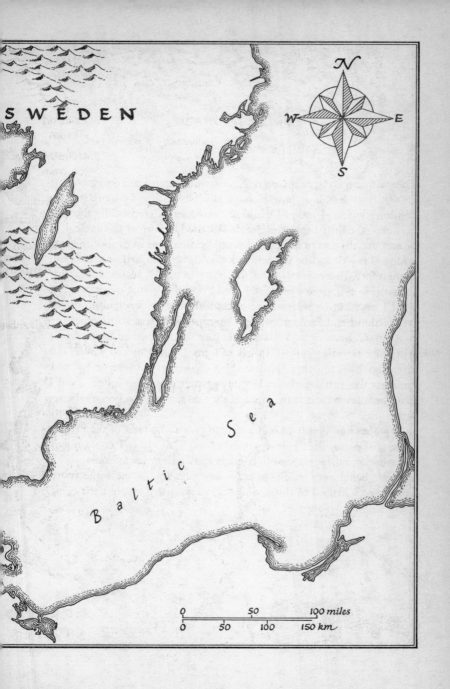

Advertisement

The writing travels, or memoirs, has ever been a pleasant employment; for vanity or sensibility always renders it interesting. In writing these desultory letters, I found I could not avoid being continually the first person – 'the little hero of each tale.'[1] I tried to correct this fault, if it be one, for they were designed for publication; but in proportion as I arranged my thoughts, my letter, I found, became stiff and affected: I, therefore, determined to let my remarks and reflections flow unrestrained, as I perceived that I could not give a just description of what I saw, but by relating the effect different objects had produced on my mind and feelings, whilst the impression was still fresh.

A person has a right, I have sometimes thought, when amused by a witty or interesting egotist, to talk of himself when he can win on our attention by acquiring our affection. Whether I deserve to rank amongst this privileged number, my readers alone can judge – and I give them leave to shut the book, if they do not wish to become better acquainted with me.

My plan was simply to endeavour to give a just view of the present state of the countries I have passed through, as far as I could obtain information during so short a residence; avoiding those details which, without being very useful to travellers who follow the same route, appear very insipid to those who only accompany you in their chair.

Letter One

Eleven days of weariness on board a vessel not intended for the accommodation of passengers have so exhausted my spirits, to say nothing of the other causes, with which you are already sufficiently acquainted, that it is with some difficulty I adhere to my determination of giving you my observations, as I travel through new scenes, whilst warmed with the impression they have made on me.

The captain, as I mentioned to you, promised to put me on shore at Arendal,* or Gothenburg, in his way to Elsinore; but contrary winds obliged us to pass both places during the night. In the morning, however, after we had lost sight of the entrance of the latter bay, the vessel was becalmed; and the captain, to oblige me, hanging out a signal for a pilot, bore down towards the shore.

My attention was particularly directed to the light-house;[2] and you can scarcely imagine with what anxiety I watched two long hours for a boat to emancipate me – still no one appeared. Every cloud that flitted on the horizon was hailed as a liberator, till approaching nearer, like most of the prospects sketched by hope, it dissolved under the eye into disappointment.

Weary of expectation, I then began to converse with the captain on the subject; and, from the tenor of the information my questions drew forth, I soon concluded, that, if I waited for a boat, I had little chance of getting on shore at this place. Despotism, as is usually the case, I found had here cramped the industry of man. The pilots being paid by the king, and scantily, they will not run into any danger, or even quit their hovels, if they can possibly avoid it, only to fulfil what is termed their duty. How different is it on the English coast, where, in the most stormy weather, boats immediately hail you, brought out by the expectation of extraordinary profit.

Disliking to sail for Elsinore, and still more to lie at anchor, or

* In Norway. [All footnotes to *A Short Residence* are Mary Wollstonecraft's.]

cruise about the coast for several days, I exerted all my rhetoric to prevail on the captain to let me have the ship's boat; and though I added the most forcible of arguments, I for a long time addressed him in vain.[3]

It is a kind of rule at sea, not to send out a boat. The captain was a good-natured man; but men with common minds seldom break through general rules. Prudence is ever the resort of weakness; and they rarely go as far as they may in any undertaking, who are determined not to go beyond it on any account. If, however, I had some trouble with the captain, I did not lose much time with the sailors; for they, all alacrity, hoisted out the boat, the moment I obtained permission, and promised to row me to the light-house.

I did not once allow myself to doubt of obtaining a conveyance from thence round the rocks – and then away for Gothenburg – confinement is so unpleasant.

The day was fine; and I enjoyed the water till, approaching the little island, poor Marguerite,[4] whose timidity always acts as a feeler before her adventuring spirit, began to wonder at our not seeing any inhabitants. I did not listen to her. But when, on landing, the same silence prevailed, I caught the alarm, which was not lessened by the sight of two old men, whom we forced out of their wretched hut. Scarcely human in their appearance, we with difficulty obtained an intelligible reply to our questions – the result of which was, that they had no boat, and were not allowed to quit their post, on any pretence. But, they informed us, that there was at the other side, eight or ten miles over, a pilot's dwelling; two guineas tempted the sailors to risk the captain's displeasure, and once more embark to row me over.

The weather was pleasant, and the appearance of the shore so grand, that I should have enjoyed the two hours it took to reach it, but for the fatigue which was too visible in the countenances of the sailors who, instead of uttering a complaint, were, with the thoughtless hilarity peculiar to them, joking about the possibility of the captain's taking advantage of a slight westerly breeze, which was springing up, to sail without them. Yet, in spite of their good humour, I could not help growing uneasy when the shore, receding, as it were, as we advanced, seemed to promise no end to their toil. This anxiety increased when, turning into the most picturesque bay I ever saw, my eyes sought in vain for the vestige of a human habitation. Before I could determine what step to take in such a dilemma, for I could not bear to think of returning to the ship, the sight of a barge relieved me, and we hastened towards it for information. We were immediately directed to pass some jutting rocks when we should see a pilot's hut.

There was a solemn silence in this scene, which made itself be felt. The sun-beams that played on the ocean, scarcely ruffled by the lightest breeze, contrasted with the huge, dark rocks, that looked like the rude materials of creation forming the barrier of unwrought space, forcibly struck me; but I should not have been sorry if the cottage had not appeared equally tranquil. Approaching a retreat where strangers, especially women, so seldom appeared, I wondered that curiosity did not bring the beings who inhabited it to the windows or door. I did not immediately recollect that men who remain so near the brute creation, as only to exert themselves to find the food necessary to sustain life, have little or no imagination to call forth the curiosity necessary to fructify the faint glimmerings of mind which entitles them to rank as lords of the creation. – Had they either, they could not contentedly remain rooted in the clods they so indolently cultivate.

Whilst the sailors went to seek for the sluggish inhabitants, these conclusions occurred to me; and, recollecting the extreme fondness which the Parisians ever testify for novelty, their very curiosity appeared to me a proof of the progress they had made in refinement. Yes; in the art of living – in the art of escaping from the cares which embarrass the first steps towards the attainment of the pleasures of social life.

The pilots informed the sailors that they were under the direction of a lieutenant retired from the service, who spoke English; adding, that they could do nothing without his orders; and even the offer of money could hardly conquer their laziness, and prevail on them to accompany us to his dwelling. They would not go with me alone which I wanted them to have done, because I wished to dismiss the sailors as soon as possible. Once more we rowed off, they following tardily, till, turning round another bold protuberance of the rocks, we saw a boat making towards us, and soon learnt that it was the lieutenant himself, coming with some earnestness to see who we were.

To save the sailors any further toil, I had my baggage instantly removed into his boat; for, as he could speak English, a previous parley was not necessary; though Marguerite's respect for me could hardly keep her from expressing the fear, strongly marked on her countenance, which my putting ourselves into the power of a strange man excited. He pointed out his cottage; and, drawing near to it, I was not sorry to see a female figure, though I had not, like Marguerite, been thinking of robberies, murders, or the other evil which instantly, as the sailors would have said, runs foul of a woman's imagination.[5]

On entering, I was still better pleased to find a clean house, with some degree of rural elegance. The beds were of muslin, coarse it is true, but dazzlingly white; and the floor was strewed over with little sprigs of juniper (the custom, as I afterwards found, of the country), which formed a contrast with the curtains and produced an agreeable sensation of freshness, to soften the ardour of noon. Still nothing was so pleasing as the alacrity of hospitality – all that the house afforded was quickly spread on the whitest linen. – Remember I had just left the vessel, where, without being fastidious, I had continually been disgusted. Fish, milk, butter, and cheese, and I am sorry to add, brandy, the bane of this country, were spread on the board. After we had dined, hospitality made them with some degree of mystery, bring us some excellent coffee. I did not then know that it was prohibited.

The good man of the house apologized for coming in continually, but declared that he was so glad to speak English, he could not stay out. He need not have apologized; I was equally glad of his company. With the wife I could only exchange smiles; and she was employed observing the make of our clothes. My hands, I found, had first led her to discover that I was the lady. I had, of course, my quantum of reverences; for the politeness of the north seems to partake of the coldness of the climate, and the rigidity of its iron sinewed rocks. Amongst the peasantry, there is, however, so much of the simplicity of the golden age [6] in this land of flint – so much overflowing of heart, and fellow-feeling, that only benevolence, and the honest sympathy of nature, diffused smiles over my countenance when they kept me standing, regardless of my fatigue, whilst they dropt courtesy after courtesy.

The situation of this house was beautiful, though chosen for convenience. The master [7] being the officer who commanded all the pilots on the coast, and the person appointed to guard wrecks, it was necessary for him to fix on a spot that would overlook the whole bay. As he had seen some service, he wore, not without a pride I thought becoming, a badge to prove that he had merited well of his country. It was happy, I thought, that he had been paid in honour; for the stipend he received was little more than twelve pounds a year. – I do not trouble myself or you with the calculation of Swedish ducats. Thus, my friend, you perceive the necessity of *perquisites*. This same narrow policy runs through every thing. I shall have occasion further to animadvert on it.

Though my host amused me with an account of himself, which gave me an idea of the manners of the people I was about to visit, I was eager to climb the rocks to view the country, and see whether the honest tars had regained their ship. With the help of the lieutenant's telescope I saw the vessel underway with a fair though gentle gale. The sea was calm, playful even as the most shallow stream, and on the vast basin I did not see a dark speck to indicate the boat. My conductors were consequently arrived.

Straying further, my eye was attracted by the sight of some heart's ease that peeped through the rocks. I caught at it as a good omen, and going to preserve it in a letter that had not conveyed balm to my heart, a cruel remembrance suffused my eyes; but it passed away like an April shower. If you are deep read in Shakespeare, you will recollect that this was the little western flower tinged by love's dart, which 'maidens call love in idleness.' [8] The gaiety of my babe was unmixed; regardless of omens or sentiments, she found a few wild strawberries more grateful than flowers or fancies.

The lieutenant informed me that this was a commodious bay. Of that I could not judge, though I felt its picturesque beauty. Rocks were piled on rocks, forming a suitable bulwark to the ocean. Come no further, they emphatically said, turning their dark sides to the waves to augment the idle roar. The view was sterile: still little patches of earth, of the most exquisite verdure, enamelled with the sweetest wild flowers, seemed to promise the goats and a few straggling cows luxurious herbage. How silent and peaceful was the scene. I gazed around with rapture, and felt more of that spontaneous pleasure which gives credibility to our expectation of happiness, than I had for a long, long time before. I forgot the horrors I had witnessed in France,[9] which had cast a gloom over all nature, and suffering the enthusiasm of my character, too often, gracious God! damped by the tears of disappointed affection, to be lighted up afresh, care took wing while simple fellow feeling expanded my heart.

To prolong this enjoyment, I readily assented to the proposal of our host to pay a visit to a family, the master of which spoke English, who was the drollest dog in the country, he added, repeating some of his stories, with a hearty laugh.

I walked on, still delighted with the rude beauties of the scene; for the sublime often gave place imperceptibly to the beautiful, dilating the emotions which were painfully concentrated.

When we entered this abode, the largest I had yet seen, I was introduced to a numerous family; but the father, from whom I was led to expect so much entertainment, was absent. The lieutenant consequently was obliged to be the interpreter of our reciprocal compliments. The phrases were awkwardly transmitted, it is true; but looks and gestures were sufficient to make them intelligible and interesting. The girls were all vivacity, and respect for me could scarcely keep them from romping with my host, who, asking for a pinch of snuff, was presented with a box, out of which an artificial mouse, fastened to the bottom, sprung. Though this trick had doubtless been played time out of mind, yet the laughter it excited was not less genuine.

They were overflowing with civility; but to prevent their almost killing my babe with kindness, I was obliged to shorten my visit; and two or three of the girls accompanied us, bringing with them a part of whatever the house afforded to contribute towards rendering my supper more plentiful; and plentiful in fact it was, though I with difficulty did honour to some of the dishes, not relishing the quantity of sugar and spices put into every thing. At supper my host told me bluntly that I was a woman of observation, for I asked him *men's questions.*

The arrangements for my journey were quickly made; I could only have a car with post-horses, as I did not chuse to wait till a carriage could be sent for to Gothenburg. The expense of my journey, about one or two and twenty English miles, I found would not amount to more than eleven or twelve shillings, paying, he assured me, generously. I gave him a guinea and a half. But it was with the greatest difficulty that I could make him take so much, indeed any thing for my lodging and fare. He declared that it was next to robbing me, explaining how much I ought to pay on the road. However, as I was positive, he took the guinea for himself; but, as a condition, insisted on accompanying me, to prevent my meeting with any trouble or imposition on the way.

I then retired to my apartment with regret. The night was so fine, that I would gladly have rambled about much longer; yet recollecting that I must rise very early, I reluctantly went to bed: but my senses had been so awake, and my imagination still continued so busy, that I sought for rest in vain. Rising before six, I scented the sweet morning air; I had long before heard the birds twittering to hail the dawning day, though it could scarcely have been allowed to have departed.

Nothing, in fact, can equal the beauty of the northern summer's evening and night; if night it may be called that only wants the glare of day, the full light, which frequently seems so impertinent; for I could write at midnight very well without a candle. I contemplated all nature at rest; the rocks, even grown darker in their appearance, looked as if they partook of the general repose, and reclined more heavily on their foundation. – What, I exclaimed, is this active principle which keeps me still awake? – Why fly my thoughts abroad when every thing around me appears at home? My child was sleeping with equal calmness – innocent and sweet as the closing flowers. – Some recollections, attached to the idea of home, mingled with reflections respecting the state of society I had been contemplating that evening, made a tear drop on the rosy cheek I had just kissed; and emotions that trembled on the brink of extacy and agony gave a poignancy to my sensations, which made me feel more alive than usual.

What are these imperious sympathies? How frequently has melancholy and even mysanthropy taken possession of me, when the world has disgusted me, and friends have proved unkind. I have then considered myself as a particle broken off from the grand mass of mankind;[10] – I was alone, till some involuntary sympathetic emotion, like the attraction of adhesion, made me feel that I was still a part of a mighty whole, from which I could not sever myself – not, perhaps, for the reflection has been carried very far, by snapping the thread of an existence which loses its charms in proportion as the cruel experience of life stops or poisons the current of the heart. Futurity, what hast thou not to give to those who know that there is such a thing as happiness! I speak not of philosophical contentment, though pain has afforded them the strongest conviction of it.

After our coffee and milk, for the mistress of the house had been roused long before us by her hospitality, my baggage was taken forward in a boat by my host, because the car could not safely have been brought to the house.

The road at first was very rocky and troublesome; but our driver was careful, and the horses accustomed to the frequent and sudden acclivities and descents; so that not apprehending any danger, I played with my girl, whom I would not leave to Marguerite's care, on account of her timidity.

Stopping at a little inn to bait the horses, I saw the first countenance in Sweden that displeased me, though the man was better dressed than any one who had as yet fallen in my way. An altercation took place between him and my host, the purport of which I could not guess, excepting that I was the occasion of it, be it what it would. The sequel was his leaving the house angrily; and I was immediately informed that he was the custom-house officer. The professional had indeed effaced the national character, for living as he did with these frank hospitable people, still only the exciseman appeared, – the counterpart of some I had met with in England and France. I was unprovided with a passport, not having entered any great town. At Gothenburg I knew I could immediately obtain one, and only the trouble made me object to the searching my trunks. He blustered for money; but the lieutenant was determined to guard me, according to promise, from imposition.

To avoid being interrogated at the town-gate, and obliged to go in the rain to give an account of myself, merely a form, before we could get the refreshment we stood in need of, he requested us to descend, I might have said step, from our car, and walk into town.

I expected to have found a tolerable inn, but was ushered into a most comfortless one; and, because it was about five o'clock, three or four hours after their dining hour, I could not prevail on them to give me any thing warm to eat.

The appearance of the accommodations obliged me to deliver one of my recommendatory letters, and the gentleman, to whom it was addressed, sent to look out for a lodging for me whilst I partook of his supper. As nothing passed at this supper to characterize the country, I shall here close my letter.

Yours truly

Letter Two

Gothenburg is a clean airy town, and having been built by the Dutch, has canals running through each street, and in some of them there are rows of trees that would render it very pleasant were it not for the pavement, which is intolerably bad.

There are several rich commercial houses, Scotch, French, and Swedish; but the Scotch, I believe, have been the most successful. The commerce and commission business with France since the war,[11] has been very lucrative, and enriched the merchants, I am afraid, at the expence of the other inhabitants, by raising the price of the necessaries of life.

As all the men of consequence, I mean men of the largest fortune, are merchants, their principal enjoyment is a relaxation from business at the table, which is spread at, I think, too early an hour (between one and two) for men who have letters to write and accounts to settle after paying due respect to the bottle. However, when numerous circles are to be brought together, and when neither literature nor public amusements furnish topics for conversation, a good dinner appears to be the only centre to rally round, especially as scandal, the zest of more select parties, can only be whispered. As for politics, I have seldom found it a subject of continual discussion in a country town in any part of the world. The politics of the place being on a smaller scale, suits better with the size of their faculties; for, generally speaking, the sphere of observation determines the extent of the mind.

The more I see of the world, the more I am convinced that civilization is a blessing not sufficiently estimated by those who have not traced its progress; for it not only refines our enjoyments, but produces a variety which enables us to retain the primitive delicacy of our sensations. Without the aid of the imagination all the pleasures of the senses must sink into grossness, unless continual novelty serve as a substitute for the imagination, which being impossible, it was to this weariness, I suppose, that Solomon alluded when he declared that there was nothing new under the sun![12] – nothing for the common sensations excited by the senses. Yet who will deny that the imagination and understanding have made many, very many discoveries since those days, which only seem harbingers of others still more noble and beneficial. I never met with much imagination amongst people who had not acquired a habit of reflection; and in that state of society in which the judgment and taste are not called forth, and formed by the cultivation of the arts and sciences, little of that delicacy of feeling and thinking is to be found characterized by the word sentiment. The want of scientific pursuits perhaps accounts for the hospitality, as well as for the cordial reception which strangers receive from the inhabitants of small towns.

Hospitality has, I think, been too much praised by travellers as a proof of goodness of heart, when in my opinion indiscriminate hospitality is rather a criterion by which you may form a tolerable estimate of the indolence or vacancy of a head; or, in other words, a fondness for social pleasures in which the mind not having its proportion of exercise, the bottle must be pushed about.

These remarks are equally applicable to Dublin, the most hospitable city I ever passed through.[13] But I will try to confine my observations more particularly to Sweden.

It is true I have only had a glance over a small part of it; yet of its present state of manners and acquirements I think I have formed a distinct idea, without having visited the capital, where, in fact, less of a national character is to be found than in the remote parts of the country.

The Swedes pique themselves on their politeness; but far from being the polish of a cultivated mind, it consists merely of tiresome forms and ceremonies. So far indeed from entering immediately into your character, and making you feel instantly at your ease, like the well-bred French, their over-acted civility is a continual restraint on all your actions. The sort of superiority which a fortune gives when there is no superiority of education, excepting what consists in the observance of senseless forms, has a contrary effect than what is intended; so that I could not help reckoning the peasantry the politest people of Sweden, who only aiming at pleasing you, never think of being admired for their behaviour.

Their tables, like their compliments, seem equally a caricature of the French. The dishes are composed, as well as theirs, of a variety of mixtures to destroy the native taste of the food without being as relishing. Spices and sugar are put into every thing, even into the bread; and the only way I can account for their partiality to high-seasoned dishes, is the constant use of salted provisions. Necessity obliges them to lay up a store of dried fish, and salted meat, for the winter; and in summer, fresh meat and fish taste insipid after them. To which may be added the constant use of spirits. Every day, before dinner and supper, even whilst the dishes are cooling on the table, men and women repair to a side-table, and to obtain an appetite, eat bread and butter, cheese, raw salmon, or anchovies,[14] drinking a glass of brandy. Salt fish or meat then immediately follows, to give a further whet to the stomach. As the dinner advances, pardon me for taking up a few minutes to describe what, alas! has detained me two or three hours on the stretch, observing, dish after dish is changed, in endless rotation, and handed round with solemn pace to each guest: but should you happen not to like the first dishes, which was often my case, it is a gross breach of politeness to ask for part of any other till its turn comes. But have patience, and there will be eating enough. Allow me to run over the acts of a visiting day, not overlooking the interludes.

Prelude a luncheon – then a succession of fish, flesh and fowl for two hours; during which time the desert, I was sorry for the strawberries and cream, rests on the table to be impregnated by the fumes of the viands. Coffee immediately follows in the drawing-room; but does not preclude punch, ale, tea and cakes, raw salmon, &c. A supper brings up the rear, not forgetting the introductory luncheon, almost equalling in removes the dinner. A day of this kind you would imagine sufficient – but a to-morrow and a to-morrow – A never ending, still beginning feast may be bearable, perhaps, when stern winter frowns, shaking with chilling aspect his hoary locks; but during a summer, sweet as fleeting, let me, my kind strangers, escape sometimes into your fir groves, wander on the margin of your beautiful lakes, or climb your rocks to view still others in endless perspective;

which, piled by more than giant's hand, scale the heavens to intercept its rays, or to receive the parting tinge of lingering day – day that, scarcely softened into twilight, allows the freshening breeze to wake, and the moon to burst forth in all her glory to glide with solemn elegance through the azure expanse.

The cow's bell has ceased to tinkle the herd to rest; they have all paced across the heath. Is not this the witching time of night? The waters murmur, and fall with more than mortal music, and spirits of peace walk abroad to calm the agitated breast. Eternity is in these moments: worldly cares melt into the airy stuff that dreams are made of; and reveries, mild and enchanting as the first hopes of love, or the recollection of lost enjoyment, carry the hapless wight into futurity, who, in bustling life, has vainly strove to throw off the grief which lies heavy at the heart. Good night! A crescent hangs out in the vault before, which woos me to stray abroad: – it is not a silvery reflection of the sun, but glows with all its golden splendour. Who fears the falling dew? It only makes the mown grass smell more fragrant.[15]

Adieu!

Letter Three

The population of Sweden has been estimated from two millions and a half to three millions; a small number for such an immense tract of country: of which only so much is cultivated, and that in the simplest manner, as is absolutely necessary to supply the necessaries of life; and near the seashore, from whence herrings are easily procured, there scarcely appears a vestige of cultivation. The scattered huts that stand shivering on the naked rocks, braving the pitiless elements, are formed of logs of wood, rudely hewn; and so little pains are taken with the craggy foundation, that nothing like a pathway points out the door.

Gathered into himself by cold, lowering his visage to avoid the cutting blast, is it surprising that the churlish pleasure of drinking drams [16] takes place of social enjoyments amongst the poor, especially if we take into the account, that they mostly live on high-seasoned provisions and rye bread? Hard enough, you may imagine, as it is only baked once a year. The servants also, in most families, eat this kind of bread, and have a different kind of food from their masters, which, in spite of all the arguments I have heard to vindicate the custom, appears to me a remnant of barbarism.

In fact, the situation of the servants in every respect, particularly that of the women, shews how far the Swedes are from having a just conception of rational equality. They are not *termed* slaves; yet a man may strike a man with impunity because he pays him wages, though these wages are so low, that necessity must teach them to pilfer, whilst servility renders them false and boorish. Still the men stand up for the dignity of man, by oppressing the women. The most menial, and even laborious offices, are therefore left to these poor drudges. Much of this I have seen. In the winter, I am told, they take the linen down to the river, to wash it in the cold water; and though their hands, cut by the ice, are cracked and bleeding, the men, their fellow servants, will not disgrace their manhood by carrying a tub to lighten their burden.[17]

You will not be surprised to hear that they do not wear shoes or stockings, when I inform you that their wages are seldom more than twenty or thirty shillings per annum. It is the custom, I know, to give them a new year's gift, and a present at some other period; but can it all amount to a just indemnity for their labour? The treatment of servants in most countries, I grant, is very unjust; and in England, that boasted land of freedom, it is often extremely tyrannical. I have frequently, with indignation, heard gentlemen declare that they would never allow a servant to answer them; and ladies of the most exquisite sensibility, who were continually exclaiming against the cruelty of the vulgar to the brute creation, have in my presence forgot that their attendants had human feelings, as well as forms. I do not know a more agreeable sight than to see servants part of a family. By taking an interest, generally speaking, in their concerns, you inspire them with one for yours. We must love our servants, or we shall never be sufficiently attentive to their happiness; and how can those masters be attentive to their happiness, who living above their fortunes, are more anxious to outshine their neighbours than to allow their household the innocent enjoyments they earn.

It is, in fact, much more difficult for servants who are tantalized by seeing and preparing the dainties of which they are not to partake, to remain honest, than the poor, whose thoughts are not led from their homely fare; so that, though the servants here are commonly thieves, you seldom hear of house-breaking, or robbery on the highway. The country is, perhaps, too thinly inhabited to produce many of that description of thieves termed footpads, or highwaymen. They are usually the spawn of great cities; the effect of the spurious desires generated by wealth, rather than the desperate struggles of poverty to escape from misery.

The enjoyment of the peasantry was drinking brandy and coffee, before the latter was prohibited, and the former not allowed to be privately distilled. The wars carried on by the late king rendering it necessary to increase the revenue, and retain the specie in the country by every possible means.[18]

The taxes before the reign of Charles the twelfth were inconsiderable.[19] Since then, the burden has continually been growing heavier, and the price of provisions has proportionably increased; nay, the advantage accruing from the exportation of corn to France, and rye to Germany, will probably produce a scarcity in both Sweden and Norway, should not a peace put a stop to it this autumn, for speculations of various kinds have already almost doubled the price.

Such are the effects of war, that it saps the vitals even of the neutral countries, who, obtaining a sudden influx of wealth, appear to be rendered flourishing by the destruction which ravages the hapless nations who are sacrificed to the ambition of their governors. I shall not, however, dwell on the vices, though they be of the most contemptible and embruting cast, to which a sudden accession of fortune gives birth, because I believe it may be delivered as an axiom that it is only in proportion to the industry necessary to acquire wealth, that a nation is really benefited by it.

The prohibition of drinking coffee, under a penalty, and the encouragement given to public distilleries, tend to impoverish the poor, who are not affected by the sumptuary laws; for the regent has lately laid very severe restraints on the article of dress, which the middling class of people found grievous because it obliged them to throw aside finery that might have lasted them for their lives.*

These may be termed vexations; still the death of the king, by saving them from the consequences his ambition would naturally have entailed on them, may be reckoned a blessing.

Besides, the French revolution has not only rendered all the crowned heads more cautious, but has so decreased every where (excepting amongst themselves) a respect for nobility, that the peasantry have not only lost their blind reverence for their seigniors, but complain, in a manly style, of oppressions which before they did not think of denominating such, because they were taught to consider themselves as a different order of beings. And, perhaps, the efforts which the aristocrats are making here, as well as in every other part of Europe, to secure their sway, will be the most effectual mode of undermining it; taking into the calculation, that the king

* The ladies are only allowed to wear black and white silks, and plain muslins, besides other restrictions of a like nature.

of Sweden, like most of the potentates of Europe, has continually been augmenting his power by encroaching on the privileges of the nobles.

The well-bred Swedes of the capital are formed on the ancient French model; and they in general speak that language; for they have a knack at acquiring languages, with tolerable fluency. This may be reckoned an advantage in some respects; but it prevents the cultivation of their own, and any considerable advance in literary pursuits.

A sensible writer * has lately observed (I have not his work by me, therefore cannot quote his exact words), 'that the Americans very wisely let the Europeans make their books and fashions for them.' [20] But I cannot coincide with him in this opinion. The reflection necessary to produce a certain number even of tolerable productions, augments, more than he is aware of, the mass of knowledge in the community. Desultory reading is commonly merely a pastime. But we must have an object to refer our reflections to, or they will seldom go below the surface. As in traveling, the keeping of a journal [21] excites to many useful enquiries that would not have been thought of, had the traveller only determined to see all he could see, without ever asking himself for what purpose. Besides, the very dabbling in literature furnishes harmless topics of conversation; for the not having such subjects at hand, though they are often insupportably fatiguing, renders the inhabitants of little towns prying and censorious. Idleness, rather than ill-nature, gives birth to scandal, and to the observation of little incidents which narrows the mind. It is frequently only the fear of being talked of, which produces that puerile scrupulosity about trifles incompatible with an enlarged plan of usefulness, and with the basis of all moral principles – respect for the virtues which are not merely the virtues of convention.

I am, my friend, more and more convinced that a metropolis, or an abode absolutely solitary, is the best calculated for the improvement of the heart, as well as the understanding; whether we desire to become acquainted with man, nature, or ourselves. Mixing with mankind, we are obliged to examine our prejudices, and often imperceptibly lose, as we analyze them. And in the country, growing intimate with nature, a thousand little circumstances, unseen by vulgar

* See Mr Cooper's *Account of America*.

eyes, give birth to sentiments dear to the imagination, and inquiries which expand the soul, particularly when cultivation has not smoothed into insipidity all its originality of character.

I love the country; yet whenever I see a picturesque situation chosen on which to erect a dwelling, I am always afraid of the improvements. It requires uncommon taste to form a whole, and to introduce accommodations and ornaments analogous with the surrounding scene.*

I visited, near Gothenburg, a house with improved land about it, with which I was particularly delighted. It was close to a lake embosomed in pine clad rocks. In one part of the meadows, your eye was directed to the broad expanse; in another, you were led into a shade, to see a part of it, in the form of a river, rush amongst the fragments of rocks and roots of trees; nothing seemed forced. One recess, particularly grand and solemn, amongst the towering cliffs, had a rude stone table, and seat, placed in it, that might have served for a druid's haunt; whilst a placid stream below enlivened the flowers on its margin, where light-footed elves would gladly have danced their airy rounds.

Here the hand of taste was conspicuous, though not obtrusive, and formed a contrast with another abode in the same neighbourhood, on

---

* With respect to gardening in England, I think we often make an egregious blunder by introducing too much shade; not considering that the shade which our climate requires need not be very thick. If it keep off the intense heat of the sun, and afford a solitary retirement, it is sufficient. But in many great gardens, or pleasure-grounds, the sun's rays can scarcely ever penetrate. These may amuse the eye; yet they are not *home walks* to which the owner can retire to enjoy air and solitude; for, excepting during an extraordinary dry summer, they are damp and chill. For the same reason, grottoes are absurd in this temperate climate. An umbrageous tree will afford sufficient shelter from the most ardent heat, that we ever feel. To speak explicitly, the usefulness of a garden ought to be conspicuous, because it ought not to be planted for the season when nature wantons in her prime; for the whole country is then a garden – far sweeter. If not very extensive, I think a garden should contain more shrubs and flowers than lofty trees; and in order to admit the sun-beams to enliven our spring, autumn and winter, serpentine walks, the rage for the line of beauty, should be made to submit to convenience. Yet, in this country, a broad straight gravel walk is a great convenience for those who wish to take exercise in all seasons, after rain particularly. When the weather is fine, the meadows offer winding paths, far superior to the formal turnings that interrupt reflection, without amusing the fancy.[22]

which much money had been lavished: where Italian colonades were placed to excite the wonder of the rude crags; and a stone staircase, to threaten with destruction a wooden house. Venuses and Apollos condemned to lie hid in snow three parts of the year, seemed equally displaced, and called the attention off from the surrounding sublimity, without inspiring any voluptuous sensations. Yet even these abortions of vanity have been useful. Numberless workmen have been employed, and the superintending artist has improved the labourers whose unskilfulness tormented him, by obliging them to submit to the discipline of rules. Adieu!

Yours affectionately

Letter Four

The severity of the long Swedish winter tends to render the people sluggish; for, though this season has its peculiar pleasures, too much time is employed to guard against its inclemency. Still, as warm clothing is absolutely necessary, the women spin, and the men weave, and by these exertions get a fence to keep out the cold. I have rarely passed a knot of cottages without seeing cloth laid out to bleach; and when I entered, always found the women spinning or knitting.

A mistaken tenderness, however, for their children, makes them, even in summer, load them with flannels; and, having a sort of natural antipathy to cold water, the squalid appearance of the poor babes, not to speak of the noxious smell which flannel and rugs retain, seems a reply to a question I had often asked – Why I did not see more children in the villages I passed through? Indeed the children appear to be nipt in the bud, having neither the graces nor charms of their age. And this, I am persuaded, is much more owing to the ignorance of the mothers than to the rudeness of the climate. Rendered feeble by the continual perspiration they are kept in, whilst every pore is absorbing unwholesome moisture, they give them, even at the breast, brandy, salt fish, and every other crude substance, which air and exercise enables the parent to digest.

The women of fortune here, as well as every where else, have nurses to suckle their children; and the total want of chastity in the lower class of women frequently renders them very unfit for the trust.[23]

You have sometimes remarked to me the difference of the manners of the country girls in England and in America; attributing the reserve of the former to the climate – to the absence of genial suns. But it must be their stars, not the zephyrs gently stealing on their senses, which here lead frail women astray.[24] – Who can look at these rocks, and allow the voluptuousness of nature to be an excuse for gratifying the desires it inspires? We must, therefore, find some other cause beside voluptuousness, I believe, to account for the conduct of the Swedish and American country girls; for I am led to conclude, from all the observations I have made, that there is always a mixture of sentiment and imagination in voluptuousness, to which neither of them have much pretension.

The country girls of Ireland and Wales equally feel the first impulse of nature, which, restrained in England by fear of delicacy, proves that society is there in a more advanced state. Besides, as the mind is cultivated, and taste gains ground, the passions become stronger, and rest on something more stable than the casual sympathies of the moment. Health and idleness will always account for promiscuous amours; and in some degree I term every person idle, the exercise of whose mind does not bear some proportion to that of the body.

The Swedish ladies exercise neither sufficiently; of course, grow very fat at an early age;[25] and when they have not this downy appearance, a comfortable idea, you will say, in a cold climate, they are not remarkable for fine forms. They have, however, mostly fine complexions; but indolence makes the lily soon displace the rose. The quantity of coffee, spices, and other things of that kind, with want of care, almost universally spoil their teeth, which contrast but ill with their ruby lips.

The manners of Stockholm are refined, I hear, by the introduction of gallantry; but in the country, romping and coarse freedoms, with coarser allusions, keep the spirits awake. In the article of cleanliness, the women, of all descriptions, seem very deficient; and their dress shews that vanity is more inherent in women than taste.

The men appear to have paid still less court to the graces. They are a robust, healthy race, distinguished for their common sense and turn for humour, rather than for wit or sentiment. I include not, as you may suppose, in this general character, some of the nobility and officers, who having travelled, are polite and well informed.

I must own to you, that the lower class of people here amuse and interest me much more than the middling, with their apish good breeding and prejudices. The sympathy and frankness of heart conspicuous in the peasantry produces even a simple gracefulness of deportment, which has frequently struck me as very picturesque; I have often also been touched by their extreme desire to oblige me, when I could not explain my wants, and by their earnest manner of expressing that desire. There is such a charm in tenderness! – It is so delightful to love our fellow-creatures, and meet the honest affections as they break forth. Still, my good friend, I begin to think that I should not like to live continually in the country, with people whose minds have such a narrow range. My heart would frequently be interested; but my mind would languish for more companionable society.

The beauties of nature appear to me now even more alluring than in my youth, because my intercourse with the world has formed, without vitiating my taste. But, with respect to the inhabitants of the country, my fancy has probably, when disgusted with artificial manners, solaced itself by joining the advantages of cultivation with the interesting sincerity of innocence, forgetting the lassitude that ignorance will naturally produce. I like to see animals sporting, and sympathize in their pains and pleasures. Still I love sometimes to view the human face divine, and trace the soul, as well as the heart, in its varying lineaments.[26]

A journey to the country, which I must shortly make, will enable me to extend my remarks. – Adieu!

Letter Five

Had I determined to travel in Sweden merely for pleasure, I should probably have chosen the road to Stockholm, though convinced, by repeated observation, that the manners of a people are best discriminated in the country. The inhabitants of the capital are all of the same genus; for the varieties in the species we must, therefore, search where the habitations of men are so separated as to allow the difference of climate to have its natural effect. And with this difference we are, perhaps, most forcibly struck at the first view, just as we form an estimate of the leading traits of a character at the first glance, of which intimacy afterwards makes us almost lose sight.

As my affairs called me to Strömstad [27] (the frontier town of Sweden) in my way to Norway, I was to pass over, I hear, the most uncultivated part of the country. Still I believe that the grand features of Sweden are the same every where, and it is only the grand features that admit of description. There is an individuality in every prospect, which remains in the memory as forcibly depicted as the particular features that have arrested our attention; yet we cannot find words to discriminate that individuality so as to enable a stranger to say, this is the face, that the view. We may amuse by setting the imagination to work; but we cannot store the memory with a fact.

As I wish to give you a general idea of this country, I shall continue in my desultory manner to make such observations and reflections as the circumstances draw forth, without losing time, by endeavouring to arrange them.

Travelling in Sweden is very cheap, and even commodious, if you make but the proper arrangements. Here, as in other parts of the continent, it is necessary to have your own carriage, and to have a servant who can speak the language, if you are unacquainted with it. Sometimes a servant who can drive would be found very useful, which was our case, for I travelled in company with two gentlemen, one of whom had a German servant who drove very well. This was all the party; for not intending to make a long stay, I left my little girl behind me.[28]

As the roads are not much frequented, to avoid waiting three or four hours for horses, we sent, as is the constant custom, an *avant courier* the night before, to order them at every post, and we constantly found them ready. Our first set I jokingly termed *requisition* horses; but afterwards we had almost always little spirited animals that went on at a round pace.

The roads, making allowance for the ups and downs, are uncommonly good and pleasant. The expence, including the postillions and other incidental things, does not amount to more than a shilling the Swedish mile.*

The inns are tolerable; but not liking the rye bread, I found it necessary to furnish myself with some wheaten before I set out. The beds too were particularly disagreeable to me. It seemed to me that I was sinking into a grave when I entered them; for, immersed in down placed in a sort of box, I expected to be suffocated before morning. The sleeping between two down beds,[29] they do so even in summer, must be very unwholesome during any season; and I cannot conceive how the people can bear it, especially as the summers are very warm. But warmth they seem not to feel; and, I should think were afraid of the air, by always keeping their windows shut. In the winter, I am persuaded, I could not exist in rooms thus closed up, with stoves heated in their manner, for they only put wood into them twice a day; and, when the stove is thoroughly heated, they shut the flue, not admitting any air to renew its elasticity, even when the rooms are crowded with company. These stoves are made of earthenware, and often in a form that ornaments an apartment, which is never the case with the heavy iron ones I have seen elsewhere. Stoves may be economical; but I like a fire, a wood one, in preference; and I am convinced that the current of air which it attracts renders this the best mode of warming rooms.

We arrived early the second evening at a little village called Kvistram, where we had determined to pass the night; having been informed that we should not afterwards find a tolerable inn until we reached Strömstad.

* A Swedish mile is nearly six English miles.

Advancing towards Kvistram, as the sun was beginning to decline, I was particularly impressed by the beauty of the situation. The road was on the declivity of a rocky mountain, slightly covered with a mossy herbage and vagrant firs. At the bottom, a river, straggling amongst the recesses of stone, was hastening forward to the ocean and its grey rocks, of which we had a prospect on the left, whilst on the right it stole peacefully forward into the meadows, losing itself in a thickly wooded rising ground. As we drew near, the loveliest banks of wild flowers variegated the prospect, and promised to exhale odours to add to the sweetness of the air, the purity of which you could almost see, alas! not smell, for the putrifying herrings, which they use as manure, after the oil has been extracted, spread over the patches of earth, claimed by cultivation, destroyed every other.

It was intolerable, and entered with us into the inn, which was in other respects a charming retreat.

Whilst supper was preparing I crossed the bridge, and strolled by the river, listening to its murmurs. Approaching the bank, the beauty of which had attracted my attention in the carriage, I recognized many of my old acquaintance growing with great luxuriancy.

Seated on it, I could not avoid noting an obvious remark. Sweden appeared to me the country in the world most proper to form the botanist and natural historian: every object seemed to remind me of the creation of things, of the first efforts of sportive nature.[30] When a country arrives at a certain state of perfection, it looks as if it were made so; and curiosity is not excited. Besides, in social life too many objects occur for any to be distinctly observed by the generality of mankind; yet a contemplative man, or poet, in the country, I do not mean the country adjacent to cities, feels and sees what would escape vulgar eyes, and draws suitable inferences. This train of reflections might have led me further, in every sense of the word; but I could not escape from the detestable evaporation of the herrings, which poisoned all my pleasure.

After making a tolerable supper, for it is not easy to get fresh provisions on the road, I retired, to be lulled to sleep by the murmuring of a stream, of which I with great difficulty obtained sufficient to perform my daily ablutions.

The last battle between the Danes and Swedes, which gave new life to their ancient enmity, was fought at this place 1788: only seventeen or eighteen were killed; for the great superiority of the Danes and Norwegians obliged the Swedes to submit; but sickness, and a scarcity of provisions, proved very fatal to their opponents, on their return.[31]

It would be very easy to search for the particulars of this engagement in the publications of the day; but as this manner of filling my pages does not come within my plan, I probably should not have remarked that the battle was fought here, were it not to relate an anecdote which I had from good authority.

I noticed, when I first mentioned this place to you that we descended a steep before we came to the inn; an immense ridge of rocks stretching out on one side. The inn was sheltered under them; and about a hundred yards from it was a bridge that crossed the river, whose murmurs I have celebrated; it was not fordable. The Swedish general received orders to stop at the bridge, and dispute the passage; a most advantageous post for an army so much inferior in force: but the influence of beauty is not confined to courts. The mistress of the inn was handsome: when I saw her there were still some remains of beauty; and, to preserve her house, the general gave up the only tenable station. He was afterwards broke for contempt of orders.[32]

Approaching the frontiers, consequently the sea, nature resumed an aspect ruder and ruder, or rather seemed the bones of the world waiting to be clothed with every thing necessary to give life and beauty. Still it was sublime.

The clouds caught their hue of the rocks that menaced them. The sun appeared afraid to shine, the birds ceased to sing, and the flowers to bloom; but the eagle fixed his nest high amongst the rocks, and the vulture hovered over this abode of desolation. The farm houses, in which only poverty resided, were formed of logs scarcely keeping off the cold and drifting snow; out of them the inhabitants seldom peeped, and the sports or prattling of children was neither seen nor heard. The current of life seemed congealed at the source: all were not frozen; for it was summer, you remember; but every thing appeared so dull, that I waited to see ice, in order to reconcile me to the absence of gaiety.

The day before, my attention had frequently been attracted by the wild beauties of the country we passed through.

The rocks which tossed their fantastic heads so high were often covered with pines and firs, varied in the most picturesque manner. Little woods filled up the recesses, when forests did not darken the scene; and vallies and glens, cleared of the trees, displayed a dazzling verdure which contrasted with the gloom of the shading pines. The eye stole into many a covert where tranquillity seemed to have taken up her abode, and the number of little lakes that continually presented themselves added to the peaceful composure of the scenery. The little cultivation which appeared did not break the enchantment, nor did castles rear their turrets aloft to crush the cottages, and prove that man is more savage than the natives of the woods. I heard of the bears, but never saw them stalk forth, which I was sorry for; I wished to have seen one in its wild state. In the winter, I am told, they sometimes catch a stray cow, which is a heavy loss to the owner.

The farms are small. Indeed most of the houses we saw on the road indicated poverty, or rather that the people could just live. Towards the frontiers they grew worse and worse in their appearance, as if not willing to put sterility itself out of countenance. No gardens smiled round the habitations, not a potatoe or cabbage to eat with the fish drying on a stick near the door. A little grain here and there appeared, the long stalks of which you might almost reckon. The day was gloomy when we passed over this rejected spot, the wind bleak, and winter seemed to be contending with nature, faintly struggling to change the season. Surely, thought I, if the sun ever shines here, it cannot warm these stones; moss only cleaves to them, partaking of their hardness; and nothing like vegetable life appears to cheer with hope the heart.

So far from thinking that the primitive inhabitants of the world lived in a southern climate, where Paradise spontaneously arose, I am led to infer, from various circumstances, that the first dwelling of man happened to be a spot like this which led him to adore a sun so seldom seen; for this worship, which probably preceded that of demons or demi-gods, certainly never began in a southern climate, where the continual presence of the sun prevented its being considered as a good; or rather the want of it never being felt, this glorious luminary would carelessly have diffused its blessings without being hailed as a benefactor. Man must therefore have been placed in the north, to tempt him to run after the sun, in order that the different parts of the earth might be peopled.[33] Nor do I wonder that hordes of barbarians always poured out of these regions to seek for milder climes, when nothing like cultivation attached them to the soil; especially when we take into the view that the adventuring spirit, common to man, is naturally stronger and more general during the infancy of society. The conduct of the followers of Mahomet, and the crusaders, will sufficiently corroborate my assertion.

Approaching nearer to Strömstad, the appearance of the town proved to be quite in character with the country we had just passed through. I hesitated to use the word country, yet could not find another; still it would sound absurd to talk of fields of rocks.

The town was built on, and under them. Three or four weather-beaten trees were shrinking from the wind; and the grass grew so sparingly, that I could not avoid thinking Dr Johnson's hyperbolical assertion 'that the man merited well of his country who made a few blades of grass grow where they never grew before', might here have been uttered with strict propriety.[34] The steeple likewise towered aloft; for what is a church, even amongst the Lutherans, without a steeple? But to prevent mischief in such an exposed situation, it is wisely placed on a rock at some distance, not to endanger the roof of the church.

Rambling about, I saw the door open, and entered, when to my great surprise I found the clergyman reading prayers, with only the clerk attending. I instantly thought of Swift's 'Dearly beloved Roger';[35] but on enquiry I learnt that some one had died that morning, and in Sweden it is customary to pray for the dead.

The sun, who I suspected never dared to shine, began now to convince me that he came forth only to torment; for though the wind was still cutting, the rocks became intolerably warm under my feet; whilst the herring effluvia, which I before found so very offensive, once more assailed me. I hastened back to the house of a merchant, the little sovereign of the place, because he was by far the richest, though not the mayor.

Here we were most hospitably received, and introduced to a very fine and numerous family. I have before mentioned to you the lillies of the north, I might have added, water lillies, for the complexion of many, even of the young women seem to be bleached on the bosom of snow. But in this youthful circle the roses bloomed with all their wonted freshness, and I wondered from whence the fire was stolen which sparkled in their fine blue eyes.

Here we slept; and I rose early in the morning to prepare for my little voyage to Norway. I had determined to go by water, and was to leave my companions behind; but not getting a boat immediately, and the wind being high and unfavourable, I was told that it was not safe to go to sea during such boisterous weather; I was therefore obliged to wait for the morrow, and had the present day on my hands; which I feared would be irksome, because the family, who possessed about a dozen French words amongst them, and not an English phrase, were anxious to amuse me, and would not let me remain alone in my room. The town we had already walked round and round; and if we advanced farther on the coast, it was still to view the same unvaried immensity of water, surrounded by barrenness.

The gentlemen wishing to peep into Norway, proposed going to Halden, the first town, the distance was only three Swedish miles. There, and back again, was but a day's journey, and would not, I thought, interfere with my voyage. I agreed, and invited the eldest and prettiest of the girls[36] to accompany us. I invited her, because I liked to see a beautiful face animated by pleasure, and to have an opportunity of regarding the country, whilst the gentlemen were amusing themselves with her.

I did not know, for I had not thought of it, that we were to scale some of the most mountainous cliffs of Sweden, in our way to the ferry which separates the two countries.

Entering amongst the cliffs, we were sheltered from the wind; warm sun-beams began to play, streams to flow, and groves of pines diversified the rocks. Sometimes they became suddenly bare and sublime. Once, in particular, after mounting the most terrific precipice, we had to pass through a tremendous defile, where the closing chasm seemed to threaten us with instant destruction, when turning quickly, verdant meadows and a beautiful lake relieved and charmed my eyes.

I have never travelled through Switzerland; but one of my companions assured me, that I should not there find any thing superior, if equal to the wild grandeur of these views.

As we had not taken this excursion into our plan, the horses had not been previously ordered, which obliged us to wait two hours at the first post. The day was wearing away. The road was so bad, that walking up the precipices consumed the time insensibly. But as we desired horses at each post ready at a certain hour, we reckoned on returning more speedily.

We stopt to dine at a tolerable farm. They brought us out ham, butter, cheese, and milk; and the charge was so moderate, that I scattered a little money amongst the children who were peeping at us, in order to pay them for their trouble.

Arrived at the ferry, we were still detained; for the people who attend at the ferries have a stupid kind of sluggishness in their manner, which is very provoking when you are in haste. At present I did not feel it; for scrambling up the cliffs, my eye followed the river as it rolled between the grand rocky banks; and to complete the scenery, they were covered with firs and pines, through which the wind rustled, as if it were lulling itself to sleep with the declining sun.

Behold us now in Norway; and I could not avoid feeling surprise at observing the difference in the manners of the inhabitants of the two sides of the river; for every thing shows that the Norwegians are more industrious and more opulent. The Swedes, for neighbours are seldom the best friends, accuse the Norwegians of knavery, and they retaliate by bringing a charge of hypocrisy against the Swedes. Local circumstances probably render both unjust, speaking from their feelings, rather than reason: and is this astonishing when we consider that most writers of travels have done the same, whose works have served as materials for the compilers of universal histories. All are eager to give a national character; which is rarely just, because they do not discriminate the natural from the acquired difference. The natural, I believe, on due consideration, will be found to consist merely in the degree of vivacity or thoughtfulness, pleasure, or pain, inspired by the climate, whilst the varieties which the forms of government, including religion, produce, are much more numerous and unstable.

A people have been characterized as stupid by nature; what a paradox! because they did not consider that slaves, having no object to stimulate industry, have not their faculties sharpened by the only thing that can exercise them, self-interest. Others have been brought forward as brutes, having no aptitude for the arts and sciences, only because the progress of improvement had not reached that stage which produces them.

Those writers who have considered the history of man, or of the human mind, on a more enlarged scale, have fallen into similar errors, not reflecting that the passions are weak where the necessaries of life are too hardly or too easily obtained.

Travellers who require that every nation should resemble their native country, had better stay at home. It is, for example, absurd to blame a people for not having that degree of personal cleanliness and elegance of manners which only refinement of taste produces, and will produce every where in proportion as society attains a general polish. The most essential service, I presume, that authors could render to society, would be to promote inquiry and discussion, instead of making those dogmatical assertions which only appear calculated to gird the human mind round with imaginary circles, like the paper globe which represents the one he inhabits.

This spirit of inquiry is the characteristic of the present century, from which the succeeding will, I am persuaded, receive a great accumulation of knowledge; and doubtless its diffusion will in a great measure destroy the factitious national characters which have been supposed permanent, though only rendered so by the permanency of ignorance.[37]

Arriving at Halden, at the siege of which Charles XII lost his life,[38] we had only time to take a transient view of it, whilst they were preparing us some refreshment.

Poor Charles! I thought of him with respect. I have always felt the same for Alexander; with whom he has been classed as a madman, by several writers, who have reasoned superficially, confounding the morals of the day with the few grand principles on which unchangeable morality rests. Making no allowance for the ignorance and prejudices of the period, they do not perceive how much they themselves are indebted to general improvement for the acquirements, and even the virtues, which they would not have had the force of mind to attain, by their individual exertions in a less advanced state of society.

The evening was fine, as is usual at this season; and the refreshing odour of the pine woods became more perceptible; for it was nine o'clock when we left Halden. At the ferry we were detained by a dispute relative to our Swedish passport, which we did not think of getting countersigned in Norway. Midnight was coming on; yet it might with such propriety have been termed the noon of night, that had Young[39] ever travelled towards the north, I should not have wondered at his becoming enamoured of the moon. But it is not the queen of night alone who reigns here in all her splendor, though the sun, loitering just below the horizon, decks her with a golden tinge from his car, illuminating the cliffs that hide him; the heavens also, of a clear softened blue, throw her forward, and the evening star appears a lesser moon to the naked eye. The huge shadows of the rocks, fringed with firs, concentrating the views, without darkening them, excited that tender melancholy which, sublimating the imagination, exalts, rather than depresses the mind.

My companions fell asleep: – fortunately they did not snore; and I contemplated, fearless of idle questions, a night such as I had never before seen or felt to charm the senses, and calm the heart. The very air was balmy, as it freshened into morn, producing the most voluptuous sensations. A vague pleasurable sentiment absorbed me, as I opened my bosom to the embraces of nature; and my soul rose to its author, with the chirping of the solitary birds, which began to feel, rather than see, advancing day. I had leisure to mark its progress. The grey morn, streaked with silvery rays, ushered in the orient beams, – how beautifully varying into purple! – yet, I was sorry to lose the soft watery clouds which preceded them, exciting a kind of expectation that made me almost afraid to breathe, lest I should break the charm. I saw the sun – and sighed.

One of my companions, now awake, perceiving that the postillion had mistaken the road, began to swear at him, and roused the other two, who reluctantly shook off sleep.

We had immediately to measure back our steps, and did not reach Strömstad before five in the morning.

The wind had changed in the night, and my boat was ready.

A dish of coffee, and fresh linen, recruited my spirits; and I directly set out again for Norway; purposing to land much higher up the coast.

Wrapping my great coat round me, I lay down on some sails at the bottom of the boat, its motion rocking me to rest, till a discourteous wave interrupted my slumbers, and obliged me to rise and feel a solitariness which was not so soothing as that of the past night.[40]

Adieu!

Letter Six

The sea was boisterous; but, as I had an experienced pilot, I did not apprehend any danger. Sometimes I was told, boats are driven far out and lost. However, I seldom calculate chances so nicely – sufficient for the day is the obvious evil!

We had to steer amongst islands and huge rocks, rarely losing sight of the shore, though it now and then appeared only a mist that bordered the water's edge. The pilot assured me that the numerous harbours on the Norway coast were very safe, and the pilot-boats were always on the watch. The Swedish side is very dangerous, I am also informed; and the help of experience is not often at hand, to enable strange vessels to steer clear of the rocks, which lurk below the water, close to the shore.

There are no tides here, nor in the Kattegat; [41] and, what appeared to me a consequence, no sandy beach. Perhaps this observation has been made before; but it did not occur to me till I saw the waves continually beating against the bare rocks, without ever receding to leave a sediment to harden.

The wind was fair, till we had to tack about in order to enter Larvik, where we arrived towards three o'clock in the afternoon. It is a clean, pleasant town, with a considerable iron-work, which gives life to it.

As the Norwegians do not frequently see travellers, they are very curious to know their business, and who they are – so curious that I was half tempted to adopt Dr Franklin's [42] plan, when travelling in America, where they are equally prying, which was to write on a paper, for public inspection, my name, from whence I came, where I was going, and what was my business. But if I were importuned by their curiosity, their friendly gestures gratified me. A woman, coming alone, interested them. And I know not whether my weariness gave me a look of peculiar delicacy; but they approached to assist me, and

enquire after my wants, as if they were afraid to hurt, and wished to
protect me. The sympathy I inspired, thus dropping down from the
clouds in a strange land, affected me more than it would have done,
had not my spirits been harassed by various causes – by much thinking
– musing almost to madness – and even by a sort of weak melancholy
that hung about my heart at parting with my daughter for the first
time.

You know that as a female I am particularly attached to her – I feel
more than a mother's fondness and anxiety, when I reflect on the
dependent and oppressed state of her sex. I dread lest she should be
forced to sacrifice her heart to her principles, or principles to her
heart. With trembling hand I shall cultivate sensibility, and cherish
delicacy of sentiment, lest, whilst I lend fresh blushes to the rose, I
sharpen the thorns that will wound the breast I would fain guard – I
dread to unfold her mind, lest it should render her unfit for the
world she is to inhabit – Hapless woman! what a fate is thine!

But whither am I wandering? I only meant to tell you that the
impression the kindness of the simple people made visible on my
countenance increased my sensibility to a painful degree. I wished to
have had a room to myself; for their attention, and rather distressing
observation, embarrassed me extremely. Yet, as they would bring me
eggs, and make my coffee, I found I could not leave them without
hurting their feelings of hospitality.

It is customary here for the host and hostess to welcome their
guests as master and mistress of the house.

My clothes, in their turn, attracted the attention of the females;
and I could not help thinking of the foolish vanity which makes many
women so proud of the observation of strangers as to take wonder
very gratuitously for admiration. This error they are very apt to fall
into; when arrived in a foreign country, the populace stare at them as
they pass; yet the make of a cap, or the singularity of a gown, is often
the cause of the flattering attention, which afterwards supports a
fantastic superstructure of self-conceit.

Not having brought a carriage over with me, expecting to have met
a person where I landed, who was immediately to have procured me
one, I was detained whilst the good people of the inn sent round to all
their acquaintance to search for a vehicle. A rude sort of *cabriole* [43]

was at last found, and a driver half drunk, who was not less eager to make a good bargain on that account. I had a Danish captain of a ship and his mate with me: the former was to ride on horseback, at which he was not very expert, and the latter to partake of my seat. The driver mounted behind to guide the horses, and flourish the whip over our shoulders; he would not suffer the reins out of his own hands. There was something so grotesque in our appearance, that I could not avoid shrinking into myself when I saw a gentleman-like man in the group which crowded round the door to observe us. I could have broken the driver's whip for cracking to call the women and children together; but seeing a significant smile on the face, I had before remarked, I burst into a laugh, to allow him to do so too, – and away we flew. This is not a flourish of the pen; for we actually went on full gallop a long time, the horses being very good; indeed I have never met with better, if so good, post-horses, as in Norway; they are of a stouter make than the English horses, appear to be well fed, and are not easily tired.

I had to pass over, I was informed, the most fertile and best cultivated tract of country in Norway. The distance was three Norwegian miles, which are longer than the Swedish. The roads were very good; the farmers are obliged to repair them; and we scampered through a great extent of country in a more improved state than any I had viewed since I left England. Still there was sufficient of hills, dales, and rocks, to prevent the idea of a plain from entering the head, or even of such scenery as England and France afford. The prospects were also embellished by water, rivers, and lakes, before the sea proudly claimed my regard; and the road running frequently through lofty groves, rendered the landscapes beautiful, though they were not so romantic as those I had lately seen with such delight.

It was late when I reached Tønsberg; and I was glad to go to bed at a decent inn. The next morning, the 17th July, conversing with the gentlemen with whom I had business to transact,[44] I found that I should be detained at Tønsberg three weeks; and I lamented that I had not brought my child with me.

The inn was quiet, and my room so pleasant, commanding a view of the sea, confined by an amphitheatre of hanging woods, that I wished to remain there, though no one in the house could speak

English or French. The mayor, my friend, however, sent a young woman to me who spoke a little English, and she agreed to call on me twice a day, to receive my orders, and translate them to my hostess.

My not understanding the language was an excellent pretext for dining alone, which I prevailed on them to let me do at a late hour; for the early dinners in Sweden had entirely deranged my day. I could not alter it there, without disturbing the economy of a family where I was as a visitor; necessity having forced me to accept of an invitation from a private family, the lodgings were so incommodious.

Amongst the Norwegians I had the arrangement of my own time; and I determined to regulate it in such a manner, that I might enjoy as much of their sweet summer as I possibly could; – short, it is true; but 'passing sweet.'⁴⁵

I never endured a winter in this rude clime; consequently it was not the contrast, but the real beauty of the season which made the present summer appear to me the finest I had ever seen. Sheltered from the north and eastern winds, nothing can exceed the salubrity, the soft freshness of the western gales. In the evening they also die away; the aspen leaves tremble into stillness, and reposing nature seems to be warmed by the moon, which here assumes a genial aspect: and if a light shower has chanced to fall with the sun, the juniper the underwood of the forest, exhales a wild perfume, mixed with a thousand nameless sweets, that, soothing the heart, leave images in the memory which the imagination will ever hold dear.

Nature is the nurse of sentiment, – the true source of taste; – yet what misery, as well as rapture, is produced by a quick perception of the beautiful and sublime, when it is exercised in observing animated nature, when every beauteous feeling and emotion excites responsive sympathy, and the harmonized soul sinks into melancholy, or rises to extasy, just as the chords are touched, like the aeolian harp⁴⁶ agitated by the changing wind. But how dangerous is it to foster these sentiments in such an imperfect state of existence; and how difficult to eradicate them when an affection for mankind, a passion for an individual, is but the unfolding of that love which embraces all that is great and beautiful.

When a warm heart has received strong impressions, they are not to be effaced. Emotions become sentiments; and the imagination renders even transient sensations permanent, by fondly retracing them. I cannot, without a thrill of delight, recollect views I have seen, which are not to be forgotten, – nor looks I have felt in every nerve which I shall never more meet. The grave has closed over a dear friend, the friend of my youth;[47] still she is present with me, and I hear her soft voice warbling as I stray over the heath. Fate has separated me from another, the fire of whose eyes, tempered by infantine tenderness, still warms my breast; even when gazing on these tremendous cliffs, sublime emotions absorb my soul. And, smile not, if I add, that the rosy tint of morning reminds me of a suffusion, which will never more charm my senses, unless it reappears on the cheeks of my child. Her sweet blushes I may yet hide in my bosom, and she is still too young to ask why starts the tear, so near akin to pleasure and pain?

I cannot write any more at present. Tomorrow we will talk of Tønsberg.

Letter Seven

Though the king of Denmark be an absolute monarch, yet the Norwegians appear to enjoy all the blessings of freedom. Norway may be termed a sister kingdom; but the people have no viceroy to lord it over them, and fatten his dependants with the fruit of their labour.[48]

There are only two counts in the whole country, who have estates, and exact some feudal observances from their tenantry. All the rest of the country is divided into small farms, which belong to the cultivator. It is true, some few, appertaining to the church, are let; but always on a lease for life, generally renewed in favour of the eldest son, who has this advantage, as well as a right to a double portion of the property. But the value of the farm is estimated; and after this portion is assigned to him, he must be answerable for the residue to the remaining part of the family.

Every farmer, for ten years, is obliged to attend annually about twelve days, to learn the military exercise; but it is always at a small distance from his dwelling, and does not lead him into any new habits of life.

There are about six thousand regulars also, garrisoned at Christiania[49] and Halden, which are equally reserved, with the militia, for the defence of their own country. So that when the prince royal[50] passed into Sweden, in 1788, he was obliged to request, not command, them to accompany him on this expedition.

These corps are mostly composed of the sons of the cottagers, who being labourers on the farms, are allowed a few acres to cultivate for themselves. These men voluntarily enlist; but it is only for a limited period, (six years), at the expiration of which they have the liberty of retiring. The pay is only two-pence a day, and bread; still, considering the cheapness of the country, it is more than sixpence in England.

The distribution of landed property into small farms, produces a degree of equality which I have seldom seen elsewhere; and the rich being all merchants, who are obliged to divide their personal fortune amongst their children, the boys always receiving twice as much as the girls, property has not a chance of accumulating till overgrown wealth destroys the balance of liberty.

You will be surprised to hear me talk of liberty; yet the Norwegians appear to me to be the most free community I have ever observed.

The mayor of each town or district, and the judges in the country, exercise an authority almost patriarchal. They can do much good, but little harm, as every individual can appeal from their judgment: and as they may always be forced to give a reason for their conduct, it is generally regulated by prudence. 'They have not time to learn to be tyrants,' said a gentleman to me, with whom I discussed the subject.

The farmers not fearing to be turned out of their farms, should they displease a man in power, and having no vote to be commanded at an election for a mock representative, are a manly race; for not being obliged to submit to any debasing tenure, in order to live, or advance themselves in the world, they act with an independent spirit. I never yet have heard of any thing like domineering, or oppression, excepting such as has arisen from natural causes. The freedom the people enjoy may, perhaps, render them a little litigious, and subject them to the impositions of cunning practitioners of the law; but the authority of office is bounded, and the emoluments of it do not destroy its utility.

Last year a man, who had abused his power, was cashiered, on the representation of the people to the bailiff of the district.

There are four in Norway, who might with propriety be termed sheriffs; and, from their sentence, an appeal, by either party, may be made to Copenhagen.[51]

Near most of the towns are commons, on which the cows of all the inhabitants, indiscriminately, are allowed to graze. The poor, to whom a cow is necessary, are almost supported by it. Besides, to render living more easy, they all go out to fish in their own boats; and fish is their principal food.

The lower class of people in the towns are in general sailors; and the industrious have usually little ventures of their own that serve to render the winter comfortable.

With respect to the country at large, the importation is considerably in favour of Norway.

They are forbidden, at present, to export corn or rye, on account of the advanced price.

The restriction which most resembles the painful subordination of Ireland, is that vessels, trading to the West Indies, are obliged to pass by their own ports, and unload their cargoes at Copenhagen, which they afterwards re-ship.[52] The duty is indeed inconsiderable; but the navigation being dangerous, they run a double risk.

There is an excise on all articles of consumption brought to the towns; but the officers are not strict; and it would be reckoned invidious to enter a house to search, as in England.

The Norwegians appear to me a sensible, shrewd people, with little scientific knowledge, and still less taste for literature: but they are arriving at the epoch which precedes the introduction of the arts and sciences.

Most of the towns are sea-ports, and sea-ports are not favourable to improvement. The captains acquire a little superficial knowledge by travelling, which their indefatigable attention to the making of money prevents their digesting; and the fortune that they thus laboriously acquire, is spent, as it usually is in towns of this description, in show and good living. They love their country, but have not much public spirit.* Their exertions are, generally speaking, only for their families; which I conceive will always be the case, till politics, becoming a subject of discussion, enlarges the heart by opening the understanding. The French revolution will have this effect.[53] They sing at present, with great glee, many republican songs, and seem earnestly to wish that the republic may stand; yet they appear very much attached to their prince royal; and, as far as rumour can give an idea of a character, he appears to merit their attachment. When I am at Copenhagen, I shall be able to ascertain on what foundation their good opinion is built; at present I am only the echo of it.

In the year 1788 he[54] travelled through Norway; and acts of mercy gave dignity to the parade, and interest to the joy, his presence

* The grand virtues of the heart particularly the enlarged humanity which extends to the whole human race, depend more on the understanding, I believe, than is generally imagined.

inspired. At this town he pardoned a girl condemned to die for murdering an illegitimate child, a crime seldom committed in this country. She is since married, and become the careful mother of a family. This might be given as an instance, that a desperate act is not always a proof of an incorrigible depravity of character; the only plausible excuse that has been brought forward to justify the infliction of capital punishments.

I will relate two or three other anecdotes to you; for the truth of which I will not vouch, because the facts were not of sufficient consequence for me to take much pains to ascertain them; and, true or false, they evince that the people like to make a kind of mistress of their prince.

An officer, mortally wounded at the ill-advised battle of Kvistram, desired to speak with the prince; and, with his dying breath, earnestly recommended to his care a young woman of Christiania, to whom he was engaged. When the prince returned there, a ball was given by the chief inhabitants. He inquired whether this unfortunate girl was invited, and requested that she might, though of the second class. The girl came; she was pretty; and finding herself amongst her superiors, bashfully sat down as near the door as possible, nobody taking notice of her. Shortly after, the prince entering, immediately inquired for her, and asked her to dance, to the mortification of the rich dames. After it was over he handed her to the top of the room, and placing himself by her, spoke of the loss she had sustained, with tenderness, promising to provide for any one she should marry, – as the story goes. She is since married, and he has not forgotten his promise.

A little girl, during the same expedition, in Sweden, who informed him that the logs of a bridge were cut underneath, was taken by his orders to Christiania, and put to school at his expence.

Before I retail other beneficial effects of his journey, it is necessary to inform you that the laws here are mild, and do not punish capitally for any crime but murder, which seldom occurs. Every other offence merely subjects the delinquent to imprisonment and labour in the castle, or rather arsenal, at Christiania, and the fortress at Halden. The first and second conviction produces a sentence for a limited number of years, – two, three, five, or seven, proportioned to the atrocity of the crime. After the third he is whipped, branded in the forehead, and condemned to perpetual slavery. This is the ordinary march of justice. For some flagrant breaches of trust, or acts of wanton cruelty, criminals have been condemned to slavery for life, the first time of conviction, but not frequently. The number of these slaves do not, I am informed, amount to more than an hundred, which is not considerable, compared with the population, upwards of eight hundred thousand. Should I pass through Christiania, on my return to Gothenburg, I shall probably have an opportunity of learning other particulars.

There is also a house of correction at Christiania for trifling misdemeanors, where the women are confined to labour and imprisonment even for life. The state of the prisoners was represented to the prince; in consequence of which, he visited the arsenal and house of correction. The slaves at the arsenal were loaded with irons of a great weight; he ordered them to be lightened as much as possible.

The people in the house of correction were commanded not to speak to him; but four women, condemned to remain there for life, got into the passage, and fell at his feet. He granted them a pardon; and inquiring respecting the treatment of the prisoners, he was informed that they were frequently whipt going in, and coming out; and for any fault, at the discretion of the inspectors. This custom he humanely abolished; though some of the principal inhabitants, whose situation in life had raised them above the temptation of stealing, were of opinion that these chastisements were necessary and wholesome.

In short, every thing seems to announce that the prince really cherishes the laudable ambition of fulfilling the duties of his station. This ambition is cherished and directed by the count Bernstorff,[55] the prime minister of Denmark, who is universally celebrated for his abilities and virtue. The happiness of the people is a substantial eulogium; and, from all I can gather, the inhabitants of Denmark and Norway are the least oppressed people of Europe. The press is free. They translate any of the French publications of the day, deliver their opinion on the subject, and discuss those it leads to with great freedom, and without fearing to displease the government.

On the subject of religion they are likewise becoming tolerant, at least, and perhaps have advanced a step further in free-thinking. One writer has ventured to deny the divinity of Jesus Christ, and to question the necessity or utility of the christian system, without being considered universally as a monster, which would have been the case a few years ago. They have translated many German works on education; and though they have not adopted any of their plans, it is become a subject of discussion. There are some grammar and free schools; but, from what I hear, not very good ones. All the children learn to read, write, and cast accounts, for the purposes of common life. They have no university;[56] and nothing that deserves the name of science is taught; nor do individuals, by pursuing any branch of knowledge, excite a degree of curiosity which is the forerunner of improvement. Knowledge is not absolutely necessary to enable a considerable portion of the community to live; and, till it is, I fear, it never becomes general.

In this country, where minerals abound, there is not one collection: and, in all probability, I venture a conjecture, the want of mechanical and chemical knowledge renders the silver mines unproductive; for the quantity of silver obtained every year is not sufficient to defray the expenses. It has been urged, that the employment of such a number of hands is very beneficial. But a positive loss is never to be done away; and the men, thus employed, would naturally find some other means of living, instead of being thus a dead weight on government, or rather on the community from whom its revenue is drawn.

About three English miles from Tønsberg there is a salt work, belonging, like all their establishments, to government, in which they employ above an hundred and fifty men, and maintain nearly five hundred people, who earn their living. The clear profit, an increasing one, amounts to two thousand pounds sterling. And as the eldest son of the inspector, an ingenious young man, has been sent by the government to travel, and acquire some mathematical and chemical knowledge in Germany, it has a chance of being improved. He is the only person I have met with here, who appears to have a scientific turn of mind. I do not mean to assert that I have not met with others, who have a spirit of inquiry.

The salt-works at St Ubes are basins in the sand, and the sun produces the evaporation; but here there is no beach. Besides, the heat of summer is so short-lived, that it would be idle to contrive machines for such an inconsiderable portion of the year. They therefore always use fires; and the whole establishment appears to be regulated with judgment.

The situation is well chosen and beautiful. I do not find, from the observation of a person who has resided here for forty years, that the sea advances or recedes on this coast.

I have already remarked, that little attention is paid to education, excepting reading, writing, and the rudiments of arithmetic; I ought to have added, that a catechism is carefully taught, and the children obliged to read in the churches, before the congregation, to prove that they are not neglected.

Degrees, to enable any one to practise any profession, must be taken at Copenhagen; and the people of this country, having the good sense to perceive that men who are to live in a community should at least acquire the elements of their knowledge, and form their youthful attachments there, are seriously endeavouring to establish an university in Norway. And Tønsberg, as a centrical place in the best part of the country, had the most suffrages; for, experiencing the bad effects of a metropolis, they have determined not to have it in or near Christiania. Should such an establishment take place, it will promote inquiry throughout the country, and give a new face to society. Premiums have been offered, and prize questions written, which I am told have merit. The building college-halls, and other appendages of the seat of science, might enable Tønsberg to recover its pristine consequence; for it is one of the most ancient towns of Norway, and once contained nine churches. At present there are only two. One is a very old structure, and has a gothic respectability about it, which scarcely amounts to grandeur, because, to render a gothic pile grand, it must have a huge unwieldiness of appearance. The chapel of Windsor may be an exception to this rule; I mean before it was in its present *nice*, *clean* state. When I first saw it, the pillars within had acquired, by time, a sombre hue, which accorded with the architecture; and the gloom increased its dimensions to the eye by hiding its parts; but now it all bursts on the view at once; and the sublimity has vanished before the brush and broom; for it has been whitewashed and scraped till it is become as bright and neat as the pots and pans in a notable house-wife's kitchen – yes; the very spurs on the recumbent knights were deprived of their venerable rust, to give a striking proof that a love of order in trifles, and taste for proportion and arrangement, are very distinct. The glare of light thus introduced, entirely destroys the sentiment these piles are calculated to inspire; so that, when I heard something like a jig from the organ-loft, I thought it an excellent hall for dancing or feasting. The measured pace of thought with which I had entered the cathedral, changed into a trip; and I bounded on the terrace, to see the royal family, with a number of ridiculous images in my head, that I shall not now recall.[57]

The Norwegians are fond of music; and every little church has an organ. In the church I have mentioned, there is an inscription importing that a king,* James the sixth, of Scotland, and first of England, who came with more than princely gallantry, to escort his bride home, stood there, and heard divine service.

There is a little recess full of coffins, which contains bodies embalmed long since – so long, that there is not even a tradition to lead to a guess at their names.

A desire of preserving the body seems to have prevailed in most countries of the world, futile as it is to term it a preservation, when the noblest parts are immediately sacrificed merely to save the muscles, skin and bone from rottenness. When I was shewn these human petrifactions, I shrunk back with disgust and horror. 'Ashes to ashes!' thought I – 'Dust to dust!' – If this be not dissolution, it is something

---

* 'Anno 1589, St Martin's Day, which was the 11th Day of November, on a Tuesday, came the high-born Prince and Lord Jacob Stuart, King in Scotland, to this Town, and the 25th Sunday after Trinity which was the 16th Day of November, stood his Grace in this Pew, and heard Scotch Preaching from the 23rd Psalm, "The Lord is my Shepherd," &c. which M. David Lentz, Preacher in Leith, then preached between 10 and 12.'

The above is an inscription which stands in St Mary's church, in Tønsberg.

It is known that king James the sixth went to Norway, to marry Princess Anna, the daughter of Frederick the second, and sister to Christian the fourth; and that the wedding was performed at Opslo (now Christiania), where the princess, by contrary winds, was detained; but that the king, during this voyage, was at Tønsberg, nobody would have known, if an inscription, in remembrance of it, had not been placed in this church.

worse than natural decay. It is treason against humanity, thus to lift up the awful veil which would fain hide its weakness. The grandeur of the active principle is never more strongly felt than at such a sight; for nothing is so ugly as the human form when deprived of life, and thus dried into stone, merely to preserve the most disgusting image of death. The contemplation of noble ruins produces a melancholy that exalts the mind. – We take a retrospect of the exertions of man, the fate of empires and their rulers; and marking the grand destruction of ages, it seems the necessary change of time leading to improvement. – Our very soul expands, and we forget our littleness; how painfully brought to our recollection by such vain attempts to snatch from decay what is destined so soon to perish. Life, what art thou? Where goes this breath? this *I*, so much alive? In what element will it mix, giving or receiving fresh energy? – What will break the enchantment of animation? – For worlds, I would not see a form I loved – embalmed in my heart – thus sacrilegiously handled! – Pugh! my stomach turns. – Is this all the distinction of the rich in the grave? – They had better quietly allow the scythe of equality to mow them down with the common mass, than struggle to become a monument of the instability of human greatness.

The teeth, nails and skin were whole, without appearing black like the Egyptian mummies; and some silk, in which they had been wrapt, still preserved its colour, pink, with tolerable freshness.

I could not learn how long the bodies had been in this state, in which they bid fair to remain till the day of judgment, if there is to be such a day; and before that time, it will require some trouble to make them fit to appear in company with angels, without disgracing humanity. – God bless you! I feel a conviction that we have some perfectible principle in our present vestment, which will not be destroyed just as we begin to be sensible of improvement; and I care not what habit it next puts on, sure that it will be wisely formed to suit a higher state of existence. Thinking of death makes us tenderly cling to our affections – with more than usual tenderness, I therefore assure you that I am your's, wishing that the temporary death of absence may not endure longer than is absolutely necessary.

Letter Eight

Tønsberg was formerly the residence of one of the little sovereigns of Norway; and on an adjacent mountain the vestiges of a fort remain which was battered down by the Swedes; the entrance of the bay lying close to it.

Here I have frequently strayed, sovereign of the waste, I seldom met any human creature; and sometimes, reclining on the mossy down, under the shelter of a rock, the prattling of the sea amongst the pebbles has lulled me to sleep – no fear of any rude satyr's approaching to interrupt my repose. Balmy were the slumbers, and soft the gales, that refreshed me, when I awoke to follow, with an eye vaguely curious, the white sails, as they turned the cliffs, or seemed to take shelter under the pines which covered the little islands that so gracefully rose to render the terrific ocean beautiful. The fishermen were calmly casting their nets; whilst the seagulls hovered over the unruffled deep. Every thing seemed to harmonize into tranquillity – even the mournful call of the bittern was in cadence with the tinkling bells on the necks of the cows, that, pacing slowly one after the other, along an inviting path in the vale below, were repairing to the cottages to be milked. With what ineffable pleasure have I not gazed – and gazed again, losing my breath through my eyes – my very soul diffused itself in the scene – and, seeming to become all senses, glided in the scarcely-agitated waves, melted in the freshening breeze, or, taking its flight with fairy wing, to the misty mountains which bounded the prospect, fancy tript over new lawns, more beautiful even than the lovely slopes on the winding shore before me. – I pause, again breathless, to trace, with renewed delight, sentiments which entranced me, when, turning my humid eyes from the expanse below to the vault above, my sight pierced the fleecy clouds that softened the azure brightness; and, imperceptibly recalling the reveries of childhood, I bowed before the awful throne of my Creator, whilst I rested on its footstool.[58]

You have sometimes wondered, my dear friend, at the extreme affection of my nature – But such is the temperature of my soul – It is not the vivacity of youth, the hey-day of existence. For years have I endeavoured to calm an impetuous tide – labouring to make my feelings take an orderly course. – It was striving against the stream. – I must love and admire with warmth, or I sink into sadness. Tokens of love which I have received have rapt me in elysium – purifying the heart they enchanted. – My bosom still glows. – Do not saucily ask, repeating Sterne's question, 'Maria, is it still so warm!'[59] Sufficiently, O my God! has it been chilled by sorrow and unkindness – still nature will prevail – and if I blush at recollecting past enjoyment, it is the rosy hue of pleasure heightened by modesty; for the blush of modesty and shame are as distinct as the emotions by which they are produced.

I need scarcely inform you, after telling you of my walks, that my constitution has been renovated here; and that I have recovered my activity, even whilst attaining a little *embonpoint*. My imprudence last winter, and some untoward accidents just at the time I was weaning my child, had reduced me to a state of weakness which I never before experienced. A slow fever preyed on me every night, during my residence in Sweden, and after I arrived at Tønsberg. By chance I found a fine rivulet filtered through the rocks, and confined in a basin for the cattle. It tasted to me like a chalybeate;[60] at any rate it was pure; and the good effect of the various waters which invalids are sent to drink, depends, I believe, more on the air, exercise and change of scene, than on their medicinal qualities. I therefore determined to turn my morning walks towards it, and seek for health from the nymph of the fountain; partaking of the beverage offered to the tenants of the shade.

Chance likewise led me to discover a new pleasure, equally beneficial to my health. I wished to avail myself of my vicinity to the sea, and bathe;[61] but it was not possible near the town; there was no convenience. The young woman whom I mentioned to you, proposed rowing me across the water, amongst the rocks; but as she was pregnant, I insisted on taking one of the oars, and learning to row. It was not difficult; and I do not know a pleasanter exercise. I soon became expert, and my train of thinking kept time, as it were, with the oars, or I suffered the boat to be carried along by the current, indulging a pleasing forgetfulness, or fallacious hopes. – How fallacious! yet, without hope, what is to sustain life, but the fear of annihilation – the only thing of which I have ever felt a dread – I cannot bear to think of being no more – of losing myself – though existence is often but a painful consciousness of misery; nay, it appears to me impossible that I should cease to exist, or that this active, restless spirit, equally alive to joy and sorrow, should only be organized dust – ready to fly abroad the moment the spring snaps, or the spark goes out, which kept it together. Surely something resides in this heart that is not perishable – and life is more than a dream.

Sometimes, to take up my oar, once more, when the sea was calm, I was amused by disturbing the innumerable young star fish [62] which floated just below the surface: I had never observed them before; for they have not a hard shell, like those which I have seen on the sea-shore. They look like thickened water, with a white edge; and four purple circles, of different forms, were in the middle, over an incredible number of fibres, or white lines. Touching them, the cloudy substance would turn or close, first on one side, then on the other, very gracefully; but when I took one of them up in the ladle with which I heaved the water out of the boat, it appeared only a colourless jelly.

I did not see any of the seals, numbers of which followed our boat when we landed in Sweden; for though I like to sport in the water, I should have had no desire to join in their gambols.

Enough, you will say, of inanimate nature, and of brutes, to use the lordly phrase of man; let me hear something of the inhabitants.

The gentleman with whom I had business, is the mayor of Tønsberg; he speaks English intelligibly; and, having a sound understanding, I was sorry that his numerous occupations prevented my gaining as much information from him as I could have drawn forth, had we frequently conversed. The people of the town, as far as I had an opportunity of knowing their sentiments, are extremely well satisfied with his manner of discharging his office. He has a degree of information and good sense which excites respect, whilst a chearfulness, almost amounting to gaiety, enables him to reconcile differences, and keep his neighbours in good humour. – 'I lost my horse,' said a woman to me; 'but ever since, when I want to send to the mill, or go out, the mayor lends me one. – He scolds if I do not come for it.'

A criminal was branded, during my stay here, for the third offence; but the relief he received made him declare that the judge was one of the best men in the world.

I sent this wretch a trifle, at different times, to take with him into slavery. As it was more than he expected, he wished very much to see me; and this wish brought to my remembrance an anecdote I heard when I was in Lisbon.[63]

A wretch who had been imprisoned several years, during which period lamps had been put up, was at last condemned to a cruel death; yet, in his way to execution, he only wished for one night's respite, to see the city lighted.

Having dined in company at the mayor's, I was invited with his family to spend the day at one of the richest merchant's houses. – Though I could not speak Danish, I knew that I could see a great deal: yes, I am persuaded that I have formed a very just opinion of the character of the Norwegians, without being able to hold converse with them.

I had expected to meet some company; yet was a little disconcerted at being ushered into an apartment full of well-dressed people; and, glancing my eyes round, they rested on several very pretty faces. Rosy cheeks, sparkling eyes, and light brown or golden locks; for I never saw so much hair with a yellow cast; and, with their fine complexions, it looked very becoming.

These women seem a mixture of indolence and vivacity; they scarcely ever walk out, and were astonished that I should, for pleasure; yet they are immoderately fond of dancing. Unaffected in their manners, if they have no pretensions to elegance, simplicity often produces a gracefulness of deportment, when they are animated by a particular desire to please – which was the case at present. The solitariness of my situation, which they thought terrible, interested them very much in my favour. They gathered round me – sung to me – and one of the prettiest, to whom I gave my hand, with some degree of cordiality, to meet the glance of her eyes, kissed me very affectionately.[64]

At dinner, which was conducted with great hospitality, though we remained at table too long, they sung several songs, and, amongst the rest, translations of some patriotic French ones. As the evening advanced, they became playful, and we kept up a sort of conversation of gestures. As their minds were totally uncultivated, I did not lose much, perhaps gained, by not being able to understand them; for fancy probably filled up, more to their advantage, the void in the picture. Be that as it may, they excited my sympathy; and I was very much flattered when I was told, the next day, that they said it was a pleasure to look at me, I appeared so good-natured.

The men were generally captains of ships. Several spoke English very tolerably; but they were merely matter of fact men, confined to a very narrow circle of observation. I found it difficult to obtain from them any information respecting their own country, when the fumes of tobacco did not keep me at a distance.

I was invited to partake of some other feasts, and always had to complain of the quantity of provision, and the length of time taken to consume it; for it would not have been proper to have said devour, all went on so fair and softly. The servants wait as slowly as their mistresses carve.

The young women here, as well as in Sweden, have commonly bad teeth, which I attribute to the same causes. They are fond of finery, but do not pay the necessary attention to their persons, to render beauty less transient than a flower; and that interesting expression which sentiment and accomplishments give, seldom supplies its place.

The servants have likewise an inferior sort of food here; but their masters are not allowed to strike them with impunity. I might have added mistresses; for it was a complaint of this kind, brought before the mayor, which led me to a knowledge of the fact.

The wages are low, which is particularly unjust, because the price of clothes is much higher than provisions. A young woman, who is wet nurse to the mistress of the inn where I lodge, receives only twelve dollars a year, and pays ten for the nursing of her own child; the father had run away to get clear of the expense. There was something in this most painful state of widowhood which excited my compassion, and led me to reflections on the instability of the most flattering plans of happiness, that were painful in the extreme, till I was ready to ask whether this world was not created to exhibit every possible combination of wretchedness. I asked these questions of a heart writhing with anguish, whilst I listened to a melancholy ditty sung by this poor girl. It was too early for thee to be abandoned, thought I, and I hastened out of the house, to take my solitary evening's walk – And here I am again, to talk of any thing, but the pangs arising from the discovery of estranged affection, and the lonely sadness of a deserted heart.[65]

The father and mother, if the father can be ascertained, are obliged to maintain an illegitimate child at their joint expense; but, should the father disappear, go up the country or to sea, the mother must maintain it herself. However, accidents of this kind do not prevent their marrying; and then it is not unusual to take the child or children home; and they are brought up very amicably with the marriage progeny.

I took some pains to learn what books were written originally in their language; but for any certain information respecting the state of Danish literature, I must wait till I arrive at Copenhagen.

The sound of the language is soft, a great proportion of the words ending in vowels; and there is a simplicity in the turn of some of the phrases which have been translated to me, that pleased and interested me. In the country, the farmers use the *thou* and *thee*; and they do not acquire the polite plurals of the towns by meeting at market. The not having markets established in the large towns appears to me a great inconvenience. When the farmers have any thing to sell, they bring it to the neighbouring town, and take it from house to house. I am surprised that the inhabitants do not feel how very incommodious this usage is to both parties, and redress it. They indeed perceive it; for when I have introduced the subject, they acknowledged that they were often in want of necessaries, there being no butchers, and they were often obliged to buy what they did not want; yet it was the *custom*; and the changing of customs of a long standing requires more energy than they yet possess. I received a similar reply, when I attempted to persuade the women that they injured their children by keeping them too warm. The only way of parrying off my reasoning was, that they must do as other people did. In short, reason on any subject of change, and they stop you by saying that 'the town would talk.' A person of sense, with a large fortune, to insure respect, might be very useful here, by inducing them to treat their children, and manage their sick properly, and eat food dressed in a simpler manner: the example, for instance, of a count's lady.

Reflecting on these prejudices made me revert to the wisdom of those legislators who established institutions for the good of the body, under the pretext of serving heaven for the salvation of the soul. These might with strict propriety be termed pious frauds; and I admire the Peruvian pair for asserting that they came from the sun,[66] when their conduct proved that they meant to enlighten a benighted country, whose obedience, or even attention, could only be secured by awe.

Thus much for conquering the *inertia* of reason; but, when it is once in motion, fables, once held sacred, may be ridiculed; and sacred they were, when useful to mankind. – Prometheus[67] alone stole fire to animate the first man; his posterity need not supernatural aid to preserve the species, though love is generally termed a flame; and it may not be necessary much longer to suppose men inspired by heaven to inculcate the duties which demand special grace, when reason convinces them that they are the happiest who are the most nobly employed.

In a few days I am to set out for the western part of Norway, and then shall return by land to Gothenburg. I cannot think of leaving this place without regret. I speak of the place before the inhabitants, though there is a tenderness in their artless kindness which attaches me to them; but it is an attachment that inspires a regret very different from that I felt at leaving Hull, in my way to Sweden. The domestic happiness, and good-humoured gaiety, of the amiable family where I and my Frances were so hospitably received, would have been sufficient to insure the tenderest remembrance, without the recollection of the social evenings to stimulate it, when good-breeding gave dignity to sympathy, and wit, zest to reason.

Adieu! – I am just informed that my horse has been waiting this quarter of an hour. I now venture to ride out alone. The steeple serves as a land-mark. I once or twice lost my way, walking alone, without being able to inquire after a path. I was therefore obliged to make to the steeple, or wind-mill, over hedge and ditch.

Your's truly

Letter Nine

I have already informed you that there are only two noblemen who have estates of any magnitude in Norway. One of these has a house near Tønsberg, at which he has not resided for some years, having been at court, or on embassies. He is now the Danish ambassador in London. The house is pleasantly situated, and the grounds about it fine; but their neglected appearance plainly tells that there is nobody at home.

A stupid kind of sadness, to my eye, always reigns in a huge habitation where only servants live to put cases on the furniture and open the windows. I enter as I would into the tomb of the Capulets,[68] to look at the family pictures that here frown in armour, or smile in ermine. The mildew respects not the lordly robe; and the worm riots unchecked on the cheek of beauty.

There was nothing in the architecture of the building, or the form of the furniture, to detain me from the avenue where the aged pines stretched along majestically. Time had given a greyish cast to their ever-green foliage; and they stood, like sires of the forest, sheltered on all sides by a rising progeny. I had not ever seen so many oaks together in Norway, as in these woods, nor such large aspens as here were agitated by the breeze, rendering the wind audible – nay, musical; for melody seemed on the wing around me. How different was the fresh odour that re-animated me in the avenue, from the damp chillness of the apartments; and as little did the gloomy thoughtfulness excited by the dusty hangings, and worm-eaten pictures, resemble the reveries inspired by the soothing melancholy of their shade. In the winter, these august pines, towering above the snow, must relieve the eye beyond measure, and give life to the white waste.

The continual recurrence of pine and fir groves, in the day, sometimes wearies the sight; but, in the evening, nothing can be more picturesque, or, more properly speaking, better calculated to produce poetical images. Passing through them, I have been struck with a mystic kind of reverence, and I did, as it were, homage to their venerable shadows. Not nymphs, but philosophers, seemed to inhabit them – ever musing; I could scarcely conceive that they were without some consciousness of existence – without a calm enjoyment of the pleasure they diffused.

How often do my feelings produce ideas that remind me of the origin of many poetical fictions. In solitude, the imagination bodies forth its conceptions unrestrained, and stops enraptured to adore the beings of its own creation. These are moments of bliss; and the memory recalls them with delight.

But I have almost forgotten the matters of fact I meant to relate, respecting the counts. They have the presentation of the livings on their estates, appoint the judges, and different civil officers, the crown reserving to itself the privilege of sanctioning them. But, though they appoint, they cannot dismiss. Their tenants also occupy their farms for life, and are obliged to obey any summons to work on the part he reserves for himself; but they are paid for their labour. In short, I have seldom heard of any noblemen so innoxious.

Observing that the gardens round the count's estate were better cultivated than any I had before seen, I was led to reflect on the advantages which naturally accrue from the feudal tenures. The tenants of the count are obliged to work at a stated price, in his grounds and garden; and the instruction which they imperceptibly receive from the head gardener, tends to render them useful, and makes them, in the common course of things, better husbandmen and gardeners on their own little farms. Thus the great, who alone travel, in this period of society, for the observation of manners and customs made by sailors is very confined, bring home improvement to promote their own comfort, which is gradually spread abroad amongst the people, till they are stimulated to think for themselves.

The bishops have not large revenues; and the priests are appointed by the king before they come to them to be ordained. There is commonly some little farm annexed to the parsonage; and the inhabitants subscribe voluntarily, three times a year, in addition to the church fees, for the support of the clergyman. The church lands were seized when lutheranism was introduced; the desire of obtaining them being probably the real stimulus of reformation. The tithes, which are never required in kind, are divided into three parts; one to the king, another to the incumbent, and the third to repair the delapidations of the parsonage. They do not amount to much. And the stipend allowed to the different civil officers is also too small, scarcely deserving to be termed an independence; that of the custom-house officers is not sufficient to procure the necessaries of life – no wonder, then, if necessity leads them to knavery. Much public virtue cannot be expected till every employment, putting perquisites out of the question, has a salary sufficient to reward industry, whilst none are so great as to permit the possessor to remain idle. It is this want of proportion between profit and labour [69] which debases men, producing the sycophantic appellations of patron and client; and that pernicious *esprit du corps*, proverbially vicious.

The farmers are hospitable, as well as independent. Offering once to pay for some coffee I drank when taking shelter from the rain, I was asked, rather angrily, if a little coffee was worth paying for. They smoke, and drink drams; but not so much as formerly. Drunkenness, often the attendant disgrace of hospitality,will here, as well as every where else, give place to gallantry and refinement of manners; but the change will not be suddenly produced.

The people of every class are constant in their attendance at church; they are very fond of dancing: and the Sunday evenings in Norway, as in catholic countries, are spent in exercises which exhilerate the spirits, without vitiating the heart. The rest of labour ought to be gay; and the gladness I have felt in France on a Sunday, or decadi,[70] which I caught from the faces around me, was a sentiment more truly religious than all the stupid stillness which the streets of London ever inspired where the sabbath is so decorously observed. I recollect, in the country parts of England the churchwardens used to go out, during the service, to see if they could catch any luckless wight playing at bowls or skittles; yet what could be more harmless? It would even, I think, be a great advantage to the English, if feats of activity, I do not include boxing matches, were encouraged on a Sunday, as it might stop the progress of methodism, and of that fanatical spirit which appears to be gaining ground. I was surprised when I visited Yorkshire in my way to Sweden, to find that sullen narrowness of thinking had made such a progress since I was an inhabitant of the country. I could hardly have supposed that sixteen or seventeen years could have produced such an alteration for the worse in the morals of a place; yes, I say morals; for observance of forms, and avoiding of practices, indifferent in themselves, often supplies the place of that regular attention to duties which are so natural, that they seldom are vauntingly exercised, though they are worth all the precepts of the law and the prophets. Besides, many of these deluded people, with the best meaning, actually lose their reason, and become miserable, the dread of damnation throwing them into a state which merits the term: and still more, in running after their preachers, expecting to promote their salvation, they disregard their welfare in this world, and neglect the interest and comfort of their families: so that in proportion as they attain a reputation for piety, they become idle.

Aristocracy and fanaticism seem equally to be gaining ground in England, particularly in the place I have mentioned: I saw very little of either in Norway. The people are regular in their attendance on public worship; but religion does not interfere with their employments.

As the farmers cut away the wood, they clear the ground. Every year, therefore, the country is becoming fitter to support the inhabitants. Half a century ago the Dutch, I am told, only paid for the cutting down of the wood, and the farmers were glad to get rid of it without giving themselves any trouble. At present they form a just estimate of its value; nay, I was surprised to find even fire wood so dear, when it appears to be in such plenty. The destruction, or gradual reduction, of their forests, will probably meliorate the climate; and their manners will naturally improve in the same ratio as industry requires ingenuity. It is very fortunate that men are, a long time, but just above the brute creation, or the greater part of the earth would never have been rendered habitable; because it is the patient labour of men, who are only seeking for a subsistence, which produces whatever embellishes existence, affording leisure for the cultivation of the arts and sciences, that lift man so far above his first state. I never, my friend, thought so deeply of the advantages obtained by human industry as since I have been in Norway. The world requires, I see, the hand of man to perfect it; and as this task naturally unfolds the faculties he exercises, it is physically impossible that he should have remained in Rousseau's golden age of stupidity.[71] And, considering the question of human happiness, where, oh! where does it reside? Has it taken up its abode with unconscious ignorance, or with the high-wrought mind? Is it the offspring of thoughtless animal spirits, or the elf of fancy continually flitting round the expected pleasure?

The increasing population of the earth must necessarily tend to its improvement, as the means of existence are multiplied by invention.

You have probably made similar reflections in America, where the face of the country, I suppose, resembles the wilds of Norway. I am delighted with the romantic views I daily contemplate, animated by the purest air; and I am interested by the simplicity of manners which reigns around me. Still nothing so soon wearies out the feelings as unmarked simplicity. I am, therefore, half convinced, that I could not live very comfortably exiled from the countries where mankind are so much further advanced in knowledge, imperfect as it is, and unsatisfactory to the thinking mind. Even now I begin to long to hear what you are doing in England and France. My thoughts fly from this wilderness to the polished circles of the world, till recollecting its vices and follies, I bury myself in the woods, but find it necessary to emerge again, that I may not lose sight of the wisdom and virtue which exalts my nature.

What a long time it requires to know ourselves; and yet almost every one has more of this knowledge than he is willing to own, even to himself. I cannot immediately determine whether I ought to rejoice at having turned over in this solitude a new page in the history of my own heart, though I may venture to assure you that a further acquaintance with mankind only tends to increase my respect for your judgment, and esteem for your character.

Farewell!

Letter Ten

I have once more, my friend, taken flight; for I left Tønsberg yesterday; but with an intention of returning, in my way back to Sweden.

The road to Larvik is very fine, and the country the best cultivated in Norway. I never before admired the beech tree; and when I met stragglers here, they pleased me still less. Long and lank, they would have forced me to allow that the line of beauty requires some curves, if the stately pine, standing near, erect, throwing her vast arms around, had not looked beautiful, in opposition to such narrow rules.

In these respects my very reason obliges me to permit my feelings to be my criterion. Whatever excites emotion has charms for me; though I insist that the cultivation of the mind, by warming, nay almost creating the imagination, produces taste, and an immense variety of sensations and emotions, partaking of the exquisite pleasure inspired by beauty and sublimity. As I know of no end to them, the word infinite, so often misapplied, might, on this occasion, be introduced with something like propriety.

But I have rambled away again. I intended to have remarked to you the effect produced by a grove of towering beech. The airy lightness of their foliage admitting a degree of sunshine, which, giving a transparency to the leaves, exhibited an appearance of freshness and elegance that I had never before remarked, I thought of descriptions of Italian scenery. But these evanescent graces seemed the effect of enchantment; and I imperceptibly breathed softly, lest I should destroy what was real, yet looked so like the creation of fancy. Dryden's fable of the flower and the leaf was not a more poetical reverie.[72]

Adieu, however, to fancy, and to all the sentiments which ennoble our nature. I arrived at Larvik, and found myself in the midst of a group of lawyers, of different descriptions. My head turned round, my heart grew sick, as I regarded visages deformed by vice; and listened to accounts of chicanery that were continually embroiling the ignorant. These locusts will probably diminish, as the people become more enlightened. In this period of social life the commonalty are always cunningly attentive to their own interest; but their faculties, confined to a few objects, are so narrowed, that they cannot discover it in the general good. The profession of the law renders a set of men still shrewder and more selfish than the rest; and it is these men, whose wits have been sharpened by knavery, who here undermine morality, confounding right and wrong.

The count of Bernstorff, who really appears to me, from all I can gather, to have the good of the people at heart, aware of this, has lately sent to the mayor of each district to name, according to the size of the place, four or six of the best-informed inhabitants, not men of the law, out of which the citizens were to elect two, who are to be termed *mediators*. Their office is to endeavour to prevent litigious suits, and conciliate differences. And no suit is to be commenced before the parties have discussed the dispute at their weekly meeting. If a reconciliation should, in consequence, take place, it is to be registered, and the parties are not allowed to retract.

By these means ignorant people will be prevented from applying for advice to men who may justly be termed stirrers-up of strife. They have, for a long time, to use a significant vulgarism, set the people by the ears, and lived by the spoil they caught up in the scramble. There is some reason to hope that this regulation will diminish their number, and restrain their mischievous activity. But till trials by jury are established, little justice can be expected in Norway.[73] Judges who cannot be bribed are often timid, and afraid of offending bold knaves, lest they should raise a set of hornets about themselves. The fear of censure undermines all energy of character; and, labouring to be prudent, they lose sight of rectitude. Besides, nothing is left to their conscience, or sagacity; they must be governed by evidence, though internally convinced that it is false.

There is a considerable iron manufactory at Larvik, for coarse work, and a lake near the town supplies the water necessary for working several mills belonging to it.

This establishment belongs to the count of Larvik. Without a fortune, and influence equal to his, such a work could not have been set afloat; personal fortunes are not yet sufficient to support such undertakings; nevertheless the inhabitants of the town speak of the size of his estate as an evil, because it obstructs commerce. The occupiers of small farms are obliged to bring their wood to the neighbouring sea-ports, to be shipped; but he, wishing to increase the value of his, will not allow it to be thus gradually cut down; which turns the trade into another channel. Added to this, nature is against them, the bay being open and insecure. I could not help smiling when I was informed that in a hard gale a vessel had been wrecked in the main street. When there are such a number of excellent harbours on the coast, it is a pity that accident has made one of the largest towns grow up in a bad one.

The father of the present count was a distant relation of the family; he resided constantly in Denmark; and his son follows his example. They have not been in possession of the estate many years; and their predecessor lived near the town, introducing a degree of profligacy of manners which has been ruinous to the inhabitants in every respect, their fortunes not being equal to the prevailing extravagance.

What little I have seen of the manners of the people does not please me so well as those of Tønsberg. I am forewarned that I shall find them still more cunning and fraudulent as I advance towards the westward, in proportion as traffic takes place of agriculture; for their towns are built on naked rocks; the streets are narrow bridges; and the inhabitants are all seafaring men, or owners of ships, who keep shops.

The inn I was at in Larvik, this journey, was not the same that I was at before. It is a good one; the people civil, and the accommodations decent. They seem to be better provided in Sweden; but in justice I ought to add, that they charge more extravagantly. My bill at Tønsberg was also much higher than I had paid in Sweden, and much higher than it ought to have been where provisions are so cheap. Indeed they seem to consider foreigners as strangers whom they should never see again, and might fairly pluck. And the inhabitants of the western coast, insulated, as it were, regard those of the east almost as strangers. Each town in that quarter seems to be a great family, suspicious of every other, allowing none to cheat them, but themselves; and, right or wrong, they support one another in the face of justice.

On this journey I was fortunate enough to have one companion with more enlarged views than the generality of his countrymen, who spoke English tolerably.

I was informed that we might still advance a mile and a quarter in our *cabrioles*; afterwards there was no choice, but of a single horse and wretched path, or a boat, the usual mode of travelling.

We therefore sent our baggage forward in the boat, and followed rather slowly, for the road was rocky and sandy. We passed, however, through several beech groves, which still delighted me by the freshness of their light green foliage, and the elegance of their assemblage, forming retreats to veil, without obscuring the sun.

I was surprised, at approaching the water, to find a little cluster of houses pleasantly situated, and an excellent inn. I could have wished to have remained there all night; but as the wind was fair, and the evening fine, I was afraid to trust to the wind, the uncertain wind of to-morrow. We therefore left Helgeroa immediately, with the declining sun.

Though we were in the open sea, we sailed more amongst the rocks and islands than in my passage from Strömstad; and they often formed very picturesque combinations. Few of the high ridges were entirely bare; the seeds of some pines or firs had been wafted by the winds or waves, and they stood to brave the elements.

Sitting then in a little boat on the ocean, amidst strangers, with sorrow and care pressing hard on me, – buffeting me about from clime to clime, – I felt

> *Like the lone shrub at random cast,*
> *That sighs and trembles at each blast!* [74]

On some of the largest rocks there were actually groves, the retreat of foxes and hares, which, I suppose, had tript over the ice during the winter, without thinking to regain the main land before the thaw.

Several of the islands were inhabited by pilots; and the Norwegian pilots are allowed to be the best in the world; perfectly acquainted with their coast, and ever at hand to observe the first signal or sail.

They pay a small tax to the king, and to the regulating officer, and enjoy the fruit of their indefatigable industry.

One of the islands, called Virgin Land, is a flat, with some depth of earth, extending for half a Norwegian mile, with three farms on it, tolerably well cultivated.

On some of the bare rocks I saw straggling houses; they rose above the denomination of huts inhabited by fishermen. My companions assured me that they were very comfortable dwellings, and that they have not only the necessaries, but even what might be reckoned the superfluities of life. It was too late for me to go on shore, if you will allow me to give that name to shivering rock, to ascertain the fact.

But rain coming on, and the night growing dark, the pilot declared that it would be dangerous for us to attempt to go to the place of our destination, East Risør, a Norwegian mile and a half further; and we determined to stop for the night at a little haven; some half dozen houses scattered under the curve of a rock. Though it became darker and darker, our pilot avoided the blind rocks with great dexterity.

It was about ten o'clock when we arrived; and the old hostess quickly prepared me a comfortable bed – a little too soft, or so; but I was weary; and opening the window to admit the sweetest of breezes to fan me to sleep, I sunk into the most luxurious rest: it was more than refreshing. The hospitable sprites of the grots surely hovered round my pillow; and if I woke, it was to listen to the melodious whispering of the wind amongst them, or to feel the mild breath of morn. Light slumbers produced dreams, where Paradise was before me. My little cherub was again hiding her face in my bosom. I heard her sweet cooing beat on my heart from the cliffs, and saw her tiny footsteps on the sands. New-born hopes seemed, like the rainbow, to appear in the clouds of sorrow, faint, yet sufficient to amuse away despair.

Some refreshing but heavy showers have detained us; and here I am writing quite alone – something more than gay, for which I want a name.

I could almost fancy myself in Nootka Sound,[75] or on some of the islands on the north west coast of America. We entered by a narrow pass through the rocks, which from this abode appear more romantic than you can well imagine; and seal-skins, hanging at the door to dry, add to the illusion.

It is indeed a corner of the world; but you would be surprised to see the cleanliness and comfort of the dwelling. The shelves are not only shining with pewter and queen's ware,[76] but some articles in silver, more ponderous, it is true, than elegant. The linen is good, as well as white. All the females spin; and there is a loom in the kitchen. A sort of individual taste appeared in the arrangement of the furniture (this is not the place for imitation), and a kindness in their desire to oblige – how superior to the apish politeness of the towns! where the people, affecting to be well bred, fatigue with their endless ceremony.

The mistress is a widow; her daughter is married to a pilot, and has three cows. They have a little patch of land at about the distance of two English miles, where they make hay for the winter, which they bring home in a boat. They live here very cheap, getting money from the vessels which stress of weather, or other causes, bring into their harbour. I suspect, by their furniture, that they smuggle a little. I can now credit the account of the other houses, which I last night thought exaggerated.

I have been conversing with one of my companions respecting the laws and regulations of Norway. He is a man with a great portion of common sense, and heart, – yes, a warm heart. This is not the first time I have remarked heart without sentiment: they are distinct. The former depends on the rectitude of the feelings, on truth of sympathy: these characters have more tenderness than passion; the latter has a higher source; call it imagination, genius, or what you will, it is something very different. I have been laughing with these simple, worthy *folk*, to give you one of my half score Danish words, and letting as much of my heart flow out in sympathy as they can take. Adieu! I must trip up the rocks. The rain is over. Let me catch pleasure on the wing – I may be melancholy to-morrow. Now all my nerves keep time with the melody of nature. Ah! let me be happy whilst I can. The tear starts as I think of it. I must fly from thought, and find refuge from sorrow in a strong imagination – the only solace for a feeling heart. Phantoms of bliss! ideal forms of excellence!

again enclose me in your magic circle, and wipe clear from my remembrance the disappointments which render the sympathy painful,
which experience rather increases than damps; by giving the indulgence of feeling the sanction of reason.

Once more farewell!

Letter Eleven

I left Portør, the little haven I mentioned, soon after I finished my last letter. The sea was rough; and I perceived that our pilot was right not to venture farther during a hazy night. We had agreed to pay four dollars for a boat from Helgeroa. I mention the sum, because they would demand twice as much from a stranger. I was obliged to pay fifteen for the one I hired at Strömstad.[77] When we were ready to set out, our boatman offered to return a dollar, and let us go in one of the boats of the place, the pilot who lived there being better acquainted with the coast. He only demanded a dollar and half, which was reasonable. I found him a civil and rather intelligent man: he was in the American service several years, during the revolution.

I soon perceived that an experienced mariner was necessary to guide us; for we were continually obliged to tack about, to avoid the rocks, which, scarcely reaching to the surface of the water, could only be discovered by the breaking of the waves over them.

The view of this wild coast, as we sailed along it, afforded me a continual subject for meditation. I anticipated the future improvement of the world, and observed how much man had still to do, to obtain of the earth all it could yield. I even carried my speculations so far as to advance a million or two of years to the moment when the earth would perhaps be so perfectly cultivated, and so completely peopled, as to render it necessary to inhabit every spot; yes; these bleak shores. Imagination went still farther, and pictured the state of man when the earth could no longer support him. Where was he to fly to from universal famine? Do not smile: I really became distressed for these fellow creatures, yet unborn.[78] The images fastened on me, and the world appeared a vast prison. I was soon to be in a smaller one — for no other name can I give to Risør. It would be difficult to form an idea of the place, if you have never seen one of these rocky coasts.

We were a considerable time entering amongst the islands, before we saw about two hundred houses crowded together, under a very high rock – still higher appearing above. Talk not of bastilles! To be born here, was to be bastilled [79] by nature – shut out from all that opens the understanding, or enlarges the heart. Huddled one behind another, not more than a quarter of the dwellings even had a prospect of the sea. A few planks formed passages from house to house, which you must often scale, mounting steps like a ladder, to enter.

The only road across the rocks leads to a habitation, sterile enough, you may suppose, when I tell you that the little earth on the adjacent ones was carried there by the late inhabitant. A path, almost impracticable for a horse, goes on to Arendal, still further to the westward.

I enquired for a walk, and mounting near two hundred steps made round a rock, walked up and down for about a hundred yards, viewing the sea, to which I quickly descended by steps that cheated the declivity. The ocean, and these tremendous bulwarks, enclosed me on every side. I felt the confinement, and wished for wings to reach still loftier cliffs, whose slippery sides no foot was so hardy as to tread; yet what was it to see? – only a boundless waste of water – not a glimpse of smiling nature – not a patch of lively green to relieve the aching sight, or vary the objects of meditation.

I felt my breath oppressed, though nothing could be clearer than the atmosphere. Wandering there alone, I found the solitude desirable; my mind was stored with ideas, which this new scene associated with astonishing rapidity. But I shuddered at the thought of receiving existence, and remaining here, in the solitude of ignorance, till forced to leave a world of which I had seen so little; for the character of the inhabitants is as uncultivated, if not as picturesquely wild, as their abode.

Having no employment but traffic, of which a contraband trade makes the basis of their profit, the coarsest feelings of honesty are quickly blunted. You may suppose that I speak in general terms; and that, with all the disadvantages of nature and circumstances, there are still some respectable exceptions, the more praiseworthy, as tricking is a very contagious mental disease that dries up all the generous juices of the heart. Nothing genial, in fact, appears around this place, or within the circle of its rocks. And, now I recollect, it seems to me that the most genial and humane characters I have met with in life, were most alive to the sentiments inspired by tranquil country scenes. What, indeed, is to humanise these beings, who rest shut up, for they seldom even open their windows, smoking, drinking brandy, and driving bargains? I have been almost stifled by these smokers. They begin in the morning, and are rarely without their pipe till they go to bed. Nothing can be more disgusting than the rooms and men towards the evening: breath, teeth, clothes, and furniture, all are spoilt. It is well that the women are not very delicate, or they would only love their husbands because they were their husbands. Perhaps, you may add, that the remark need not be confined to so small a part of the world; and, *entre nous*, I am of the same opinion. You must not term this inuendo fancy, for it does not come home.[80]

If I had not determined to write, I should have found my confinement here, even for three or four days, tedious. I have no books; and to pace up and down a small room, looking at tiles, overhung by rocks, soon becomes wearisome. I cannot mount two hundred steps, to walk a hundred yards, many times in the day. Besides, the rocks, retaining the heat of the sun, are intolerably warm. I am nevertheless very well; for though there is a shrewdness in the character of these people, depraved by a sordid love of money which repels me, still the comparisons they force me to make keep my heart calm, by exercising my understanding.

Every where wealth commands too much respect; but here, almost exclusively; and it is the only object pursued – not through brake and briar, but over rocks and waves – yet of what use would riches be to me? I have sometimes asked myself, were I confined to live in such a spot. I could only relieve a few distressed objects, perhaps render them idle, and all the rest of life would be a blank.

My present journey has given fresh force to my opinion, that no place is so disagreeable and unimproving as a country town. I should like to divide my time between the town and country; in a lone house, with the business of farming and planting, where my mind would gain strength by solitary musing; and in a metropolis to rub off the rust of thought, and polish the taste which the contemplation of nature had rendered just.[81] Thus do we wish as we float down the stream of life, whilst chance does more to gratify a desire of know-

ledge than our best-laid plans. A degree of exertion, produced by
some want, more or less painful, is probably the price we must all pay
for knowledge. How few authors or artists have arrived at eminence
who have not lived by their employment?

I was interrupted yesterday by business, and was prevailed upon to
dine with the English vice-consul.[82] His house being open to the sea,
I was more at large; and the hospitality of the table pleased me,
though the bottle was rather too freely pushed about. Their manner
of entertaining was such as I have frequently remarked when I have
been thrown in the way of people without education, who have more
money than wit, that is, than they know what to do with. The women
were unaffected, but had not the natural grace which was often
conspicuous at Tønsberg. There was even a striking difference in their
dress; these having loaded themselves with finery, in the style of the
sailors' girls of Hull or Portsmouth. Taste has not yet taught them to
make any but an ostentatious display of wealth: yet I could perceive
even here the first steps of the improvement which I am persuaded
will make a very obvious progress in the course of half a century; and
it ought not to be sooner, to keep pace with the cultivation of the
earth. Improving manners will introduce finer moral feelings. They
begin to read translations of some of the most useful German productions lately published; and one of our party sung a song, ridiculing
the powers coalesced against France, and the company drank confusion to those who had dismembered Poland.[83]

The evening was extremely calm and beautiful. Not being able to
walk, I requested a boat, as the only means of enjoying free air.

The view of the town was now extremely fine. A huge rocky
mountain stood up behind it; and a vast cliff stretched on each side,
forming a semicircle. In a recess of the rocks was a clump of pines,
amongst which a steeple rose picturesquely beautiful.

The church-yard is almost the only verdant spot in the place. Here,
indeed, friendship extends beyond the grave; and, to grant a sod of
earth, is to accord a favour. I should rather chuse, did it admit of a
choice, to sleep in some of the caves of the rocks; for I am become
better reconciled to them since I climbed their craggy sides, last
night, listening to the finest echoes I ever heard. We had a French-
horn with us; and there was an enchanting wildness in the dying away

of the reverberation, that quickly transported me to Shakspeare's magic island.[84] Spirits unseen seemed to walk abroad, and flit from cliff to cliff, to sooth my soul to peace.

I reluctantly returned to supper, to be shut up in a warm room, only to view the vast shadows of the rocks extending on the slumbering waves. I stood at the window some time before a buzz filled the drawing-room; and now and then the dashing of a solitary oar rendered the scene still more solemn.

Before I came here, I could scarcely have imagined that a simple object, rocks, could have admitted of so many interesting combinations – always grand, and often sublime.

                                        Good night! God bless you!

Letter Twelve

I left East Risør the day before yesterday. The weather was very fine; but so calm that we loitered on the water near fourteen hours, only to make about six and twenty miles.

It seemed to me a sort of emancipation when we landed at Helgeroa. The confinement which every where struck me whilst sojourning amongst the rocks, made me hail the earth as a land of promise; and the situation shone with fresh lustre from the contrast – from appearing to be a free abode. Here it was possible to travel by land – I never thought this a comfort before, and my eyes, fatigued by the sparkling of the sun on the water, now contentedly reposed on the green expanse, half persuaded that such verdant meads had never till then regaled them.

I rose early to pursue my journey to Tønsberg. The country still wore a face of joy – and my soul was alive to its charms. Leaving the most lofty, and romantic of the cliffs behind us, we were almost continually descending to Tønsberg, through elysian scenes; for not only the sea, but mountains, rivers, lakes, and groves, gave an almost endless variety to the prospect. The cottagers were still leading home the hay; and the cottages, on this road, looked very comfortable. Peace and plenty – I mean not abundance, seemed to reign around – still I grew sad as I drew near my old abode. I was sorry to see the sun so high; it was broad noon. Tønsberg was something like a home – yet I was to enter without lighting-up pleasure in any eye – I dreaded the solitariness of my apartment, and wished for night to hide the starting tears, or to shed them on my pillow, and close my eyes on a world where I was destined to wander alone. Why has nature so many charms for me – calling forth and cherishing refined sentiments, only to wound the breast that fosters them? How illusive, perhaps the most so, are the plans of happiness founded on virtue and principle; what inlets of misery do they not open in a half civilized society? The satisfaction arising from conscious rectitude, will not calm an injured heart, when tenderness is ever finding excuses; and self-applause is a cold solitary feeling, that cannot supply the place of disappointed affection, without throwing a gloom over every prospect, which, banishing pleasure, does not exclude pain. I reasoned and reasoned; but my heart was too full to allow me to remain in the house, and I walked, till I was wearied out, to purchase rest – or rather forget-fulness.

Employment has beguiled this day, and tomorrow I set out for Moss, in my way to Strömstad. At Gothenburg I shall embrace my *Fannikin*; probably she will not know me again – and I shall be hurt if she do not. How childish is this! still it is a natural feeling. I would not permit myself to indulge the 'thick coming fears'[85] of fondness, whilst I was detained by business. – Yet I never saw a calf bounding in a meadow, that did not remind me of my little frolicker. A calf, you say. Yes; but a *capital* one, I own.

I cannot write composedly – I am every instant sinking into reveries – my heart flutters, I know not why. Fool! It is time thou wert at rest.

Friendship and domestic happiness are continually praised; yet how little is there of either in the world, because it requires more cultivation of mind to keep awake affection, even in our own hearts, than the common run of people suppose. Besides, few like to be seen as they really are; and a degree of simplicity, and of undisguised confidence, which, to uninterested observers, would almost border on weakness, is the charm, nay the essence of love or friendship: all the bewitching graces of childhood again appearing.[86] As objects merely to exercise my taste, I therefore like to see people together who have an affection for each other; every turn of their features touches me, and remains pictured on my imagination in indelible characters. The zest of novelty is, however, necessary to rouse the languid sympathies which have been hacknied in the world; as is the factitious behaviour, falsely termed good-breeding, to amuse those, who, defective in taste, continually rely for pleasure on their animal spirits, which not being maintained by the imagination, are unavoidably sooner exhausted than the sentiments of the heart. Friendship is in general sincere at the commencement, and lasts whilst there is any thing to support it; but as a mixture of novelty and vanity is the usual prop, no wonder if it fall with the slender stay. The fop in the play,[87] payed a greater compliment than he was aware of, when he said to a person, whom he meant to flatter, 'I like you almost as well as a *new acquaintance.*' Why am I talking of friendship, after which I have had such a wild-goose chase. — I thought only of telling you that the crows, as well as wild-geese, are here birds of passage.

Letter Thirteen

I left Tønsberg yesterday, the 22nd of August. It is only twelve or thirteen English miles to Moss, through a country, less wild than any tract I had hitherto passed over in Norway. It was often beautiful; but seldom afforded those grand views, which fill, rather than sooth the mind.

We glided along the meadows, and through the woods, with sunbeams playing around us; and though no castles adorned the prospects, a greater number of comfortable farms met my eyes, during this ride, than I have ever seen, in the same space, even in the most cultivated part of England. And the very appearance of the cottages of the labourers, sprinkled amidst them, excluded all those gloomy ideas inspired by the contemplation of poverty.

The hay was still bringing in; for one harvest in Norway, treads on the heels of the other. The woods were more variegated; interspersed with shrubs. We no longer passed through forests of vast pines, stretching along with savage magnificence. Forests that only exhibited the slow decay of time, or the devastation produced by warring elements. No; oaks, ashes, beech; and all the light and graceful tenants of our woods here sported luxuriantly. I had not observed many oaks before; for the greater part of the oak planks, I am informed, come from the westward.

In France the farmers generally live in villages, which is a great disadvantage to the country; but the Norwegian farmers, always owning their farms, or being tenants for life, reside in the midst of them; allowing some labourers a dwelling, rent free, who have a little land appertaining to the cottage, not only for a garden, but for crops of different kinds, such as rye, oats, buck-wheat, hemp, flax, beans, potatoes, and hay, which are sown in strips about it; reminding a stranger of the first attempts at culture, when every family was obliged to be an independent community.

These cottagers work at a certain price, ten-pence per day, for the farmers on whose ground they live; and they have spare time enough to cultivate their own land; and lay in a store of fish for the winter. The wives and daughters spin; and the husbands and sons weave; so that they may fairly be reckoned independent; having also a little money in hand to buy coffee, brandy, and some other superfluities.

The only thing I disliked was the military service, which trammels them more than I at first imagined. It is true that the militia is only called out once a year – yet, in case of war, they have no alternative, but must abandon their families. Even the manufacturers are not exempted, though the miners are, in order to encourage undertakings which require a capital at the commencement. And what appears more tyrannical, the inhabitants of certain districts are appointed for the land, others for the sea service. Consequently, a peasant, born a soldier, is not permitted to follow his inclination, should it lead him to go to sea: a natural desire near so many sea ports.

In these regulations the arbitrary government, the king of Denmark being the most absolute monarch in Europe, appears, which in other respects, seeks to hide itself in a lenity that almost renders the laws nullities. If any alteration of old customs is thought of, the opinion of the whole country is required, and maturely considered. I have several times had occasion to observe, that fearing to appear tyrannical, laws are allowed to become obsolete, which ought to be put in force, or better substituted in their stead; for this mistaken moderation, which borders on timidity, favours the least respectable part of the people.

I saw on my way not only good parsonage houses, but comfortable dwellings, with glebe land for the clerk: always a consequential man in every country: a being proud of a little smattering of learning, to use the appropriate epithet, and vain of the stiff good-breeding reflected from the vicar; though the servility practised in his company gives it a peculiar cast.

The widow of the clergyman is allowed to receive the benefit of the living for a twelve-month, after the death of the incumbent.

Arriving at the ferry, the passage over to Moss is about six or eight English miles; I saw the most level shore I had yet seen in Norway. The appearance of the circumjacent country had been preparing me for the change of scene, which was to greet me, when I reached the coast. For the grand features of nature had been dwindling into prettiness as I advanced; yet the rocks, on a smaller scale, were finely wooded to the water's edge. Little art appeared, yet sublimity every where gave place to elegance. The road had often assumed the appearance of a graveled one, made in pleasure grounds, whilst the trees excited only an idea of embellishment. Meadows, like lawns, in an endless variety, displayed the careless graces of nature; and the ripening corn gave a richness to the landscape, analogous with the other objects.

Never was a southern sky more beautiful, nor more soft its gales. Indeed, I am led to conclude, that the sweetest summer in the world, is the northern one. The vegetation being quick and luxuriant, the moment the earth is loosened from its icy fetters, and the bound streams regain their wonted activity. The balance of happiness, with respect to climate, may be more equal than I at first imagined; for the inhabitants described with warmth the pleasures of a winter, at the thoughts of which I shudder. Not only their parties of pleasure but of business are reserved for this season, when they travel with astonishing rapidity, the most direct way, skimming over the hedge and ditch.

On entering Moss I was struck by the animation which seemed to result from industry. The richest of the inhabitants keep shops, resembling in their manners, and even the arrangement of their houses, the trades people of Yorkshire; with an air of more independence, or rather consequence, from feeling themselves the first people in the place. I had not time to see the iron works, belonging to Mr Anker,[88] of Christiania, a man of fortune and enterprise; and I was not very anxious to see them, after having viewed those at Larvik.

Here I met with an intelligent literary man, who was anxious to gather information from me, relative to the past and present situation of France. The newspapers printed at Copenhagen, as well as those in England, give the most exaggerated accounts of their atrocities and distresses; but the former without any apparent comments or inferences. Still the Norwegians, though more connected with the English, speaking their language, and copying their manners, wish well to the republican cause; and follow, with the most lively interest, the successes of the French arms. So determined were they, in fact, to excuse every thing, disgracing the struggle of freedom, by admitting the tyrant's plea necessity, that I could hardly persuade them that Robespierre was a monster.[89]

The discussion of this subject is not so general as in England, being confined to the few, the clergy and physician, with a small portion of people who have a literary turn and leisure: the greater part of the inhabitants, having a variety of occupations, being owners of ships, shopkeepers and farmers, have employment enough at home. And their ambition to become rich may tend to cultivate the common sense, which characterizes and narrows both their hearts and views; confining the former to their families, taking the *handmaids* of it into the circle of pleasure, if not of interest; and the latter to the inspection of their workmen, including the noble science of bargain-making – that is getting every thing at the cheapest, and selling it at the dearest rate. I am now more than ever convinced, that it is an intercourse with men of science and artists, which not only diffuses taste, but gives that freedom to the understanding, without which I have seldom met with much benevolence of character, on a large scale.

Besides, though you do not hear of much pilfering and stealing in Norway, yet they will, with a quiet conscience, buy things at a price which must convince them they were stolen. I had an opportunity of knowing that two or three reputable people had purchased some articles of vagrants, who were detected. How much of the virtue, which appears in the world, is put on for the world! And how little dictated by self respect – so little, that I am ready to repeat the old question – and ask, where is truth or rather principle to be found? These are, perhaps, the vapourings of a heart ill at ease – the effusions of a sensibility wounded almost to madness. But enough of this – we will discuss the subject in another state of existence – where truth and justice will reign. How cruel are the injuries which make us quarrel with human nature! – At present black melancholy hovers round my footsteps; and sorrow sheds a mildew over all the future prospects, which hope no longer gilds.[90]

A rainy morning prevented my enjoying the pleasure the view of a picturesque country would have afforded me; for though this road passed through a country, a greater extent of which was under cultivation, than I had usually seen here, it nevertheless retained all the wild charms of Norway. Rocks still enclosed the valleys, whose grey sides enlivened their verdure. Lakes appeared like branches of the sea, and branches of the sea assumed the appearance of tranquil lakes; whilst streamlets prattled amongst the pebbles, and the broken mass of stone which had rolled into them; giving fantastic turns to the trees whose roots they bared.

It is not, in fact, surprising that the pine should be often undermined, it shoots its fibres in such an horizontal direction, merely on the surface of the earth, requiring only enough to cover those that cling to the crags. Nothing proves to me, so clearly, that it is the air which principally nourishes trees and plants, as the flourishing appearance of these pines. – The firs demanding a deeper soil, are seldom seen in equal health, or so numerous on the barren cliffs. They take shelter in the crevices, or where, after some revolving ages, the pines have prepared them a footing.

Approaching, or rather descending, to Christiania, though the weather continued a little cloudy, my eyes were charmed with the view of an extensive undulated valley, stretching out under the shelter of a noble amphitheatre of pine-covered mountains. Farm houses scattered about animated, nay, graced a scene which still retained so much of its native wildness, that the art which appeared, seemed so necessary it was scarcely perceived. Cattle were grazing in the shaven meadows; and the lively green, on their swelling sides, contrasted with the ripening corn and rye. The corn that grew on the slopes, had not, indeed, the laughing luxuriance of plenty, which I have seen in more genial climes. A fresh breeze swept across the grain, parting its slender stalks; but the wheat did not wave its head with its wonted, careless dignity, as if nature had crowned it the king of plants.

The view, immediately on the left, as we drove down the mountain, was almost spoilt by the depredations committed on the rocks to make alum. I did not know the process. – I only saw that the rocks looked red after they had been burnt; and regretted that the operation should leave a quantity of rubbish, to introduce an image of human industry in the shape of destruction.[91] The situation of Christiania is certainly uncommonly fine; and I never saw a bay that so forcibly gave me an idea of a place of safety from the storms of the ocean – all the surrounding objects were beautiful, and even grand. But neither the rocky mountains, nor the woods that graced them, could be compared with the sublime prospects I had seen towards the westward; and as for the hills, 'capped with *eternal* snow', Mr Coxe's [92] description led me to look for them; but they had flown; for I looked vainly around for this noble back-ground.

A few months ago the people of Christiania rose, exasperated by the scarcity, and consequent high price of grain. The immediate cause was the shipping of some, said to be for Moss; but which they suspected was only a pretext to send it out of the country: and I am not sure that they were wrong in their conjecture. – Such are the tricks of trade! They threw stones at Mr Anker, the owner of it, as he rode out of town to escape from their fury; they assembled about his house. And the people demanded afterwards, with so much impetuosity, the liberty of those who were taken up in consequence of the tumult, that the Grand Bailiff thought it prudent to release them without further altercation.

You may think me too severe on commerce; but from the manner it is at present carried on, little can be advanced in favour of a pursuit that wears out the most sacred principles of humanity and rectitude. What is speculation, but a species of gambling, I might have said fraud, in which address generally gains the prize? I was led into these reflections when I heard of some tricks practised by merchants, miscalled reputable, and certainly men of property, during the present war, in which common honesty was violated: damaged goods, and provisions, having been shipped for the express purpose of falling into the hands of the English, who had pledged themselves to reimburse neutral nations, for the cargoes they seized: cannon also, sent back as unfit for service, have been shipped as a *good speculation*; the captain receiving orders to cruise about till he fell in with an English frigate. [93] Many individuals, I believe, have suffered by the seizures of their vessels; still I am persuaded that the English government has been very much imposed upon in the charges made by merchants, who contrived to get their ships taken. This censure is not confined to the Danes. Adieu! For the present, I must take advantage of a moment of fine weather to walk out and see the town.

At Christiania I met with that polite reception, which rather characterises the progress of manners in the world, than of any particular portion of it. The first evening of my arrival I supped with some of the most fashionable people of the place; and almost imagined myself in a circle of English ladies, so much did they resemble them in manners, dress, and even in beauty; for the fairest of my country-women would not have been sorry to rank with the Grand Bailiff's lady. There were several pretty girls present, but she outshone them all; and what interested me still more, I could not avoid observing that in acquiring the easy politeness which distinguishes people of quality, she had preserved her Norwegian simplicity. There was, in fact, a graceful timidity in her address, inexpressibly charming. This surprised me a little, because her husband was quite a Frenchman of the *ancien régime*, or rather a courtier, the same kind of animal in every country.

Here I saw the cloven foot of despotism. I boasted, to you, that they had no viceroy in Norway; but these grand bailiffs, particularly the superior one, who resides at Christiania, are political monsters of the same species. Needy sycophants are provided for by their relations and connexions at Copenhagen, as at other courts. And though the Norwegians are not in the abject state of the Irish, yet this second-hand government is still felt by their being deprived of several natural advantages to benefit the domineering state.

The grand bailiffs are mostly noblemen from Copenhagen, who act as men of common minds will always act in such situations – aping a degree of courtly parade which clashes with the independent character of a magistrate. Besides, they have a degree of power over the country judges, which some of them who exercise a jurisdiction truly patriarchal, most painfully feel. I can scarcely say why, my friend, but in this city, thoughtfulness seemed to be sliding into melancholy, or rather dullness. – The fire of fancy, which had been kept alive in the country, was almost extinguished by reflections on the ills that harass such a large portion of mankind. – I felt like a bird fluttering on the ground unable to mount; yet unwilling to crawl tranquilly like a reptile, whilst still conscious it had wings.

I walked out, for the open air is always my remedy when an aching-head proceeds from an oppressed heart. Chance directed my steps towards the fortress, and the sight of the slaves, working with chains on their legs, only served to embitter me still more against the regulations of society, which treated knaves in such a different manner, especially as there was a degree of energy in some of their countenances which unavoidably excited my attention, and almost created respect.

I wished to have seen, through an iron grate, the face of a man who has been confined six years,[94] for having induced the farmers to revolt against some impositions of the government. I could not obtain a clear account of the affair; yet, as the complaint was against some farmers of taxes, I am inclined to believe, that it was not totally without foundation. He must have possessed some eloquence, or have had truth on his side; for the farmers rose by hundreds to support him, and were very much exasperated at his imprisonment; which will probably last for life, though he has sent several very spirited remonstrances to the upper court, which makes the judges so averse to giving a sentence which may be cavilled at, that they take advantage of the glorious uncertainty of the law, to protract a decision which is only to be regulated by reasons of state.

The greater number of the slaves, I saw here, were not confined for life. Their labour is not hard; and they work in the open air, which prevents their constitutions from suffering by imprisonment. Still as they are allowed to associate together, and boast of their dexterity, not only to each other but to the soldiers around them, in the garrison, they commonly, it is natural to conclude, go out more confirmed, and more expert knaves than when they entered.

It is not necessary to trace the origin of the association of ideas, which led me to think that the stars and gold keys, which surrounded me the evening before, disgraced the wearers, as much as the fetters I was viewing – perhaps more. I even began to investigate the reason which led me to suspect that the former produced the latter.

The Norwegians are extravagantly fond of courtly distinction, and of titles, though they have no immunities annexed to them, and are easily purchased. The proprietors of mines have many privileges: they are almost exempt from taxes, and the peasantry born on their estates, as well as those on the count's, are not born soldiers or sailors.

One distinction, or rather trophy of nobility, which might have occurred to the Hottentots, amused me; it was a bunch of hog's bristles placed on the horses' heads; surmounting that part of the harness to which a round piece of brass often dangles, fatiguing the eye with its idle motion.

From the fortress I returned to my lodging, and quickly was taken out of town to be shewn a pretty villa, and English garden.[95] To a Norwegian both might have been objects of curiosity, and of use, by exciting to the comparison which leads to improvement. But whilst I gazed, I was employed in restoring the place to nature, or taste, by giving it the character of the surrounding scene. Serpentine walks, and flowering shrubs, looked trifling in a grand recess of the rocks, shaded by towering pines. Groves of lesser trees might have been sheltered under them, which would have melted into the landscape, displaying only the art which ought to point out the vicinity of a human abode, furnished with some elegance. But few people have sufficient taste to discern, that the art of embellishing, consists in interesting, not in astonishing.

Christiania is certainly very pleasantly situated; and the environs I passed through, during this ride, afforded many fine, and cultivated prospects; but, excepting the first view approaching to it, rarely present any combination of objects so strikingly new, or picturesque, as to command remembrance.

Adieu!

Letter Fourteen

Christiania is a clean, neat city; but it has none of the graces of architecture, which ought to keep pace with the refining manners of a people – or the outside of the house will disgrace the inside; giving the beholder an idea of overgrown wealth devoid of taste. Large square wooden houses offend the eye, displaying more than gothic barbarism. Huge gothic piles, indeed, exhibit a characteristic sublimity, and a wildness of fancy peculiar to the period when they were erected; but size, without grandeur or elegance, has an emphatical stamp of meanness, of poverty of conception, which only a commercial spirit could give.

The same thought has struck me, when I have entered the meeting-house of my respected friend, Dr Price.[96] I am surprised that the dissenters, who have not laid aside all the pomps and vanities of life, should imagine a noble pillar, or arch, unhallowed. Whilst men have senses, whatever sooths them lends wings to devotion; else why do the beauties of nature, where all that charm them are spread around with a lavish hand, force even the sorrowing heart to acknowledge that existence is a blessing; and this acknowledgement is the most sublime homage we can pay to the Deity.

The argument of convenience is absurd. Who would labour for wealth, if it were to procure nothing but conveniencies? If we wish to render mankind moral from principle, we must, I am persuaded, give a greater scope to the enjoyments of the senses, by blending taste with them. This has frequently occurred to me since I have been in the north, and observed that there sanguine characters always take refuge in drunkenness after the fire of youth is spent.

But I have flown from Norway, to go back to the wooden houses. Farms constructed with logs, and even little villages, here erected in the same simple manner, have appeared to me very picturesque. In the more remote parts I had been particularly pleased with many cottages situated close to a brook, or bordering on a lake, with the whole farm contiguous. As the family increases, a little more land is cultivated: thus the country is obviously enriched by population. Formerly the farmers might more justly have been termed wood-cutters. But now they find it necessary to spare the woods a little; and this change will be universally beneficial; for whilst they lived entirely by selling the trees they felled, they did not pay sufficient attention to husbandry; consequently, advanced very slowly in agricultural knowledge. Necessity will in future more and more spur them on; for the ground, cleared of wood, must be cultivated, or the farm loses its value: there is no waiting for food till another generation of pines be grown to maturity.

The people of property are very careful of their timber; and, rambling through a forest near Tønsberg, belonging to the count, I have stopt to admire the appearance of some of the cottages inhabited by a woodman's family – a man employed to cut down the wood necessary for the household and the estate. A little lawn was cleared, on which several lofty trees were left which nature had grouped, whilst the encircling firs sported with wild grace. The dwelling was sheltered by the forest, noble pines spreading their branches over the roof; and before the door a cow, goat, nag, and children, seemed equally content with their lot; and if contentment be all we can attain, it is, perhaps, best secured by ignorance.

As I have been most delighted with the country parts of Norway, I was sorry to leave Christiania, without going further to the north, though the advancing season admonished me to depart, as well as the calls of business and affection.

June and July are the months to make a tour through Norway; for then the evenings and nights are the finest I have ever seen; but towards the middle, or latter end of August, the clouds begin to gather, and summer disappears almost before it has ripened the fruit of autumn – even, as it were, slips from your embraces, whilst the satisfied senses seem to rest in enjoyment.

You will ask, perhaps, why I wished to go further northward. Why? not only because the country, from all I can gather, is most romantic, abounding in forests and lakes, and the air pure, but I have heard much of the intelligence of the inhabitants, substantial farmers, who have none of that cunning to contaminate their simplicity, which displeased me so much in the conduct of the people on the sea coast. A man, who has been detected in any dishonest act, can no longer live among them. He is universally shunned, and shame becomes the severest punishment. Such a contempt have they, in fact, for every species of fraud, that they will not allow the people on the western coast to be their countrymen; so much do they despise the arts for which those traders who live on the rocks are notorious.

The description I received of them carried me back to the fables of the golden age:[97] independence and virtue; affluence without vice; cultivation of mind, without depravity of heart; with 'ever smiling liberty', the nymph of the mountain.[98] – I want faith! My imagination hurries me forward to seek an asylum in such a retreat from all the disappointments I am threatened with; but reason drags me back, whispering that the world is still the world, and man the same compound of weakness and folly, who must occasionally excite love and disgust, admiration and contempt. But this description, though it seems to have been sketched by a fairy pencil, was given me by a man of sound understanding, whose fancy seldom appears to run away with him.

A law in Norway, termed the *odels right*, has lately been modified, and probably will be abolished as an impediment to commerce. The heir of an estate had the power of re-purchasing it at the original purchase money, making allowance for such improvements as were absolutely necessary, during the space of twenty years. At present ten is the term allowed for after thought; and when the regulation was made, all the men of abilities were invited to give their opinion whether it were better to abrogate or modify it. It is certainly a convenient and safe way of mortgaging land; yet the most rational men, whom I conversed with on the subject, seemed convinced that the right was more injurious than beneficial to society; still if it contribute to keep the farms in the farmers' own hands, I should be sorry to hear that it were abolished.[99]

The aristocracy in Norway, if we keep clear of Christiania, is far from being formidable; and it will require a long time to enable the merchants to attain a sufficient monied interest to induce them to reinforce the upper class, at the expence of the yeomanry, with whom they are usually connected.

England and America owe their liberty to commerce, which created a new species of power to undermine the feudal system. But let them beware of the consequence; the tyranny of wealth is still more galling and debasing than that of rank.

Farewell! I must prepare for my departure.

Letter Fifteen

I left Christiania yesterday. The weather was not very fine; and having been a little delayed on the road, I found that it was too late to go round, a couple of miles, to see the cascade near Frederikstad, which I had determined to visit. Besides, as Frederikstad is a fortress, it was necessary to arrive there before they shut the gate.

The road along the river is very romantic, though the views are not grand; and the riches of Norway, its timber, floats silently down the stream, often impeded in its course by islands and little cataracts, the offspring, as it were, of the great one I had frequently heard described.

I found an excellent inn at Frederikstad, and was gratified by the kind attention of the hostess, who, perceiving that my clothes were wet, took great pains to procure me, as a stranger, every comfort for the night.

It had rained very hard; and we passed [100] the ferry in the dark, without getting out of our carriage, which I think wrong, as the horses are sometimes unruly. Fatigue and melancholy, however, had made me regardless whether I went down or across the stream; and I did not know that I was wet before the hostess remarked it. My imagination has never yet severed me from my griefs – and my mind has seldom been so free as to allow my body to be delicate.*

How I am altered by disappointment! – When going to Lisbon, the elasticity of my mind was sufficient to ward off weariness, and my imagination still could dip her brush in the rainbow of fancy, and sketch futurity in glowing colours. [101] Now – but let me talk of something else – will you go with me to the cascade?

The cross road to it was rugged and dreary; and though a considerable extent of land was cultivated on all sides, yet the rocks were entirely bare, which surprised me, as they were more on a level with

* 'When the mind's free,/ The body's delicate.' vid. *King Lear*.

the surface than any I had yet seen. On inquiry, however, I learnt that some years since a forest had been burnt. This appearance of desolation was beyond measure gloomy, inspiring emotions that sterility had never produced. Fires of this kind are occasioned by the wind suddenly rising when the farmers are burning roots of trees, stalks of beans, &c. with which they manure the ground. The devastation must, indeed, be terrible, when this, literally speaking, wild fire, runs along the forest, flying from top to top, and crackling amongst the branches. The soil, as well as the trees, is swept away by the destructive torrent; and the country, despoiled of beauty and riches, is left to mourn for ages.

Admiring, as I do, these noble forests, which seem to bid defiance to time, I looked with pain on the ridge of rocks that stretched far beyond my eye, formerly crowned with the most beautiful verdure.

I have often mentioned the grandeur, but I feel myself unequal to the task of conveying an idea of the beauty and elegance of the scene when the spiral tops of the pines are loaded with ripening seed, and the sun gives a glow to their light green tinge, which is changing into purple, one tree more or less advanced, contrasting with another. The profusion with which nature has decked them, with pendant honours, prevents all surprise at seeing, in every crevice, some sapling struggling for existence. Vast masses of stone are thus encircled; and roots, torn up by the storms, become a shelter for a young generation. The pine and fir woods, left entirely to nature, display an endless variety; and the paths in the wood are not entangled with fallen leaves, which are only interesting whilst they are fluttering between life and death. The grey cobweb-like appearance of the aged pines is a much finer image of decay; the fibres whitening as they lose their moisture, imprisoned life seems to be stealing away. I cannot tell why – but death, under every form, appears to me like something getting free – to expand in I know not what element; nay I feel that this conscious being must be as unfettered, have the wings of thought, before it can be happy.[102]

Reaching the cascade, or rather cataract, the roaring of which had a long time announced its vicinity, my soul was hurried by the falls into a new train of reflections. The impetuous dashing of the rebounding torrent from the dark cavities which mocked the exploring eye, produced an equal activity in my mind: my thoughts darted from earth to heaven, and I asked myself why I was chained to life and its misery? Still the tumultuous emotions this sublime object excited, were pleasurable; and, viewing it, my soul rose, with renewed dignity, above its cares – grasping at immortality – it seemed as impossible to stop the current of my thoughts, as of the always varying, still the same, torrent before me – I stretched out my hand to eternity, bounding over the dark speck of life to come.[103]

We turned with regret from the cascade. On a little hill, which commands the best view of it, several obelisks are erected to commemorate the visits of different kings. The appearance of the river above and below the falls is very picturesque, the ruggedness of the scenery disappearing as the torrent subsides into a peaceful stream. But I did not like to see a number of saw-mills crowded together close to the cataracts; they destroyed the harmony of the prospect.

The sight of a bridge erected across a deep valley, at a little distance, inspired very dissimilar sensations. It was most ingeniously supported by mast-like trunks, just stript of their branches; and logs, placed one across the other, produced an appearance equally light and firm, seeming almost to be built in the air when we were below it; the height taking from the magnitude of the supporting trees give them a slender, graceful look.

There are two noble estates in this neighbourhood, the proprietors of which seem to have caught more than their portion of the enterprising spirit that is gone abroad. Many agricultural experiments have been made; and the country appears better enclosed and cultivated; yet the cottages had not the comfortable aspect of those I had observed near Moss, and to the westward. Man is always debased by servitude, of any description; and here the peasantry are not entirely free.

Adieu!

I almost forgot to tell you, that I did not leave Norway without making some inquiries after the monsters said to have been seen in the northern sea; but though I conversed with several captains, I could not meet with one who had ever heard any traditional description of them, much less had any ocular demonstration of their existence. Till the fact be better ascertained, I should think the account of them ought to be torn out of our Geographical Grammars.[104]

Letter Sixteen

I set out from Frederikstad about three o'clock in the afternoon, and expected to reach Strömstad before the night closed in; but the wind dying away, the weather became so calm, that we scarcely made any perceptible advances toward the opposite coast, though the men were fatigued with rowing.

Getting amongst the rocks and islands as the moon rose, and the stars darted forward out of the clear expanse, I forgot that the night stole on, whilst indulging affectionate reveries, the poetical fictions of sensibility; I was not, therefore, aware of the length of time we had been toiling to reach Strömstad. And when I began to look around, I did not perceive any thing to indicate that we were in its neighbourhood. So far from it, that when I inquired of the pilot, who spoke a little English, I found that he was only accustomed to coast along the Norwegian shore; and had been, only once, across to Strömstad. But he had brought with him a fellow better acquainted, he assured me, with the rocks by which they were to steer our course; for we had not a compass on board; yet, as he was half a fool, I had little confidence in his skill. There was then great reason to fear that we had lost our way, and were straying amidst a labyrinth of rocks, without a clue.

This was something like an adventure; but not of the most agreeable cast; besides, I was impatient to arrive at Strömstad, to be able to send forward, that night, a boy to order horses on the road to be ready; for I was unwilling to remain there a day, without having any thing to detain me from my little girl; and from the letters which I was impatient to get from you.

I began to expostulate, and even to scold the pilot, for not having informed me of his ignorance, previous to my departure. This made him row with more force; and we turned round one rock only to see another, equally destitute of the tokens we were in search of to tell us where we were. Entering also into creek after creek, which promised to be the entrance of the bay we were seeking, we advanced merely to find ourselves running aground.

The solitariness of the scene, as we glided under the dark shadows of the rocks, pleased me for a while; but the fear of passing the whole night thus wandering to and fro, and losing the next day, roused me. I begged the pilot to return to one of the largest islands, at the side of which we had seen a boat moored. As we drew nearer, a light, through a window on the summit, became our beacon; but we were farther off than I supposed.

With some difficulty the pilot got on shore, not distinguishing the landing place; and I remained in the boat, knowing that all the relief we could expect, was a man to direct us. After waiting some time, for there is an insensibility in the very movements of these people,* that would weary more than ordinary patience, he brought with him a man, who, assisting them to row, we landed at Strömstad a little after one in the morning.

It was too late to send off a boy; but I did not go to bed before I had made the arrangements necessary to enable me to set out as early as possible.

The sun rose with splendour. My mind was too active to allow me to loiter long in bed, though the horses did not arrive till between seven and eight. However, as I wished to let the boy, who went forward to order the horses, get considerably the start of me, I bridled-in my impatience.

This precaution was unavailing, for after the three first posts, I had to wait two hours, whilst the people at the post-house went, fair and softly, to the farm, to bid them bring up the horses, which were carrying in the first-fruits of the harvest. I discovered here that these sluggish peasants had their share of cunning. Though they had made me pay for a horse, the boy had gone on foot, and only arrived half an hour before me. This disconcerted the whole arrangement of the day; and being detained again three hours, I reluctantly determined to sleep at Kvistram, two posts short of Uddevalla, where I had hoped to have arrived that night.

But, when I reached Kvistram, I found I could not approach the

* It is very possible that he staid to smoke a pipe, though I was waiting in the cold.

door of the inn, for men, horses, and carts, cows, and pigs huddled together. From the concourse of people, I had met on the road, I conjectured that there was a fair in the neighbourhood, this crowd convinced me that it was but too true. The boisterous merriment that almost every instant produced a quarrel or made me dread one, with the clouds of tobacco, and fumes of brandy, gave an infernal appearance to the scene. There was every thing to drive me back, nothing to excite sympathy in a rude tumult of the senses, which I foresaw would end in a gross debauch. What was to be done? No bed was to be had, or even a quiet corner to retire to for a moment – all was lost in noise, riot, and confusion.

After some debating they promised me horses, which were to go on to Uddevalla, two stages. I requested something to eat first, not having dined; and the hostess, whom I have mentioned to you before, as knowing how to take care of herself, brought me a plate of fish, for which she charged a rixdollar and a half. This was making hay whilst the sun shone. I was glad to get out of the up-roar, though not disposed to travel in an incommodious open carriage all night, had I thought that there was any chance of getting horses.

Quitting Kvistram, I met a number of joyous groups, and though the evening was fresh, many were stretched on the grass like weary cattle; and drunken men had fallen by the road side. On a rock, under the shade of lofty trees, a large party of men and women had lighted a fire, cutting down fuel around to keep it alive all night. They were drinking, smoking, and laughing, with all their might and main. I felt for the trees whose torn branches strewed the ground. – Hapless nymphs! thy haunts I fear were polluted by many an unhallowed flame; the casual burst of the moment!

The horses went on very well; but when we drew near the post-house, the postilion stopt short, and neither threats, nor promises, could prevail on him to go forward. He even began to howl and weep, when I insisted on his keeping his word. Nothing, indeed, can equal the stupid obstinacy of some of these half alive beings, who seem to have been made by Prometheus, when the fire he stole from Heaven was so exhausted, that he could only spare a spark to give life, not animation, to the inert clay.

It was some time before we could rouse any body; and, as I

expected, horses we were told could not be had in less than four or five hours. I again attempted to bribe the churlish brute, who brought us here; but I discovered, that in spite of the courteous hostess's promise, he had received orders not to go any farther.

As there was no remedy I entered, and was almost driven back by the stench – a softer phrase would not have conveyed an idea of the hot vapour that issued from an apartment, in which some eight or ten people were sleeping, not to reckon the cats and dogs stretched on the floor. Two or three of the men or women were lying on the benches, others on old chests; and one figure started half out of a trunk to look at me, whom I might have taken for a ghost, had the *chemise* been white, to contrast with the sallow visage. But the *costume* of apparitions not being preserved I passed, nothing dreading, except the effluvia, warily amongst the pots, pans, milk-pails, and washing-tubs. After scaling a ruinous staircase, I was shewn a bed-chamber. The bed did not invite me to enter; opening, therefore, the window, and taking some clean towels out of my night-sack, I spread them over the coverlid, on which tired nature found repose, in spite of the previous disgust.

With the grey of the morn the birds awoke me; and descending to enquire for the horses, I hastened through the apartment, I have already described, not wishing to associate the idea of a pigstye with that of a human dwelling.

I do not now wonder that the girls lose their fine complexions at such an early age, or that love here is merely an appetite, to fulfil the main design of nature, never enlivened by either affection or sentiment.

For a few posts we found the horses waiting; but afterwards I was retarded, as before, by the peasants, who, taking advantage of my ignorance of the language, made me pay for the fourth horse, that ought to have gone forward to have the others in readiness, though it had never been sent. I was particularly impatient at the last post, as I longed to assure myself that my child was well.

My impatience, however, did not prevent my enjoying the journey. I had six weeks before passed over the same ground, still it had sufficient novelty to attract my attention, and beguile, if not banish, the sorrow that had taken up its abode in my heart. How interesting are the varied beauties of nature; and what peculiar charms characterize each season! The purple hue which the heath now assumed, gave it a degree of richness, that almost exceeded the lustre of the young green of spring – and harmonized exquisitely with the rays of the ripening corn. The weather was uninterruptedly fine, and the people busy in the fields cutting down the corn, or binding up the sheaves, continually varied the prospect. The rocks, it is true, were unusually rugged and dreary, yet as the road runs for a considerable way by the side of a fine river, with extended pastures on the other side, the image of sterility was not the predominant object, though the cottages looked still more miserable, after having seen the Norwegian farms. The trees, likewise, appeared of the growth of yesterday, compared with those Nestors of the forest I have frequently mentioned. The women and children were cutting off branches from the beech, birch, oak, &c, and leaving them to dry – This way of helping out their fodder, injures the trees. But the winters are so long, that the poor cannot afford to lay in a sufficient stock of hay. By such means they just keep life in the poor cows, for little milk can be expected when they are so miserably fed.

It was Saturday, and the evening was uncommonly serene. In the villages I every where saw preparations for Sunday; and I passed by a little car loaded with rye, that presented, for the pencil and heart, the sweetest picture of a harvest home I had ever beheld! A little girl was mounted a straddle on a shaggy horse, brandishing a stick over its head; the father was walking at the side of the car with a child in his arms, who must have come to meet him with tottering steps, the little creature was stretching out its arms to cling around his neck; and a boy, just above petticoats, was labouring hard, with a fork, behind, to keep the sheaves from falling.

My eyes followed them to the cottage, and an involuntary sigh whispered to my heart, that I envied the mother, much as I dislike cooking, who was preparing their pottage. I was returning to my babe, who may never experience a father's care or tenderness. The bosom that nurtured her, heaved with a pang at the thought which only an unhappy mother could feel.[105]

Adieu!

Letter Seventeen

I was unwilling to leave Gothenburg, without visiting Trollhättan. I wished not only to see the cascade, but to observe the progress of the stupendous attempt to form a canal through the rocks, to the extent of an English mile and a half.[106]

This work is carried on by a company who employ daily nine hundred men; five years was the time mentioned in the proposals, addressed to the public, as necessary for the completion. A much more considerable sum than the plan requires has been subscribed, for which there is every reason to suppose the promoters will receive ample interest.

The Danes survey the progress of this work with a jealous eye, as it is principally undertaken to get clear of the Sound duty.

Arrived at Trollhättan, I must own that the first view of the cascade disappointed me: and the sight of the works, as they advanced, though a grand proof of human industry, was not calculated to warm the fancy. I, however, wandered about; and at last coming to the conflux of the various cataracts, rushing from different falls, struggling with the huge masses of rock, and rebounding from the profound cavities, I immediately retracted, acknowledging that it was indeed a grand object. A little island stood in the midst, covered with firs, which, by dividing the torrent, rendered it more picturesque; one half appearing to issue from a dark cavern, that fancy might easily imagine a vast fountain, throwing up its waters from the very centre of the earth.[107]

I gazed I know not how long, stunned with the noise; and growing giddy with only looking at the never-ceasing tumultuous motion, I listened, scarcely conscious where I was, when I observed a boy, half obscured by the sparkling foam, fishing under the impending rock on the other side. How he had descended I could not perceive; nothing like human footsteps appeared; and the horrific crags seemed to bid defiance even to the goat's activity. It looked like an abode only fit for the eagle, though in its crevices some pines darted up their spiral heads; but they only grew near the cascade; every where else sterility itself reigned with dreary grandeur; for the huge grey massy rocks which probably had been torn asunder by some dreadful convulsion of nature, had not even their first covering of a little cleaving moss. There were so many appearances to excite the idea of chaos, that, instead of admiring the canal and the works, great as they are termed, and little as they appear, I could not help regretting that such a noble scene had not been left in all its solitary sublimity. Amidst the awful roaring of the impetuous torrents, the noise of human instruments, and the bustle of workmen, even the blowing up of the rocks, when grand masses trembled in the darkened air – only resembled the insignificant sport of children.

One fall of water, partly made by art, when they were attempting to construct sluices, had an uncommonly grand effect; the water precipitated itself with immense velocity down a perpendicular, at least fifty or sixty yards, into a gulph, so concealed by the foam as to give full play to the fancy: there was a continual uproar: I stood on a rock to observe it, a kind of bridge formed by nature, nearly on a level with the commencement of the fall. After musing by it a long time, I turned towards the other side, and saw a gentle stream stray calmly out. I should have concluded that it had no communication with the torrent, had I not seen a huge log, that fell headlong down the cascade, steal peacefully into the purling stream.

I retired from these wild scenes with regret to a miserable inn, and next morning returned to Gothenburg, to prepare for my journey to Copenhagen.

I was sorry to leave Gothenburg, without travelling further into Sweden; yet I imagine I should only have seen a romantic country thinly inhabited, and these inhabitants struggling with poverty. The Norwegian peasantry, mostly independent, have a rough kind of frankness in their manner; but the Swedish, rendered more abject by misery, have a degree of politeness in their address, which, though it may sometimes border on insincerity, is oftener the effect of a broken spirit, rather softened than degraded by wretchedness.

In Norway there are no notes in circulation of less value than a

Swedish rixdollar. A small silver coin, commonly not worth more than a penny, and never more than twopence, serves for change: but in Sweden they have notes as low as sixpence. I never saw any silver pieces there; and could not without difficulty, and giving a premium, obtain the value of a rixdollar, in a large copper coin, to give away on the road to the poor who open the gates.

As another proof of the poverty of Sweden, I ought to mention that foreign merchants, who have acquired a fortune there, are obliged to deposit the sixth part when they leave the kingdom. This law, you may suppose, is frequently evaded.

In fact, the laws here, as well as in Norway, are so relaxed, that they rather favour than restrain knavery.

Whilst I was at Gothenburg, a man who had been confined for breaking open his master's desk, and running away with five or six thousand rixdollars, was only sentenced to forty days confinement on bread and water; and this slight punishment his relations rendered nugatory by supplying him with more savoury food.

The Swedes are in general attached to their families; yet a divorce may be obtained by either party, on proving the infidelity of the other, or acknowledging it themselves.[108] The women do not often recur to this equal privilege; for they either retaliate on their husbands, by following their own devices, or sink into the merest domestic drudges, worn down by tyranny to servile submission. Do not term me severe, if I add, that after youth is flown, the husband becomes a sot; and the wife amuses herself by scolding her servants. In fact, what is to be expected in any country where taste and cultivation of mind do not supply the place of youthful beauty and animal spirits? Affection requires a firmer foundation than sympathy; and few people have a principle of action sufficiently stable to produce rectitude of feeling; for, in spite of all the arguments I have heard to justify deviations from duty, I am persuaded that even the most spontaneous sensations are more under the direction of principle than weak people are willing to allow.

But adieu to moralizing. I have been writing these last sheets at an inn in Elsinore, where I am waiting for horses; and as they are not yet ready, I will give you a short account of my journey from Gothenburg; for I set out the morning after I returned from Trollhättan.

The country, during the first day's journey, presented a most barren appearance; as rocky, yet not so picturesque as Norway, because on a diminutive scale. We stopt to sleep at a tolerable inn in Falkenberg, a decent little town.

The next day beeches and oaks began to grace the prospects, the sea every now and then appearing to give them dignity. I could not avoid observing also, that even in this part of Sweden, one of the most sterile, as I was informed, there was more ground under cultivation than in Norway. Plains of varied crops stretched out to a considerable extent, and sloped down to the shore, no longer terrific. And, as far as I could judge, from glancing my eye over the country, as we drove along, agriculture was in a more advanced state; though, in the habitations, a greater appearance of poverty still remained. The cottages indeed often looked most uncomfortable, but never so miserable as those I had remarked on the road to Strömstad; and the towns were equal, if not superior to many of the little towns in Wales, or some I have passed through on my way from Calais to Paris.

The inns, as we advanced, were not to be complained of, unless I had always thought of England. The people were civil, and much more moderate in their demands than the Norwegians, particularly to the westward, where they boldly charge for what you never had, and seem to consider you, as they do a wreck, if not as lawful prey, yet as a lucky chance, which they ought not to neglect to seize.

The prospect of Elsinore, as we passed the Sound, was pleasant. I gave three rixdollars for my boat, including something to drink. I mention the sum, because they impose on strangers.

Adieu! till I arrive at Copenhagen.

Letter Eighteen

COPENHAGEN

The distance from Elsinore to Copenhagen is twenty-two miles; the road is very good, over a flat country diversified with wood, mostly beech, and decent mansions. There appeared to be a great quantity of corn land; and the soil looked much more fertile than it is in general so near the sea. The rising grounds indeed were very few; and around Copenhagen it is a perfect plain, and of course has nothing to recommend it, but cultivation, not decorations. If I say that the houses did not disgust me, I tell you all I remember of them; for I cannot recollect any pleasurable sensations they excited; or that any object, produced by nature or art, took me out of myself. The view of the city, as we drew near, was rather grand, but, without any striking feature to interest the imagination, except the trees which shade the foot-paths.

Just before I reached Copenhagen, I saw a number of tents on a wide plain, and supposed that the rage for encampments [109] had reached this city; but I soon discovered that they were the asylum of many of the poor families who had been driven out of their habitations by the late fire. [110]

Entering soon after, I passed amongst the dust and rubbish it had left, affrighted by viewing the extent of the devastation; for at least a quarter of the city had been destroyed. There was little in the appearance of fallen bricks and stacks of chimneys to allure the imagination into soothing melancholy reveries; nothing to attract the eye of taste, but much to afflict the benevolent heart. The depredations of time have always something in them to employ the fancy, or lead to musing on subjects which, withdrawing the mind from objects of sense, seem to give it new dignity: but here I was treading on live ashes. The sufferers were still under the pressure of the misery occasioned by this dreadful conflagration. I could not take refuge in the thought; *they suffered – but they are no more!* a reflection I frequently summon to calm my mind, when sympathy rises to anguish: I therefore desired the driver to hasten to the hotel recommended to me, that I might avert my eyes, and snap the train of thinking which had sent me into all the corners of the city, in search of houseless heads.

This morning I have been walking round the town, till I am weary of observing the ravages. I had often heard the Danes, even those who had seen Paris and London, speak of Copenhagen with rapture. Certainly I have seen it in a very disadvantageous light, some of the best streets having been burnt and the whole place thrown into confusion. Still the utmost that can, or could ever, I believe, have been said in its praise, might be comprised in a few words. The streets are open, and many of the houses large; but I saw nothing to rouse the idea of elegance or grandeur, if I except the circus [111] where the king and prince royal reside.

The palace, which was consumed about two years ago, must have been a handsome spacious building: the stone-work is still standing; and a great number of the poor, during the late fire, took refuge in its ruins, till they could find some other abode. Beds were thrown on the landing places of the grand stair-case, where whole families crept from the cold, and every little nook is boarded up as a retreat for some poor creatures deprived of their home. At present a roof may be sufficient to shelter them from the night air; but as the season advances, the extent of the calamity will be more severely felt, I fear, though the exertions on the part of government are very considerable. Private charity has also, no doubt, done much to alleviate the misery which obtrudes itself at every turn; still public spirit appears to me to be hardly alive here. Had it existed, the conflagration might have been smothered in the beginning, as it was at last, by tearing down several houses before the flames had reached them. To this the inhabitants would not consent; and the prince royal not having sufficient energy of character to know when he ought to be absolute, calmly let them pursue their own course, till the whole city seemed to be threatened with destruction. Adhering, with puerile scrupulosity, to the law, which he has imposed on himself, of acting exactly right, he did wrong by idly lamenting, while he marked the progress of a mischief that one decided step would have stopt. He was afterwards obliged to resort to violent measures; but then – who could blame him? And, to avoid censure, what sacrifices are not made by weak minds! [112]

A gentleman, who was a witness of the scene, assured me, likewise, that if the people of property had taken half as much pains to extinguish the fire, as to preserve their valuables and furniture, it would soon have been got under. But they who were not immediately in danger did not exert themselves sufficiently, till fear, like an electrical shock, roused all the inhabitants to a sense of the general evil. Even the fire engines were out of order, though the burning of the palace ought to have admonished them of the necessity of keeping them in constant repair. But this kind of indolence, respecting what does not immediately concern them, seems to characterize the Danes. A sluggish concentration in themselves makes them so careful to preserve their property, that they will not venture on any enterprise to increase it, in which there is a shadow of hazard.

Considering Copenhagen as the capital of Denmark and Norway, I was surprised not to see so much industry or taste as in Christiania. Indeed from every thing I have had an opportunity of observing, the Danes are the people who have made the fewest sacrifices to the graces.

The men of business are domestic tyrants, coldly immersed in their own affairs, and so ignorant of the state of other countries, that they dogmatically assert that Denmark is the happiest country in the world; the prince royal the best of all possible princes; and count Bernstorff the wisest of ministers. [113]

As for the women, they are simply notable house-wives; without accomplishments, or any of the charms that adorn more advanced social life. This total ignorance may enable them to save something in their kitchens; but it is far from rendering them better parents. On the contrary, the children are spoilt; as they usually are, when left to the care of weak, indulgent mothers, who having no principle of action to regulate their feelings, become the slaves of infants, enfeebling both body and mind by false tenderness.

I am perhaps a little prejudiced, as I write from the impression of the moment; for I have been tormented to-day by the presence of unruly children, and made angry by some invectives thrown out against the maternal character of the unfortunate Matilda. [114] She was censured, with the most cruel insinuation, for her management of her son; though, from what I could gather, she gave proofs of good sense, as well as tenderness in her attention to him. She used to bathe him herself every morning; insisted on his being loosely clad; and would not permit his attendants to injure his digestion, by humouring his appetite. She was equally careful to prevent his acquiring haughty airs, and playing the tyrant in leading-strings. The queen dowager would not permit her to suckle him; but the next child being a daughter, and not the heir apparent of the crown, less opposition was made to her discharging the duty of a mother.

Poor Matilda! thou hast haunted me ever since my arrival; and the view I have had of the manners of the country, exciting my sympathy, has increased my respect for thy memory!

I am now fully convinced that she was the victim of the party she displaced, who would have overlooked, or encouraged, her attachment, had her lover not, aiming at being useful, attempted to overturn some established abuses before the people, ripe for the change, had sufficient spirit to support him when struggling in their behalf. Such indeed was the asperity sharpened against her, that I have heard her, even after so many years have elapsed, charged with licentiousness, not only for endeavouring to render the public amusements more elegant, but for her very charities, because she erected amongst other institutions, an hospital to receive foundlings. Disgusted with many customs which pass for virtues, though they are nothing more than observances of forms, often at the expence of truth, she probably ran into an error common to innovators, in wishing to do immediately what can only be done by time.

Many very cogent reasons have been urged by her friends to prove, that her affection for Struensee was never carried to the length alledged against her, by those who feared her influence. Be that as it may, she certainly was not a woman of gallantry; and if she had an attachment [115] for him, it did not disgrace her heart or understanding, the king being a notorious debauchee, and an idiot into the bargain. As the king's conduct had always been directed by some favourite, they also endeavoured to govern him, from a principle of self-preservation, as well as a laudable ambition; but, not aware of the prejudices they had to encounter, the system they adopted displayed more benevolence of heart than soundness of judgment. As to the charge, still believed, of their giving the king drugs to injure his faculties, it is too absurd to be refuted. Their oppressors had better have accused them of dabbling in the black art; for the potent spell still keeps his wits in bondage.

I cannot describe to you the effect it had on me to see this puppet of a monarch moved by the strings which count Bernstorff holds fast; sit, with vacant eye, erect, receiving the homage of courtiers, who mock him with a shew of respect. He is, in fact, merely a machine of state, to subscribe the name of a king to the acts of the government, which, to avoid danger, have no value, unless counter-signed by the prince royal; for he is allowed to be absolutely an idiot, excepting that now and then an observation, or trick, escapes him, which looks more like madness than imbecility.

What a farce is life! This effigy of majesty is allowed to burn down to the socket, whilst the hapless Matilda was hurried into an untimely grave.

> *As flies to wanton boys, are we to the gods;*
> *They kill us for their sport.*[116]

Adieu!

Letter Nineteen

Business having obliged me to go a few miles out of town this morning, I was surprised at meeting a crowd of people of every description; and inquiring the cause, of a servant who spoke French, I was informed that a man had been executed two hours before, and the body afterwards burnt. I could not help looking with horror around – the fields lost their verdure – and I turned with disgust from the well-dressed women, who were returning with their children from this sight. What a spectacle for humanity! The seeing such a flock of idle gazers, plunged me into a train of reflections, on the pernicious effects produced by false notions of justice. And I am persuaded that till capital punishments be entirely abolished, executions ought to have every appearance of horror given to them; instead of being, as they are now, a scene of amusement for the gaping crowd, where sympathy is quickly effaced by curiosity.

I have always been of opinion that the allowing actors to die, in the presence of the audience, has an immoral tendency; but trifling when compared with the ferocity acquired by viewing the reality as a show; for it seems to me, that in all countries the common people go to executions to see how the poor wretch plays his part, rather than to commiserate his fate, much less to think of the breach of morality which has brought him to such a deplorable end. Consequently executions, far from being useful examples to the survivors, have, I am persuaded, a quite contrary effect, by hardening the heart they ought to terrify. Besides, the fear of ignominious death, I believe, never deterred any one from the commission of a crime; because, in committing it, the mind is roused to activity about present circumstances. It is a game at hazard, at which all expect the turn of the die in their own favour; never reflecting on the chance of ruin, till it comes. In fact, from what I saw, in the fortress of Norway, I am more and more convinced that the same energy of character, which renders a man a daring villain, would have rendered him useful to society, had that society been well organized. When a strong mind is not disciplined by cultivation, it is a sense of injustice that renders it unjust.[117]

Executions, however, occur very rarely at Copenhagen; for timidity, rather than clemency, palsies all the operations of the present government. The malefactor, who died this morning, would not, probably, have been punished with death at any other period; but an incendiary excites universal execration; and as the greater part of the inhabitants are still distressed by the late conflagration, an example was thought absolutely necessary; though, from what I can gather, the fire was accidental.

Not, but that I have very seriously been informed, that combustible materials were placed at proper distances, by the emissaries of Mr Pitt;[118] and, to corroborate the fact, many people insist, that the flames burst out at once in different parts of the city; not allowing the wind to have any hand in it. So much for the plot. But the fabricators of plots in all countries build their conjectures on the 'baseless fabric of a vision';[119] and, it seems even a sort of poetical justice, that whilst this minister is crushing at home, plots of his own conjuring up, that on the continent, and in the north, he should, with as little foundation, be accused of wishing to set the world on fire.

I forgot to mention, to you, that I was informed, by a man of veracity, that two persons came to the stake to drink a glass of the criminal's blood, as an infallible remedy for the apoplexy. And when I animadverted in the company, where it was mentioned, on such a horrible violation of nature, a Danish lady reproved me very severely, asking how I knew that it was not a cure for the disease? adding, that every attempt was justifiable in search of health. I did not, you may imagine, enter into an argument with a person the slave of such a gross prejudice. And I allude to it not only as a trait of the ignorance of the people, but to censure the government, for not preventing scenes that throw an odium on the human race.

Empiricism[120] is not peculiar to Denmark; and I know no way of rooting it out, though it be a remnant of exploded witchcraft, till the acquiring a general knowledge of the component parts of the human frame, become a part of public education.

Since the fire, the inhabitants have been very assiduously employed in searching for property secreted during the confusion; and it is astonishing how many people, formerly termed reputable, had availed themselves of the common calamity to purloin what the flames spared. Others, expert at making a distinction without a difference, concealed what they found, not troubling themselves to enquire for the owners, though they scrupled to search for plunder any where, but amongst the ruins.

To be honester than the laws require, is by most people thought a work of supererogation; and to slip through the grate of the law, has ever exercised the abilities of adventurers, who wish to get rich the shortest way. Knavery, without personal danger, is an art, brought to great perfection by the statesman and swindler; and meaner knaves are not tardy in following their footsteps.

It moves my gall to discover some of the commercial frauds practised during the present war. In short, under whatever point of view I consider society, it appears, to me, that an adoration of property is the root of all evil. Here it does not render the people enterprising, as in America, but thrifty and cautious. I never, therefore, was in a capital where there was so little appearance of active industry; and as for gaiety, I looked in vain for the sprightly gait of the Norwegians, who in every respect appear to me to have got the start of them. This difference I attribute to their having more liberty: a liberty which they think their right by inheritance, whilst the Danes, when they boast of their negative happiness, always mention it as the boon of the prince royal, under the superintending wisdom of count Bernstorff. Vassallage is nevertheless ceasing throughout the kingdom, and with it will pass away that sordid avarice which every modification of slavery is calculated to produce.

If the chief use of property be power, in the shape of the respect it procures, is it not among the inconsistencies of human nature most incomprehensible, that men should find a pleasure in hoarding up property which they steal from their necessities, even when they are convinced that it would be dangerous to display such an enviable superiority? Is not this the situation of serfs in every country; yet a rapacity to accumulate money seems to become stronger in proportion as it is allowed to be useless.

Wealth does not appear to be sought for, amongst the Danes, to obtain the elegant luxuries of life; for a want of taste is very conspicuous at Copenhagen; so much so, that I am not surprised to hear that poor Matilda offended the rigid lutherans, by aiming to refine their pleasures. The elegance which she wished to introduce, was termed lasciviousness: yet I do not find that the absence of gallantry renders the wives more chaste, or the husbands more constant. Love here seems to corrupt the morals, without polishing the manners, by banishing confidence and truth, the charm as well as cement of domestic life. A gentleman, who has resided in this city some time, assures me that he could not find language to give me an idea of the gross debaucheries into which the lower order of people fall; and the promiscuous amours of the men of the middling class with their female servants, debases both beyond measure, weakening every species of family affection.

I have every where been struck by one characteristic difference in the conduct of the two sexes; women, in general, are seduced by their superiors, and men jilted by their inferiors; rank and manners awe the one, and cunning and wantonness subjugate the other; ambition creeping into the woman's passion, and tyranny giving force to the man's; for most men treat their mistresses as kings do their favourites: *ergo* is not man then the tyrant of the creation?

Still harping on the same subject, you will exclaim – How can I avoid it, when most of the struggles of an eventful life have been occasioned by the oppressed state of my sex: we reason deeply, when we forcibly feel.

But to return to the straight road of observation. The sensuality so prevalent appears to me to arise rather from indolence of mind, and dull senses, than from an exuberance of life, which often fructifies the whole character when the vivacity of youthful spirits begins to subside into strength of mind.

I have before mentioned that the men are domestic tyrants, considering them as fathers, brothers, or husbands; but there is a kind of interregnum between the reign of the father and husband, which is the only period of freedom and pleasure that the women enjoy. Young people, who are attached to each other, with the consent of their friends, exchange rings, and are permitted to enjoy a degree of liberty together, which I have never noticed in any other country. The days of courtship are therefore prolonged, till it be perfectly convenient to marry: the intimacy often becomes very tender: and if the lover obtain the privilege of a husband, it can only be termed half by stealth, because the family is wilfully blind. It happens very rarely that these honorary engagements are dissolved or disregarded, a stigma being attached to a breach of faith, which is thought more disgraceful, if not so criminal, as the violation of the marriage vow.[121]

Do not forget that, in my general observations, I do not pretend to sketch a national character; but merely to note the present state of morals and manners, as I trace the progress of the world's improvement. Because, during my residence in different countries, my principal object has been to take such a dispassionate view of men as will lead me to form a just idea of the nature of man. And, to deal ingenuously with you, I believe I should have been less severe in the remarks I have made on the vanity and depravity of the French,* had I travelled towards the north before I visited France.

The interesting picture frequently drawn of the virtues of a rising people has, I fear, been fallacious, excepting the accounts of the enthusiasm which various public struggles have produced. We talk of the depravity of the French, and lay a stress on the old age of the nation; yet where has more virtuous enthusiasm been displayed than during the two last years, by the common people of France and in their armies? I am obliged sometimes to recollect the numberless instances which I have either witnessed, or heard well authenticated, to balance the account of horrors, alas! but too true. I am, therefore, inclined to believe that the gross vices which I have always seen allied with simplicity of manners, are the concomitants of ignorance.

What, for example, has piety, under the heathen or christian system, been, but a blind faith in things contrary to the principles of reason? And could poor reason make considerable advances, when it was reckoned the highest degree of virtue to do violence to its dictates? Lutherans preaching reformation, have built a reputation for sanctity on the same foundation as the catholics; yet I do not perceive that a regular attendance on public worship, and their other observances, make them a whit more true in their affections, or honest in their

---

* See *Historical and Moral View of the French Revolution.*

private transactions. It seems, indeed, quite as easy to prevaricate with religious injunctions as human laws, when the exercise of their reason does not lead people to acquire principles for themselves to be the criterion of all those they receive from others.

If travelling, as the completion of a liberal education, were to be adopted on rational grounds, the northern states ought to be visited before the more polished parts of Europe, to serve as the elements even of the knowledge of manners, only to be acquired by tracing the various shades in different countries. But, when visiting distant climes, a momentary social sympathy should not be allowed to influence the conclusions of the understanding; for hospitality too frequently leads travellers, especially those who travel in search of pleasure, to make a false estimate of the virtues of a nation; which, I am now convinced, bear an exact proportion to their scientific improvements.[122]

Adieu.

Letter Twenty

I have formerly censured the French for their extreme attachment to theatrical exhibitions, because I thought that they tended to render them vain and unnatural characters. But I must acknowledge, especially as women of the town never appear in the Parisian, as at our theatres, that the little saving of the week is more usefully expended there, every Sunday, than in porter or brandy, to intoxicate or stupify the mind. The common people of France have a great superiority over that class in every other country on this very score. It is merely the sobriety of the Parisians which renders their fêtes more interesting, their gaiety never becoming disgusting or dangerous; as is always the case when liquor circulates. Intoxication is the pleasure of savages, and of all those whose employments rather exhaust their animal spirits, than exercise their faculties. Is not this, in fact, the vice, both in England and the northern states of Europe, which appears to be the greatest impediment to general improvement?[123] Drinking is here the principal relaxation of the men, including smoking; but the women are very abstemious, though they have no public amusements as a substitute. I ought to except one theatre,[124] which appears more than is necessary; for when I was there, it was not half full; and neither the ladies nor actresses displayed much fancy in their dress.

The play was founded on the story of the Mock Doctor;[125] and, from the gestures of the servants, who were the best actors, I should imagine contained some humour. The farce, termed *ballat*, was a kind of pantomime, the childish incidents of which were sufficient to shew the state of the dramatic art in Denmark, and the gross taste of the audience. A magician, in the disguise of a tinker, enters a cottage where the women are all busy ironing, and rubs a dirty frying-pan against the linen. The women raise an hue-and-cry, and dance after him, rousing their husbands, who join in the dance, but get the start of them in the pursuit. The tinker, with the frying-pan for a shield, renders them immoveable, and blacks their cheeks. Each laughs at the other, unconscious of his own appearance; mean while the women enter to enjoy the sport, '*the rare fun*', with other incidents of the same species.

The singing was much on a par with the dancing; the one as destitute of grace, as the other of expression; but the orchestra was well filled, the instrumental being far superior to the vocal music.

I have likewise visited the public library and museum, as well as the palace of Rosenborg.[126] This palace, now deserted, displays a gloomy kind of grandeur throughout; for the silence of spacious apartments always makes itself to be felt; I at least feel it; and I listen for the sound of my footsteps, as I have done at midnight to the ticking of the death-watch, encouraging a kind of fanciful superstition. Every object carried me back to past times, and impressed the manners of the age forcibly on my mind. In this point of view the preservation of old palaces, and their tarnished furniture, is useful; for they may be considered as historical documents.

The vacuum left by departed greatness was every where observable, whilst the battles and processions, portrayed on the walls, told you who had here excited revelry after retiring from slaughter; or dismissed pageantry in search of pleasure. It seemed a vast tomb, full of the shadowy phantoms of those who had played or toiled their hour out, and sunk behind the tapestry, which celebrated the conquests of love or war. Could they be no more – to whom my imagination thus gave life? Could the thoughts, of which there remained so many vestiges, have vanished quite away? And these beings, composed of such noble materials of thinking and feeling, have they only melted into the elements to keep in motion the grand mass of life? It cannot be! – As easily could I believe that the large silver lions, at the top of the banqueting room, thought and reasoned. But avaunt! ye waking dreams! – yet I cannot describe the curiosities to you.

There were cabinets full of baubles, and gems, and swords, which must have been wielded by giant's hand. The coronation ornaments wait quietly here till wanted; and the wardrobe exhibits the vestments which formerly graced these shews. It is a pity they do not lend them to the actors, instead of allowing them to perish ingloriously.

I have not visited any other palace, excepting Hirsholm; the gardens of which are laid out with taste, and command the finest views the country affords. As they are in the modern and English style, I thought I was following the footsteps of Matilda, who wished to multiply around her the images of her beloved country. I was also gratified by the sight of a Norwegian landscape in miniature, which with great propriety makes a part of the Danish king's garden. The cottage is well imitated, and the whole has a pleasing effect, particularly so to me who love Norway – its peaceful farms and spacious wilds.

The public library [127] consists of a collection much larger than I expected to see; and it is well arranged. Of the value of the Icelandic manuscripts I could not form a judgment, though the alphabet of some of them amused me, by shewing what immense labour men will submit to, in order to transmit their ideas to posterity. I have sometimes thought it a great misfortune for individuals to acquire a certain delicacy of sentiment, which often makes them weary of the common occurrences of life; yet it is this very delicacy of feeling and thinking which probably has produced most of the performances that have benefited mankind. It might with propriety, perhaps, be termed the malady of genius; the cause of that characteristic melancholy which 'grows with its growth, and strengthens with its strength'.[128]

There are some good pictures in the royal museum – Do not start – I am not going to trouble you with a dull catalogue, or stupid criticisms on masters, to whom time has assigned their just niche in the temple of fame; had there been any by living artists of this country, I should have noticed them, as making a part of the sketches I am drawing of the present state of the place. The good pictures were mixed indiscriminately with the bad ones, in order to assort the frames. The same fault is conspicuous in the new splendid gallery forming at Paris; [129] though it seems an obvious thought that a school for artists ought to be arranged in such a manner, as to shew the progressive discoveries and improvements in the art.

A collection of the dresses, arms, and implements of the Laplanders attracted my attention, displaying that first species of ingenuity which is rather a proof of patient perseverance, than comprehension of mind. The specimens of natural history, and curiosities of art, were likewise huddled together without that scientific order which alone renders them useful; but this may partly have been occasioned by the hasty manner in which they were removed from the palace, when in flames.

There are some respectable men of science here, but few literary characters, and fewer artists. They want encouragement, and will continue, I fear, from the present appearance of things, to languish unnoticed a long time; for neither the vanity of wealth, nor the enterprising spirit of commerce, has yet thrown a glance that way.

Besides, the prince royal, determined to be economical, almost descends to parsimony; and perhaps depresses his subjects, by labouring not to oppress them; for his intentions always seem to be good — yet nothing can give a more forcible idea of the dullness which eats away all activity of mind, than the insipid routine of a court, without magnificence or elegance.

The prince, from what I can now collect, has very moderate abilities; yet is so well disposed, that count Bernstorff finds him as tractable as he could wish; for I consider the count as the real sovereign, scarcely behind the curtain; the prince having none of that obstinate self-sufficiency of youth, so often the fore-runner of decision of character. He, and the princess his wife, dine every day with the king, to save the expence of two tables. What a mummery it must be to treat as a king a being who has lost the majesty of man! But even count Bernstorff's morality submits to this standing imposition; and he avails himself of it sometimes, to soften a refusal of his own, by saying it is the *will* of the king, my master, when every body knows that he has neither will nor memory. Much the same use is made of him as, I have observed, some termagant wives make of their husbands; they would dwell on the necessity of obeying their husbands, poor passive souls, who never were allowed *to will*, when they wanted to conceal their own tyranny.

A story is told here of the king's formerly making a dog counsellor of state, because when the dog, accustomed to eat at the royal table, snatched a piece of meat off an old officer's plate, he reproved him jocosely, saying that he, *monsieur le chien*, had not the privilege of dining with his majesty; a privilege annexed to this distinction.

The burning of the palace was, in fact, a fortunate circumstance, as it afforded a pretext for reducing the establishment of the hous-

hold, which was far too great for the revenue of the crown. The
Prince Royal, at present, runs into the opposite extreme; and the
formality, if not the parsimony, of the court, seems to extend to all
the other branches of society, which I had an opportunity of
observing; though hospitality still characterizes their intercourse with
strangers.

But let me now stop; I may be a little partial, and view every thing
with the jaundiced eye of melancholy – for I am sad – and have
cause.

God bless you!

Letter Twenty-one

I have seen count Bernstorff;[130] and his conversation confirms me in the opinion I had previously formed of him; — I mean, since my arrival at Copenhagen. He is a worthy man, a little vain of his virtue *à la Necker*;[131] and more anxious not to do wrong, that is to avoid blame, than desirous of doing good; especially if any particular good demands a change. Prudence, in short, seems to be the basis of his character; and, from the tenour of the government, I should think inclining to that cautious circumspection which treads on the heels of timidity. He has considerable information, and some finesse; or he could not be a minister. Determined not to risk his popularity, for he is tenderly careful of his reputation, he will never gloriously fail like Struensee, or disturb, with the energy of genius, the stagnant state of the public mind.

I suppose that Lavater,[132] whom he invited to visit him two years ago, some say to fix the principles of the christian religion firmly in the prince royal's mind, found lines in his face to prove him a statesman of the first order; because he has a knack at seeing a great character in the countenances of men in exalted stations, who have noticed him, or his works. Besides, the count's sentiments relative to the French revolution, agreeing with Lavater's, must have ensured his applause.

The Danes, in general, seem extremely averse to innovation, and, if happiness only consist in opinion, they are the happiest people in the world; for I never saw any so well satisfied with their own situation. Yet the climate appears to be very disagreeable; the weather being dry and sultry, or moist and cold; the atmosphere never having that sharp, bracing purity, which in Norway prepares you to brave its rigours. I do not then hear the inhabitants of this place talk with delight of the winter, which is the constant theme of the Norwegians, on the contrary they seem to dread its comfortless inclemency.

The ramparts are pleasant, and must have been much more so before the fire, the walkers not being annoyed by the clouds of dust, which, at present, the slightest wind wafts from the ruins. The windmills, and the comfortable houses contiguous, belonging to the millers, as well as the appearance of the spacious barracks for the soldiers and sailors, tend to render this walk more agreeable. The view of the country has not much to recommend it to notice, but its extent and cultivation: yet as the eye always delights to dwell on verdant plains, especially when we are resident in a great city, these shady walks should be reckoned amongst the advantages procured by the government for the inhabitants. I like them better than the royal gardens, also open to the public, because the latter seem sunk in the heart of the city, to concentrate its fogs.

The canals, which intersect the streets, are equally convenient and wholesome; but the view of the sea, commanded by the town, had little to interest me whilst the remembrance of the various bold and picturesque shores, I had seen, was fresh in my memory. Still the opulent inhabitants, who seldom go abroad, must find the spots where they fix their country seats much pleasanter on account of the vicinity of the ocean.

One of the best streets in Copenhagen is almost filled with hospitals, erected by the government; and, I am assured, as well regulated as institutions of this kind are in any country; but whether hospitals, or workhouses, are any where superintended with sufficient humanity, I have frequently had reason to doubt.

The autumn is so uncommonly fine, that I am unwilling to put off my journey to Hamburg much longer, lest the weather should alter suddenly, and the chilly harbingers of winter catch me here, where I have nothing now to detain me but the hospitality of the families to whom I had recommendatory letters. I lodged at an hotel situated in a large open square, where the troops exercise, and the market is kept. My apartments were very good; and, on account of the fire, I was told that I should be charged very high; yet, paying my bill just now, I find the demands much lower in proportion than in Norway, though my dinners were in every respect better.

I have remained more at home, since I arrived at Copenhagen, than I ought to have done in a strange place; but the mind is not always equally active in search of information; and my oppressed heart too often sighs out,

> *How dull, flat, and unprofitable*
> *Are to me all the usages of this world —*
> *That it should come to this!* —[133]

Farewell! Fare thee well, I say — if thou can'st, repeat the adieu in a different tone.

Letter Twenty-two

I arrived at Korsör the night after I quitted Copenhagen, purposing to take my passage across the Great Belt the next morning, though the weather was rather boisterous. It is about four and twenty miles; but as neither I nor my little girl are ever attacked by sea sickness, though who can avoid *ennui*? I enter a boat with the same indifference as I change horses; and as for danger, come when it may, I dread it not sufficiently to have any anticipating fears.

The road from Copenhagen was very good, through an open, flat country, that had little to recommend it to notice excepting the cultivation, which gratified my heart more than my eye.

I took a barge with a German baron, who was hastening back from a tour into Denmark, alarmed by the intelligence of the French having passed the Rhine.[134] His conversation beguiled the time, and gave a sort of stimulus to my spirits, which had been growing more and more languid ever since my return to Gothenburg – you know why. I had often endeavoured to rouse myself to observation by reflecting that I was passing through scenes which I should probably never see again, and consequently ought not to omit observing; still I fell into reveries, thinking, by way of excuse, that enlargement of mind and refined feelings are of little use, but to barb the arrows of sorrow which waylay us every where, eluding the sagacity of wisdom, and rendering principles unavailing, if considered as a breast-work to secure our own hearts.

Though we had not a direct wind, we were not detained more than three hours and a half on the water, just long enough to give us an appetite for our dinner.

We travelled the remainder of the day, and the following night, in company with the same party, the German gentleman whom I have mentioned, his friend, and servant: the meetings, at the post-houses, were pleasant to me, who usually heard nothing but strange tongues around me. Marguerite and the child often fell asleep; and when they were awake, I might still reckon myself alone, as our train of thoughts had nothing in common. Marguerite, it is true, was much amused by the *costume* of the women; particularly by the *panier** which adorned both their heads and tails: and, with great glee, recounted to me the stories she had treasured up for her family, when once more within the barriers of dear Paris; not forgetting, with that arch, agreeable vanity peculiar to the French, which they exhibit whilst half ridiculing it, to remind me of the importance she should assume when she informed her friends of all her journeys by sea and land – shewing the pieces of money she had collected, and stammering out a few foreign phrases, which she repeated in a true Parisian accent. Happy thoughtlessness; aye, and enviable harmless vanity, which thus produced a *gaité du coeur* worth all my philosophy.

The man I had hired at Copenhagen advised me to go round, about twenty miles, to avoid passing the Little Belt, excepting by a ferry, as the wind was contrary. But the gentlemen over-ruled his arguments, which we were all very sorry for afterwards when we found ourselves becalmed on the Little Belt ten hours, tacking about, without ceasing, to gain on the shore.[135]

An over-sight likewise made the passage appear much more tedious, nay almost insupportable. When I went on board at the Great Belt, I had provided refreshments in case of detention, which remaining untouched, I thought not then any such precaution necessary for the second passage, misled by the epithet of little, though I have since been informed that it is frequently the longest. This mistake occasioned much vexation; for the child, at last, began to cry so bitterly for bread, that fancy conjured up before me the wretched Ugolino,[136] with his famished children; and I, literally speaking, enveloped myself in sympathetic horrors, augmented by every tear my babe shed; from which I could not escape, till we landed, and a luncheon of bread, and basin of milk, routed the spectres of fancy.

I then supped with my companions, with whom I was soon after to part for ever – always a most melancholy, death-like idea – a sort of separation of soul; for all the regret which follows those from whom fate separates us, seems to be something torn from ourselves. These

* This word in French means both basket and hoop.

were strangers I remember; yet when there is any originality in a countenance, it takes its place in our memory; and we are sorry to lose an acquaintance the moment he begins to interest us, though picked up on the highway. There was, in fact, a degree of intelligence, and still more sensibility in the features and conversation of one of the gentlemen, that made me regret the loss of his society during the rest of the journey; for he was compelled to travel post, by his desire to reach his estate before the arrival of the French.

This was a comfortable inn, as were several others I stopt at; but the heavy sandy roads were very fatiguing, after the fine ones we had lately skimmed over both in Sweden and Denmark. The country resembled the most open part of England; laid out for corn, rather than grazing: it was pleasant; yet there was little in the prospects to awaken curiosity, by displaying the peculiar characteristics of a new country, which had so frequently stole me from myself in Norway. We often passed over large unenclosed tracts, not graced with trees, or at least very sparingly enlivened by them; and the half-formed roads seemed to demand the landmarks, set up in the waste, to prevent the traveller from straying far out of his way, and plodding through the wearisome sand.

The heaths were dreary, and had none of the wild charms of those of Sweden and Norway to cheat time; neither the terrific rocks, nor smiling herbage, grateful to the sight, and scented from afar, made us forget their length; still the country appeared much more populous; and the towns, if not the farm-houses, were superior to those of Norway. I even thought that the inhabitants of the former had more intelligence, at least I am sure they had more vivacity in their coun- tenances than I had seen during my northern tour: their senses seemed awake to business and pleasure. I was, therefore, gratified by hearing once more the busy hum of industrious men in the day, and the exhilarating sounds of joy in the evening; for as the weather was still fine, the women and children were amusing themselves at their doors, or walking under the trees, which in many places were planted in the streets; and as most of the towns of any note were situated on little bays, or branches, of the Baltic, their appearance, as we approached, was often very picturesque, and, when we entered, displayed the comfort and cleanliness of easy, if not the elegance of opulent, circumstances.

But the chearfulness of the people in the streets was particularly grateful to me, after having been depressed by the deathlike silence of those of Denmark, where every house made me think of a tomb. The dress of the peasantry is suited to the climate; in short, none of that poverty and dirt appeared, at the sight of which the heart sickens.

As I only stopt to change horses, take refreshment, and sleep, I had not an opportunity of knowing more of the country than conclusions, which the information gathered by my eyes enabled me to draw; and that was sufficient to convince me that I should much rather have lived in some of the towns I now pass through, than in any I had seen in Sweden or Denmark. The people struck me, as having arrived at that period when the faculties will unfold themselves; in short, they look alive to improvement, neither congealed by indolence, nor bent down by wretchedness to servility.

From the previous impression, I scarcely can trace from whence I received it, I was agreeably surprised to perceive such an appearance of comfort in this part of Germany. I had formed a conception of the tyranny of the petty potentates that had thrown a gloomy veil over the face of the whole country, in my imagination, that cleared away like the darkness of night before the sun. As I saw the reality, I should probably have discovered much lurking misery, the consequence of ignorant oppression, no doubt, had I had time to inquire into particulars; but it did not stalk abroad, and infect the surface over which my eye glanced. Yes, I am persuaded that a considerable degree of general knowledge pervades this country; for it is only from the exercise of the mind that the body acquires the activity from which I drew these inferences. Indeed the king of Denmark's German dominions, Holstein, appeared to me far superiour to any other part of his kingdom which had fallen under my view; and the robust rustics to have their muscles braced, instead of the *as it were* lounge of the Danish peasantry.

Arriving at Schleswig, the residence of prince Charles of Hesse-Cassel, the sight of the soldiers recalled all the unpleasing ideas of German despotism, which imperceptibly vanished as I advanced into the country. I view, with a mixture of pity and horror, these beings training to be sold to slaughter, or be slaughtered, and fell into reflections, on an old opinion of mine, that it is the preservation of the species, not of individuals, which appears to be the design of the Deity throughout the whole of nature. Blossoms come forth only to be blighted; fish lay their spawn where it will be devoured: and what a large portion of the human race are born merely to be swept prematurely away. Does not this waste of budding life emphatically assert, that it is not men, but man, whose preservation is so necessary to the completion of the grand plan of the universe? Children peep into existence, suffer, and die; men play like moths about a candle, and sink into the flame: war, and 'the thousand ills which flesh is heir to',[137] mow them down in shoals, whilst the more cruel prejudices of society palsies existence, introducing not less sure, though slower decay.

The castle was heavy and gloomy; yet the grounds about it were laid out with some taste; a walk, winding under the shade of lofty trees, led to a regularly built, and animated town.

I crossed the draw-bridge, and entered to see this shell of a court in miniature, mounting ponderous stairs, it would be a solecism to say a flight, up which a regiment of men might have marched, shouldering their firelocks, to exercise in vast galleries, where all the generations of the princes of Hesse-Cassel might have been mustered rank and file, though not the phantoms of all the wretched they had bartered to support their state, unless these airy substances could shrink and expand, like Milton's devils, to suit the occasion.[138]

The sight of the presence-chamber, and of the canopy to shade the *fauteuil*, which aped a throne, made me smile. All the world is a stage, thought I; and few are there in it who do not play the part they have learnt by rote; and those who do not, seem marks set up to be pelted at by fortune; or rather as sign-posts, which point out the road to others, whilst forced to stand still themselves amidst the mud and dust.

Waiting for our horses, we were amused by observing the dress of the women, which was very grotesque and unwieldy. The false notion of beauty which prevails, here, as well as in Denmark, I should think very inconvenient in summer, as it consists in giving a rotundity to a certain part of the body, not the most slim, when nature has done her part. This Dutch prejudice often leads them to toil under the weight of some ten or a dozen petticoats, which, with an enormous basket, literally speaking, as a bonnet, or a straw hat of dimensions equally gigantic, almost completely concealing the human form, as well as face divine, often worth shewing – still they looked clean, and tript along, as it were, before the wind, with a weight of tackle that I could scarcely have lifted. Many of the country girls, I met, appeared to me pretty, that is, to have fine complexions, sparkling eyes, and a kind of arch, hoyden playfulness which distinguishes the village coquette. The swains, in their Sunday trim, attended some of these fair ones, in a more slouching pace, though their dress was not so cumbersome. The women seem to take the lead in polishing the manners every where, that being the only way to better their condition.

From what I have seen throughout my journey, I do not think the situation of the poor in England is much, if at all superior to that of the same class in different parts of the world; and in Ireland, I am sure, it is much inferior. I allude to the former state of England; for at present the accumulation of national wealth only increases the cares of the poor, and hardens the hearts of the rich, in spite of the highly extolled rage for alms-giving.

You know that I have always been an enemy to what is termed charity, because timid bigots endeavouring thus to cover their *sins*, do violence to justice, till, acting the demi-god, they forget that they are men. And there are others who do not even think of laying up a treasure in heaven, whose benevolence is merely tyranny in disguise: they assist the most worthless, because the most servile, and term them helpless only in proportion to their fawning.

After leaving Schleswig, we passed through several pretty towns; Itzehoe particularly pleased me: and the country still wearing the same aspect, was improved by the appearance of more trees and enclosures. But what gratified me most, was the population. I was weary of travelling four or five hours, never meeting a carriage, and scarcely a peasant – and then to stop at such wretched huts, as I had seen in Sweden, was surely sufficient to chill any heart, awake to sympathy, and throw a gloom over my favourite subject of contemplation, the future improvement of the world.[139]

The farm-houses, likewise, with the huge stables, into which we drove, while the horses were putting to, or baiting, were very clean and commodious. The rooms, with a door into this hall-like stable and storehouse in one, were decent; and there was a compactness in the appearance of the whole family lying thus snugly together under the same roof, that carried my fancy back to the primitive times, which probably never existed with such a golden lustre as the animated imagination lends, when only able to seize the prominent features.

At one of them, a pretty young woman,[140] with languishing eyes, of celestial blue, conducted us into a very neat parlour; and observing how loosely, and lightly, my little girl was clad, began to pity her in the sweetest accents, regardless of the rosy down of health on her cheeks. This same damsel was dressed, it was Sunday, with taste, and even coquetry, in a cotton jacket, ornamented with knots of blue ribbon, fancifully disposed to give life to her fine complexion. I loitered a little to admire her, for every gesture was graceful; and, amidst the other villagers, she looked like a garden lily suddenly rearing its head amongst grain, and corn-flowers. As the house was small, I gave her a piece of money, rather larger than it was my custom to give to the female waiters; for I could not prevail on her to sit down; which she received with a smile; yet took care to give it, in my presence, to a girl, who had brought the child a slice of bread; by which I perceived that she was the mistress, or daughter, of the house – and without doubt the *belle* of the village. There was, in short, an appearance of chearful industry, and of that degree of comfort which shut out misery, in all the little hamlets as I approached Hamburg, which agreeably surprised me.

The short jackets which the women wear here, as well as in France, are not only more becoming to the person, but much better calculated for women who have rustic or houshold employments, than the long gowns worn in England, dangling in the dirt.

All the inns on the road were better than I expected, though the softness of the beds still harassed me, and prevented my finding the rest I was frequently in want of, to enable me to bear the fatigue of the next day. The charges were moderate, and the people very civil, with a certain honest hilarity and independent spirit in their manner, which almost made me forget that they were inn-keepers, a set of men, waiters, hostesses, chamber-maids, &c. down to the ostler, whose cunning servility, in England, I think particularly disgusting.

The prospect of Hamburg, at a distance, as well as the fine road shaded with trees, led me to expect to see a much pleasanter city than I found.

I was aware of the difficulty of obtaining lodgings, even at the inns, on account of the concourse of strangers at present resorting to such a centrical situation, and determined to go to Altona the next day to seek for an abode, wanting now only rest. But even for a single night we were sent from house to house, and found at last a vacant room to sleep in, which I should have turned from with disgust, had there been a choice.

I scarcely know any thing that produces more disagreeable sensations, I mean to speak of the passing cares, the recollection of which afterwards enlivens our enjoyments, than those excited by little disasters of this kind. After a long journey, with our eyes directed to some particular spot, to arrive and find nothing as it should be, is vexatious, and sinks the agitated spirits. But I, who received the cruelest of disappointments, last spring,[141] in returning to my home, term such as these emphatically passing cares. Know you of what materials some hearts are made? I play the child, and weep at the recollection – for the grief is still fresh that stunned as well as wounded me – yet never did drops of anguish like these bedew the cheeks of infantine innocence – and why should they mine, that never were stained by a blush of guilt? Innocent and credulous as a child, why have I not the same happy thoughtlessness?

Adieu!

Letter Twenty-three

I might have spared myself the disagreeable feelings I experienced the first night of my arrival at Hamburg, leaving the open air to be shut up in noise and dirt, had I gone immediately to Altona, where a lodging had been prepared for me by a gentleman from whom I received many civilities during my journey. I wished to have travelled in company with him from Copenhagen, because I found him intelligent and friendly; but business obliged him to hurry forward; and I wrote to him on the subject of accommodations, as soon as I was informed of the difficulties I might have to encounter to house myself and brat.

It is but a short and pleasant walk from Hamburg to Altona, under the shade of several rows of trees; and this walk is the more agreeable, after quitting the rough pavement of either place.

Hamburg is an ill, close-built town, swarming with inhabitants; and, from what I could learn, like all the other free towns, governed in a manner which bears hard on the poor, whilst narrowing the minds of the rich, the character of the man is lost in the Hamburger. Always afraid of the encroachments of their Danish neighbours, that is, anxiously apprehensive of their sharing the golden harvest of commerce with them, or taking a little of the trade off their hands, though they have more than they know what to do with, they are ever on the watch, till their very eyes lose all expression, excepting the prying glance of suspicion.

The gates of Hamburg are shut at seven, in the winter, and nine in the summer, lest some strangers, who come to traffic in Hamburg, should prefer living, and consequently, so exactly do they calculate, spend their money out of the walls of the Hamburger's world. Immense fortunes have been acquired by the *per cents* arising from commissions, nominally only two and a half; but mounted to eight or ten at least, by the secret *manoeuvres* of trade, not to include the advantage of purchasing goods wholesale, in common with contractors, and that of having so much money left in their hands – not to play with, I can assure you. Mushroom fortunes have started up during the war; the men, indeed, seem of the species of the fungus; and the insolent vulgarity which a sudden influx of wealth usually produces in common minds, is here very conspicuous, which contrasts with the distresses of many of the emigrants, 'fallen – fallen from their high estate' [142] – such are the ups and downs of fortune's wheel! Many emigrants have met, with fortitude, such a total change of circumstances as scarcely can be paralleled, retiring from a palace, to an obscure lodging, with dignity; but the greater number glide about the ghosts of greatness, with the *croix de St Louis* [143] ostentatiously displayed, determined to hope, 'though heaven and earth their wishes crossed'. Still good-breeding points out the gentleman; and sentiments of honour and delicacy appear the offspring of greatness of soul, when compared with the grovelling views of the sordid accumulators of *cent per cent.*[144]

Situation seems to be the mould in which men's characters are formed; so much so, inferring from what I have lately seen, that I mean not to be severe when I add, previously asking why priests are in general cunning, and statesmen false? that men entirely devoted to commerce never acquire, or lose, all taste and greatness of mind. An ostentatious display of wealth without elegance, and a greedy enjoyment of pleasure without sentiment, embrutes them till they term all virtue, of an heroic cast, romantic attempts at something above our nature; and anxiety about the welfare of others, a search after misery, in which we have no concern. But you will say that I am growing bitter, perhaps, personal. Ah! shall I whisper to you – that you – yourself, are strangely altered, since you have entered deeply into commerce – more than you are aware of – never allowing yourself to reflect, and keeping your mind, or rather passions in a continual state of agitation – Nature has given you talents, which lie dormant, or are wasted in ignoble pursuits – You will rouse yourself, and shake off the vile dust that obscures you, or my understanding, as well as my heart, deceives, me, egregiously – only tell me when? But to go farther a-field.[145]

Madame La Fayette left Altona the day I arrived, to endeavour, at

Vienna, to obtain the enlargement of her husband, or permission to share his prison. She lived in a lodging up two pair of stairs, without a servant, her two daughters chearfully assisting; chusing, as well as herself, to descend to any thing before unnecessary obligations. During her prosperity, and consequent idleness, she did not, I am told, enjoy a good state of health, having a train of nervous complaints which, though they have not a name, unless the significant word *ennui* be borrowed, had an existence in the higher French circles; but adversity and virtuous exertions put these ills to flight, and dispossessed her of a devil, who deserves the appellation of legion.[146]

Madame Genlis,[147] also, resided at Altona some time, under an assumed name, with many other sufferers of less note, though higher rank. It is, in fact, scarcely possible to stir out without meeting interesting countenances, every lineament of which tells you that they have seen better days.

At Hamburg, I was informed, a duke had entered into partnership with his cook, who becoming a *traiteur*,[148] they were both comfortably supported by the profit arising from his industry. Many noble instances of the attachment of servants to their unfortunate masters, have come to my knowledge both here and in France, and touched my heart, the greatest delight of which is to discover human virtue.

At Altona, a president of one of the *ci-devant* parliaments keeps an ordinary,[149] in the French style; and his wife, with chearful dignity, submits to her fate, though she is arrived at an age when people seldom relinquish their prejudices. A girl who waits there brought a dozen *double louis d'or* concealed in her clothes, at the risk of her life, from France; which she preserves, lest sickness, or any other distress, should overtake her mistress, 'who,' she observed, 'was not accustomed to hardships.' This house was particularly recommended to me by an acquaintance of your's, the author of the American Farmer's Letters.[150] I generally dine in company with him: and the gentleman whom I have already mentioned, is often diverted by our declamations against commerce, when we compare notes respecting the characteristics of the Hamburgers. 'Why, madam,' said he to me one day, 'you will not meet with a man who has any calf to his leg; body and soul, muscles and heart, are equally shrivelled up by a thirst of gain. There is nothing generous even in their youthful passions;

profit is their only stimulus, and calculations the sole employment of their faculties; unless we except some gross animal gratifications which, snatched *at spare moments*, tend still more to debase the character, because, though touched by his tricking wand, they have all the arts, without the wit, of the wing-footed god.'[151]

Perhaps you may also think us too severe; but I must add, that the more I saw of the manners of Hamburg, the more was I confirmed in my opinion relative to the baleful effect of extensive speculations on the moral character. Men are strange machines; and their whole system of morality is in general held together by one grand principle, which loses its force the moment they allow themselves to break with impunity over the bounds which secured their self-respect. A man ceases to love humanity, and then individuals, as he advances in the chase after wealth; as one clashes with his interest, the other with his pleasures: to business, as it is termed, every thing must give way; nay, is sacrificed; and all the endearing charities of citizen, husband, father, brother, become empty names. But – but what? Why, to snap the chain of thought, I must say farewell. Cassandra was not the only prophetess whose warning voice has been disregarded. How much easier it is to meet with love in the world, than affection!

Your's, sincerely.

Letter Twenty-four

My lodgings at Altona are tolerably comfortable, though not in any proportion to the price I pay; but, owing to the present circumstances, all the necessaries of life are here extravagantly dear. Considering it as a temporary residence, the chief inconvenience of which, I am inclined to complain, is the rough streets that must be passed before Marguerite and the child can reach a level road.

The views of the Elbe, in the vicinity of the town, are pleasant, particularly as the prospects here afford so little variety. I attempted to descend, and walk close to the water edge; but there was no path; and the smell of glue, hanging to dry, an extensive manufactory of which is carried on close to the beach, I found extremely disagreeable. But to commerce every thing must give way; profit and profit are the only speculations – 'double – double, toil and trouble.'[152] I have seldom entered a shady walk without being soon obliged to turn aside to make room for the rope-makers; and the only tree, I have seen, that appeared to be planted by the hand of taste, is in the church-yard, to shade the tomb of the poet Klopstock's wife.[153]

Most of the merchants have country houses to retire to, during the summer; and many of them are situated on the banks of the Elbe, where they have the pleasure of seeing the packet-boats arrive, the periods of most consequence to divide their week.

The moving picture,[154] consisting of large vessels and small-craft, which are continually changing their position with the tide, renders this noble river, the vital stream of Hamburg, very interesting; and the windings have sometimes a very fine effect, two or three turns being visible, at once, intersecting the flat meadows: a sudden bend often increasing the magnitude of the river; and the silvery expanse, scarcely gliding, though bearing on its bosom so much treasure, looks for a moment, like a tranquil lake.

Nothing can be stronger than the contrast which this flat country and strand afford, compared with the mountains, and rocky coast, I have lately dwelt so much among. In fancy I return to a favourite spot, where I seemed to have retired from man and wretchedness; but the din of trade drags me back to all the care I left behind, when lost in sublime emotions. Rocks aspiring towards the heavens, and, as it were, shutting out sorrow, surrounded me, whilst peace appeared to steal along the lake to calm my bosom, modulating the wind that agitated the neighbouring poplars. Now I hear only an account of the tricks of trade, or listen to the distressful tale of some victim of ambition.

The hospitality of Hamburg is confined to Sunday invitations to the country houses I have mentioned, when dish after dish smokes upon the board; and the conversation ever flowing in the muddy channel of business, it is not easy to obtain any appropriate information. Had I intended to remain here some time, or had my mind been more alive to general inquiries, I should have endeavoured to have been introduced to some characters, not so entirely immersed in commercial affairs; though, in this whirlpool of gain, it is not very easy to find any but the wretched or supercilious emigrants, who are not engaged in pursuits which, in my eyes, appear as dishonourable as gambling. The interests of nations are bartered by speculating merchants. My God! with what *sang froid* artful trains of corruption bring lucrative commissions into particular hands, disregarding the relative situation of different countries – and can much common honesty be expected in the discharge of trusts obtained by fraud? But this, *entre nous*.

During my present journey, and whilst residing in France, I have had an opportunity of peeping behind the scenes of what are vulgarly termed great affairs, only to discover the mean machinery which has directed many transactions of moment. The sword has been merciful, compared with the depredations made on human life by contractors, and by the swarm of locusts who have battened on the pestilence they spread abroad. These men, like the owners of negro ships, never smell on their money the blood by which it has been gained, but sleep quietly in their beds, terming such occupations *lawful callings*; yet the lightning marks not their roofs, to thunder conviction on them, 'and to justify the ways of God to man.'[155]

Why should I weep for myself? – 'Take, O world! thy much indebted tear!'[156]

Adieu!

Letter Twenty-five

There is a pretty little French theatre at Altona; and the actors are much superiour to those I saw at Copenhagen. The theatres at Hamburg are not open yet, but will very shortly, when the shutting of the gates at seven o'clock forces the citizens to quit their country houses. But, respecting Hamburg, I shall not be able to obtain much more information, as I have determined to sail with the first fair wind for England.[157]

The presence of the French army would have rendered my intended tour through Germany, in my way to Switzerland, almost impracticable, had not the advancing season obliged me to alter my plan. Besides, though Switzerland is the country which for several years I have been particularly desirous to visit, I do not feel inclined to ramble any farther this year; nay, I am weary of changing the scene, and quitting people and places the moment they begin to interest me. – This also is vanity!

DOVER

I left this letter unfinished, as I was hurried on board; and now I have only to tell you, that, at the sight of Dover cliffs, I wondered how any body could term them grand; they appear so insignificant to me, after those I had seen in Sweden and Norway.

Adieu! My spirit of observation seems to be fled – and I have been wandering round this dirty place, literally speaking, to kill time; though the thoughts, I would fain fly from, lie too close to my heart to be easily shook off, or even beguiled, by any employment, except that of preparing for my journey to London. – God bless you!

Mary –

Appendix

Private business and cares have frequently so absorbed me, as to prevent my obtaining all the information, during this journey, which the novelty of the scenes would have afforded, had my attention been continually awake to inquiry. This insensibility to present objects I have often had occasion to lament, since I have been preparing these letters for the press; but, as a person of any thought naturally considers the history of a strange country to contrast the former with the present state of its manners, a conviction of the increasing knowledge and happiness of the kingdoms I passed through, was perpetually the result of my comparative reflections.

The poverty of the poor, in Sweden, renders the civilization very partial; and slavery has retarded the improvement of every class in Denmark; yet both are advancing; and the gigantic evils of despotism and anarchy have in a great measure vanished before the meliorating manners of Europe. Innumerable evils still remain, it is true, to afflict the humane investigator, and hurry the benevolent reformer into a labyrinth of error, who aims at destroying prejudices quickly which only time can root out, as the public opinion becomes subject to reason.

An ardent affection for the human race makes enthusiastic characters eager to produce alteration in laws and governments prematurely. To render them useful and permanent, they must be the growth of each particular soil, and the gradual fruit of the ripening understanding of the nation, matured by time, not forced by an unnatural fermentation.[158] And, to convince me that such a change is gaining ground, with accelerating pace, the view I have had of society, during my northern journey, would have been sufficient, had I not previously considered the grand causes which combine to carry mankind forward, and diminish the sum of human misery.

Author's Supplementary Notes

Note One

Norway, according to geometrical measure, is 202 miles in length. In breadth it is very unequal. The common Norway mile contains about 24,000 yards, English measurement.

Norway is reckoned to contain 7,558 quadrate miles: it is divided into four parts. There are four grand bailiffs, and four bishops. The four chief towns are Christiania, Trondheim, Bergen, and Christiansand. Its natural products are wood, silver, copper, and iron, a little gold has been found, fish, marble, and the skins of several animals. The exportation exceeds the importation. The balance in favour of Norway, in the year 1767, was about 476,085 rixdollars, £95,217 sterling. It has been increasing ever since. The silver mines of Kongsberg yield silver to the amount of 350,000 rixdollars, £70,000 sterling; but it is asserted, that this sum is not sufficient to defray the expences of working them. Kongsberg is the only inland town, and contains 10,000 souls.

The copper mines at Rorraas yield about 4000 ship-pound a year; a ship-pound is 320 pounds: the yearly profit amounts to 150,000 rixdollars, £30,000 sterling. There are fifteen or sixteen iron works in Norway, which produce iron to the value of 400,000 rixdollars, £80,000 per annum.

The exportation of salted and dried fish is very considerable. In the year 1786 the returns for its exportation amounted to 749,200 rixdollars, £169,840.

There are four regiments of dragoons, each consisting of 108 men, officers included; two regiments of marching infantry, 1157 men each, with five companies in garrison, amounting to 3377 men; thirteen regiments of militia, 1916 men each, making 24,908 men; 960 men, light troops, who, in winter, whilst the snow is on the ground, run along on a kind of skates – a couple of long instruments made of wood.[159]

Note Two

The Taxes in Norway consist of

1. A land tax. Farms, worth from two to three thousand dollars, pay from fifteen to twenty dollars annually.
2. A duty on all articles of provision, and on all goods carried in or out.
3. A tax on rank and office.
4. A tax on pensions and salaries; two per cent on one hundred dollars, and in proportion to ten per cent.
5. A tax on money put out to interest, with security on land or houses, of a quarter per cent. And as the allowed interest is four per cent the duty is one fourth of the interest.

WILLIAM GODWIN

Memoirs of the Author of
The Rights of Woman

NOTE ON THE TEXT OF THE 'MEMOIRS'

The text of the *Memoirs* I have chosen to reprint here is that of Godwin's first edition, published by Joseph Johnson in January 1798. It is in fact the first reprint of this edition, unamended (apart from a very few spellings, which have been modernized), to appear since that date.

As explained in the Introduction, Godwin responded to the storm of criticism it aroused, by swiftly publishing a second edition with various alterations, deletions and additions, in the summer of 1798. (The text that William Clark Durant published in 1927 is an amalgam of the two.) I have decided to maintain the integrity of the first edition, and handle the text of the second edition in the following way.

(a) Wherever Godwin added a new passage, of whatever length, it has been printed as a footnote at the place it occurs in the original text. (b) Where Godwin made small cuts, or alterations of phrase, I have indicated the most important of these in the footnotes as well. These footnotes are indicated in the text by a superior *letter*. I have ignored what I consider insignificant (often stylistic) changes, as these would unduly clutter the reader's text; but have faithfully recorded significant ones however small, even a single adjective. (c) In the three places where Godwin substantially rewrote (as explained in the Introduction, section 7), I have reprinted the two longest as an Appendix to the text, and the other in footnotes.

The reader thus has an authoritative and readable first-edition text; together with an accurate impression, from the footnotes, of what changes were made in the second edition. I hope the scholar in William Godwin would have approved.

Finally, the small *numbers* in the body of the text (as in *A Short Residence*) indicate where further information or commentary is available in my editorial notes at the back of the book. In general, I have tried to sketch in the background to contemporary names or references; and also added further observations on Godwin's technique as a biographer, which seems to me of the greatest historical interest in the development of the form itself. Once again, I have been enormously helped by the work of previous scholars in the field, notably William Clark Durant and Claire Tomalin; and by some shrewd remarks of William St Clair.

MEMOIRS

OF THE

AUTHOR

OF A

VINDICATION OF THE RIGHTS OF WOMAN.

By WILLIAM GODWIN.

LONDON:

PRINTED FOR J. JOHNSON, NO. 72, ST. PAUL'S
CHURCH-YARD; AND G. G. AND J. ROBINSON,
PATERNOSTER-ROW.
1798.

*Facsimile of the title-page
of the first edition*

PREFACE

It has always appeared to me, that to give the public some account of the life of a person of eminent merit deceased, is a duty incumbent on survivors. It seldom happens that such a person passes through life, without being the subject of thoughtless calumny, or malignant misrepresentation. It cannot happen that the public at large should be on a footing with their intimate acquaintance, and be the observer of those virtues which discover themselves principally in personal intercourse. Every benefactor of mankind is more or less influenced by a liberal passion for fame; and survivors only pay a debt due to these benefactors, when they assert and establish on their part, the honour they loved. The justice which is thus done to the illustrious dead, converts into the fairest source of animation and encouragement to those who would follow them in the same career. The human species at large is interested in this justice, as it teaches them to place their respect and affection, upon those qualities which best deserve to be esteemed and loved. I cannot easily prevail on myself to doubt, that the more fully we are presented with the picture and story of such persons as the subject of the following narrative, the more generally shall we feel in ourselves an attachment to their fate, and a sympathy in their excellencies. There are not many individuals with whose character the public welfare and improvement are more intimately connected, than the author of *A Vindication of the Rights of Woman*.

The facts detailed in the following pages, are principally taken from the mouth of the person to whom they relate; and of the veracity and ingenuousness of her habits, perhaps no one that was ever acquainted with her, entertains a doubt. The writer of this narrative, when he has met with persons, that in any degree created to themselves an interest and attachment in his mind, has always felt a curiosity to be acquainted with the scenes through which they had passed, and the incidents that had contributed to form their understandings and character.[1] Impelled by this sentiment, he repeatedly led the conversation of Mary to topics of this sort; and, once or twice, he made notes in her presence, of a few dates calculated to arrange the circumstances in his mind. To the materials thus collected, he has added an industrous enquiry among the persons most intimately acquainted with her at the different periods of her life.

Chapter One
1759–1775

Mary Wollstonecraft was born on the 27th of April 1759. Her father's name was Edward John, and the name of her mother Elizabeth, of the family of Dixons of Ballyshannon in the kingdom of Ireland: her paternal grandfather was a respectable manufacturer in Spitalfields, and is supposed to have left to his son a property of about 10,000*l*. Three of her brothers and two sisters are still living; their names, Edward, James, Charles, Eliza, and Everina. Of these, Edward only was older than herself; he resides in London. James is in Paris, and Charles in or near Philadelphia in America. Her sisters have for some years been engaged in the office of governesses in private families, and are both at present in Ireland.[a]

I am doubtful whether the father of Mary was bred to any profession; but, about the time of her birth, he resorted, rather perhaps as an amusement than a business, to the occupation of farming. He was of a very active, and somewhat versatile disposition, and so frequently changed his abode, as to throw some ambiguity upon the place of her birth. She told me, that the doubt in her mind in that respect, lay between London, and a farm upon Epping Forest, which was the principal scene of the five first years of her life.

Mary was distinguished in early youth, by some portion of that exquisite sensibility, soundness of understanding, and decision of character, which were the leading features of her mind through the whole course of her life. She experienced in the first period of her existence, but few of those indulgences and marks of affection, which are principally calculated to sooth the subjection and sorrows of our early years. She was not the favourite either of her father or mother. Her father was a man of a quick, impetuous disposition, subject to

a. Last two sentences deleted in second edition. (All lettered footnotes in *the Memoirs* indicate changes introduced in the second edition; Godwin's footnotes are indicated by asterisks.)

alternate fits of kindness and cruelty.[b] In his family he was a despot,[c] and his wife appears to have been the first, and most submissive of his subjects. The mother's partiality was fixed upon the eldest son, and her system of government relative to Mary, was characterized by considerable rigour. She, at length, became convinced of her mistake, and adopted a different plan with her younger daughters. When, in the *Wrongs of Woman*, Mary speaks of 'the petty cares which obscured the morning of her heroine's life; continual restraint in the most trivial matters; unconditional submission to orders, which, as a mere child, she soon discovered to be unreasonable, because inconsistent and contradictory; and the being often obliged to sit, in the presence of her parents, for three or four hours together, without daring to utter a word;' she is, I believe, to be considered as copying the outline of the first period of her own existence.

But it was in vain that the blighting winds of unkindness or indifference, seemed destined to counteract the superiority of Mary's mind. It surmounted every obstacle; and by degrees, from a person little considered in the family, she became in some sort its director and umpire. The despotism of her education cost her many a heart-ache. She was not formed to be the contented and unresisting subject of a despot; but I have heard her remark more than once, that, when she felt she had done wrong, the reproof or chastisement of her mother, instead of being a terror to her, she found to be the only thing capable of reconciling her to herself. The blows of her father, on the contrary, which were the mere ebullitions of a passionate temper, instead of humbling her roused her indignation. Upon such occasions she felt her superiority, and was apt to betray marks of contempt. The quickness of her father's temper, led him sometimes to threaten similar violence towards his wife. When that was the case, Mary would often throw herself between the despot and his victim, with the purpose to receive upon her own person the blows that might be directed against her mother. She has even laid whole nights upon the landing-place near their chamber-door, when, mistakenly, or with reason, she apprehended that her father might break out into paroxysms of violence. The conduct he held towards the members of his

b. '. . . kindness and severity'.
c. . . . 'he was absolute'.

family, was of the same kind as that he observed towards animals. He was for the most part extravagantly fond of them; but, when he was displeased, and this frequently happened, and for very trivial reasons, his anger was alarming. Mary was what Dr Johnson would have called, 'a very good hater.' In some instance of passion exercised by her father to one of his dogs, she was accustomed to speak of her emotions of abhorrence, as having risen to agony. In a word, her conduct during her girlish years, was such, as to extort some portion of affection from her mother, and to hold her father in considerable awe.[2]

In one respect, the system of education of the mother appears to have had merit. All her children were vigorous and healthy. This seems very much to depend upon the management of our infant years. It is affirmed by some persons of the present day, most profoundly skilled in the sciences of health and disease, that there is no period of human life so little subject to mortality, as the period of infancy. Yet, from the mismanagement to which children are exposed, many of the diseases of childhood are rendered fatal, and more persons die in that, than in any other period of human life. Mary had projected a work upon this subject, which she had carefully considered, and well understood. She has indeed left a specimen of her skill in this respect in her eldest daughter, three years and a half old, who is a singular example of vigorous constitution and florid health. Mr Anthony Carlisle,[3] surgeon, of Soho-square, whom to name is sufficiently to honour, had promised to revise her production. This is but one out of numerous projects of activity and usefulness, which her untimely death has fatally terminated.

The rustic situation in which Mary spent her infancy, no doubt contributed to confirm the stamina of her constitution. She sported in the open air, and amidst the picturesque and refreshing scenes of nature, for which she always retained the most exquisite relish. Dolls and the other amusements usually appropriated to female children, she held in contempt; and felt a much greater propensity to join in the active and hardy sports of her brothers, than to confine herself to those of her own sex.

About the time that Mary completed the fifth year of her age, her father removed to a small distance from his former habitation and took a farm near the Whalebone upon Epping Forest, a little way out of the Chelmsford road. In Michaelmas 1765, he once more changed his residence, and occupied a convenient house behind the town of Barking in Essex, eight miles from London. In this situation some of their nearest neighbours were, Bamber Gascoyne, esquire, successively member of parliament for several boroughs, and his brother, Mr Joseph Gascoyne.[d] Bamber Gascoyne resided but little on this spot; but his brother was almost a constant inhabitant, and his family in habits of the most frequent intercourse with the family of Mary.[e] Here Mr Wollstonecraft remained for three years. In September 1796, I accompanied my wife in a visit to this spot. No person reviewed with greater sensibility, the scenes of her childhood. We found the house uninhabited, and the garden in a wild and ruinous state.[4] She renewed her acquaintance with the market-place, the streets, and the wharf, the latter of which we found crowded with barges, and full of activity.

In Michaelmas 1768, Mr Wollstonecraft again removed to a farm near Beverley in Yorkshire. Here the family remained for six years,[5] and consequently, Mary did not quit this residence until she had attained the age of fifteen years and five months. The principal part of her school-education passed during this period; but it was not to any advantage of infant literature, that she was indebted for her subsequent eminence; her education in this respect was merely such, as was afforded by the day-schools of the place, in which she resided. To her recollections Beverley appeared a very handsome town, surrounded by genteel families, and with a brilliant assembly. She was surprized, when she visited it in 1795, upon her voyage to Norway, to find the reality so very much below the picture in her imagination.

Hitherto Mr Wollstonecraft had been a farmer; but the restlessness of his disposition would not suffer him to content himself with the occupation in which for some years he had been engaged, and the temptation of a commercial speculation of some sort being held out to him, he removed to a house in Queen's-Row, in Hoxton near London, for the purpose of its execution. Here he remained for a

d. Second edition adds: 'I mention this circumstance on account of its connection with the topography of the spot.'

e. 'Bamber Gascoyne . . . Mary.' – This sentence deleted in the second edition.

year and a half; but, being frustrated in his expectations of profit, he, after that term, gave up the project in which he was engaged, and returned to his former pursuits. During this residence in Hoxton, the writer of these memoirs inhabited, as a student, at the dissenting college in that place. It is perhaps a question of curious speculation to enquire, what would have been the amount of the difference in the pursuits and enjoyments of each party, if they had met, and considered each other with the same distinguishing regard in 1776, as they were afterwards impressed with in the year 1796. The writer had then completed the twentieth, and Mary the seventeenth year of her age. Which would have been predominant; the disadvantages of obscurity, and the pressure of a family; or the gratifications and improvement that might have flowed from their intercourse?

One of the acquaintances Mary formed at this time was with a Mr Clare, who inhabited the next house to that which was tenanted by her father, and to whom she was probably in some degree indebted for the early cultivation of her mind. Mr Clare was a clergyman, and appears to have been a humourist of a very singular cast. In his person he was deformed and delicate; and his figure, I am told, bore a resemblance to that of the celebrated Pope. He had a fondness for poetry, and was not destitute of taste. His manners were expressive of a tenderness and benevolence, the demonstrations of which appeared to have been somewhat too artificially cultivated. His habits were those of a perfect recluse. He seldom went out of his drawing-room, and he showed to a friend of Mary a pair of shoes, which had served him, he said, for fourteen years. Mary frequently spent days and weeks together, at the house of Mr Clare.[f][6]

f. Second edition adds: 'It is easy to perceive that this connection was of a character different from those to which she had hitherto been accustomed. It were to be desired that the biographer of persons of eminent talents, should possess the means of analysing the causes by which they were modified, and tracing methodically the progress of their minds. But though this can seldom be performed, he ought probably not to neglect to record the fragments of progress and cultivation that may have come down to him. A censurable fastidiousness only, could teach us to reject information, because that information is imperfect.'[7]

Chapter Two

1775–1783

But a connection more memorable originated about this time, between Mary and a person of her own sex, for whom she contracted a friendship so fervent,[a] as for years to have constituted the ruling passion of her mind. The name of this person was Frances Blood; she was two years older than Mary. Her residence was at that time at Newington Butts, a village near the southern extremity of the metropolis; and the original instrument for bringing these two friends acquainted, was Mrs Clare, wife of the gentleman already mentioned, who was on a footing of considerable intimacy with both parties. The acquaintance of Fanny, like that of Mr Clare, contributed to ripen the immature talents of Mary.

The situation in which Mary was introduced to her, bore a resemblance to the first interview of Werter with Charlotte.[b][8] She was conducted to the door of a small house, but furnished with peculiar neatness and propriety. The first object that caught her sight, was a young woman of a slender and elegant form, and eighteen years of age, busily employed in feeding and managing some children, born of the same parents, but considerably inferior to her in age. The impression Mary received from this spectacle was indelible;[c] and, before the interview was concluded, she had taken, in her heart, the vows of an eternal friendship.

Fanny was a young woman of extraordinary accomplishments. She sung and played with taste. She drew with exquisite fidelity and neatness; and, by the employment of this talent, for some time maintained her father, mother, and family, but ultimately ruined her health by her extraordinary exertions. She read and wrote with con-

a. 'warm'.
b. This comparison of Mary with Werther was deleted in the second edition.
c. . . . 'received from a scene, which so happily accorded with her two most cherished conceptions, the picturesque and the affectionate, was indelible'.

siderable application; and the same ideas of minute and delicate propriety followed her in these, as in her other occupations.

Mary, a wild, but animated and aspiring girl of sixteen, contemplated Fanny, in the first instance, with sentiments of inferiority and reverence. Though they were much together, yet, the distance of their habitations being considerable, they supplied the want of more frequent interviews by an assiduous correspondence. Mary found Fanny's letters better spelt and better indited than her own, and felt herself abashed. She had hitherto paid but a superficial attention to literature. She had read, to gratify the ardour of an inextinguishable thirst of knowledge; but she had not thought of writing as an art. Her ambition to excel was now awakened, and she applied herself with passion and earnestness. Fanny undertook to be her instructor; and, so far as related to accuracy and method, her lessons were given with considerable skill.

It has already been mentioned that, in the spring of the year 1776, Mr Wollstonecraft quitted his situation at Hoxton, and returned to his former agricultural pursuits. The situation upon which he now fixed was in Wales, a circumstance that was felt as a severe blow to Mary's darling spirit of friendship. The principal acquaintance of the Wollstonecrafts in this retirement, was the family of a Mr Allen, two of whose daughters are since married to the two elder sons of the celebrated English potter, Josiah Wedgwood.[d][9]

Wales however was Mr Wollstonecraft's residence for little more than a year. He returned to the neighbourhood of London; and Mary, whose spirit of independence was unalterable, had influence enough to determine his choice in favour of the village of Walworth, that she might be near her chosen friend. It was probably before this, that she had once or twice started the idea of quitting her parental roof, and providing for herself. But she was prevailed upon to resign this idea, and conditions were stipulated with her, relative to her having an apartment in the house that should be exclusively her own, and her commanding the other requisites of study. She did not however think herself fairly treated in these instances, and either the conditions abovementioned, or some others, were not observed in the sequel,

d. This reference to the Wedgwood family was deleted in the second edition.

with the fidelity she expected. In one case, she had procured an eligible situation, and every thing was settled respecting her removal to it, when the intreaties and tears of her mother led her to surrender her own inclinations, and abandon the engagement.

These however were only temporary delays. Her propensities continued the same, and the motives by which she was instigated were unabated. In the year 1778, she being nineteen years of age, a proposal was made to her of living as a companion with a Mrs Dawson of Bath, a widow lady, with one son already adult. Upon enquiry she found that Mrs Dawson was a woman of great peculiarity of temper, that she had had a variety of companions in succession, and that no one had found it practicable to continue with her. Mary was not discouraged by this information and accepted the situation, with a resolution that she would effect in this respect, what none of her predecessors had been able to do. In the sequel she had reason to consider the account she had received as sufficiently accurate, but she did not relax in her endeavours. By method, constancy and firmness, she found the means of making her situation tolerable; and Mrs Dawson would occasionally confess, that Mary was the only person that had lived with her in that situation, in her treatment of whom she had felt herself under any restraint.

With Mrs Dawson she continued to reside for two years, and only left her, summoned by the melancholy circumstance of her mother's rapidly declining health. True to the calls of humanity, Mary felt in this intelligence an irresistible motive, and eagerly returned to the paternal roof, which she had before resolutely quitted. The residence of her father at this time, was at Enfield near London. He had, I believe, given up agriculture from the time of his quitting Wales, it appearing that he now made it less a source of profit than loss, and being thought advisable that he should rather live upon the interest of his property already in possession.

The illness of Mrs Wollstonecraft was lingering, but hopeless. Mary was assiduous in her attendance upon her mother. At first, every attention was received with acknowledgments and gratitude; but, as the attentions grew habitual, and the health of the mother more and more wretched, they were rather exacted, than received. Nothing would be taken by the unfortunate patient, but from the hands of Mary; rest was denied night or day, and by the time nature was exhausted in the parent, the daughter was qualified to assume her place, and become in turn herself a patient. The last words her mother ever uttered were, 'A little patience, and all will be over!' and these words are repeatedly referred to by Mary in the course of her writings.

Upon the death of Mrs Wollstonecraft, Mary bid final adieu to the roof of her father. According to my memorandums, I find her next the inmate of Fanny at Walham Green, near the village of Fulham. Upon what plan they now lived together I am unable to ascertain; certainly not that of Mary becoming in any degree an additional burthen upon the industry of her friend. Thus situated, their intimacy ripened; they approached more nearly to a footing of equality; and their attachment became more rooted and active.

Mary was ever ready at the call of distress, and, in particular, during her whole life was eager and active to promote the welfare of every member of her family. In 1780 she attended the deathbed of her mother; in 1782 she was summoned by a not less melancholy occasion, to attend her sister Eliza, married to a Mr Bishop, who, subsequently to a dangerous lying-in, remained for some months in a very afflicting situation.[10] Mary continued with her sister without intermission, to her perfect recovery.

Chapter Three

1783–1785

Mary was now arrived at the twenty-fourth year of her age. Her project, five years before, had been personal independence; it was now usefulness. In the solitude of attendance on her sister's illness, and during the subsequent convalescence, she had had leisure to ruminate upon purposes of this sort. Her expanded mind led her to seek something more arduous than the mere removal of personal vexations; and the sensibility of her heart would not suffer her to rest in solitary gratifications. The derangement of her father's affairs daily became more and more glaring; and a small independent provision made for herself and her sisters, appears to have been sacrificed in the wreck. For ten years, from 1782 to 1792, she may be said to have been, in a great degree, the victim of a desire to promote the benefit of others.[11] She did not foresee the severe disappointment with which an exclusive purpose of this sort is pregnant; she was inexperienced enough to lay a stress upon the consequent gratitude of those she benefited; and she did not sufficiently consider that, in proportion as we involve ourselves in the interests and society of others, we acquire a more exquisite sense of their defects, and are tormented with their untractableness and folly.[a]

The project upon which she now determined, was no other than that of a day-school, to be superintended by Fanny Blood, herself, and her two sisters. They accordingly opened one in the year 1783, at the village of Islington; but in the course of a few months removed it to Newington Green.[12]

a. Second editions adds: 'Her mistakes in this respect were two: she engaged herself too minutely and too deeply in the care of their welfare; and she was too much impressed by any seeming want of ingenuous and honourable feeling on the part of those she benefited. In the mixed scene of human life, it is necessary that, while we take some care for others, we should leave scope for the display of their own prudence and reason; and that, when we have discharged our duty respecting them, we should be habituated to derive a principal consolation from the consciousness of having done so.'

Here Mary formed some acquaintances who influenced the future events of her life. The first of these in her own estimation, was Dr Richard Price,[13] well known for his political and mathematical calculations, and universally esteemed by those who knew him, for the simplicity of his manners, and the ardour of his benevolence. The regard conceived by these two persons for each other, was mutual, and partook of a spirit of the purest attachment. Mary had been bred in the principles of the church of England, but her esteem for this venerable preacher led her occasionally to attend upon his public instructions. Her religion was, in reality, little allied to any system of forms; and, as she has often told me, was founded rather in taste, than in the niceties of polemical discussion. Her mind constitutionally attached itself to the sublime and the amiable. She found an inexpressible delight in the beauties of nature, and in the splendid reveries of the imagination. But nature itself, she thought, would be no better than a vast blank, if the mind of the observer did not supply it with an animating soul. When she walked amidst the wonders of nature, she was accustomed to converse with her God. To her mind he was pictured as not less amiable, generous and kind, than great, wise and exalted. In fact, she had received few lessons of religion in her youth, and her religion was almost entirely of her own creation. But she was not on that account the less attached to it, or the less scrupulous in discharging what she considered as its duties. She could not recollect the time when she had believed the doctrine of future punishments.[b] The tenets of her system were the growth of her own moral taste, and her religion therefore had always been a gratification, never a terror, to her. She expected a future state; but she would not allow her ideas of that future state to be modified by the notions of judgment and retribution. From this sketch, it is sufficiently evident, that the pleasure she took in an occasional attendance upon the sermons of Dr Price, was not accompanied with a superstitious adherence to his doctrines. The fact is, that, as far down as the year 1787, she regularly frequented public worship, for the most part according to the forms of the church of England. After that period her attendance became less constant, and in no long time was wholly discontinued. I believe it may be admitted as a maxim, that no person

b. This sentence about Hell was deleted in the second edition.

of a well furnished mind, that has shaken off the implicit subjection
of youth, and is not the zealous partizan of a sect, can bring himself
to conform to the public and regular routine of sermons and prayers.[14]

Another of the friends she acquired at this period, was Mrs Burgh,
widow of the author of the *Political Disquisitions*,[15] a woman universally well spoken of for the warmth and purity of her benevolence.
Mary, whenever she had occasion to allude to her, to the last period
of her life, paid the tribute due to her virtues. The only remaining
friend necessary to be enumerated in this place, is the rev. John
Hewlet, now master of a boarding-school at Shacklewel near Hackney,
whom I shall have occasion to mention hereafter.

It was during her residence at Newington Green, that she was
introduced to the acquaintance of Dr Johnson, who was at that time
considered as in some sort the father of English literature. The doctor
treated her with particular kindness and attention, had a long conversation with her, and desired her to repeat her visit often. This she
firmly purposed to do; but the news of his last illness, and then of his
death, intervened to prevent her making a second visit.[16]

I have already said that Fanny's health had been materially injured
by her incessant labours for the maintenance of her family. She had
also suffered a disappointment, which preyed upon her mind. To
these different sources of ill health she became gradually a victim;
and at length discovered all the symptoms of a pulmonary consumption. By the medical men that attended her, she was advised to
try the effects of a southern climate; and, about the beginning of the
year 1785, sailed for Lisbon.

The first feeling with which Mary had contemplated her friend,
was a sentiment of inferiority and reverence; but that, from the
operation of a ten years' acquaintance was considerably changed.
Fanny had originally been far before her in literary attainments; this
disparity no longer existed. In whatever degree Mary might endeavour
to free herself from the delusions of self-esteem, this period of
observation upon her own mind and that of her friend, could not
pass, without her perceiving that there were some essential characteristics of genius, which she possessed, and in which her friend was
deficient. The principal of these was a firmness of mind, an un-

conquerable greatness of soul, by which, after a short internal struggle, she was accustomed to rise above difficulties and suffering.
Whatever Mary undertook, she perhaps in all instances accomplished;
and, to her lofty spirit, scarcely any thing she desired, appeared hard
to perform. Fanny, on the contrary, was a woman of a timid and
irresolute nature, accustomed to yield to difficulties, and probably
priding herself in this morbid softness of her temper. One instance
that I have heard Mary relate of this sort, was that, at a certain time,
Fanny, dissatisfied with her domestic situation, expressed an earnest
desire to have a home of her own. Mary, who felt nothing more
pressing than to relieve the inconveniences of her friend, determined
to accomplish this object for her. It cost her infinite exertions; but at
length she was able to announce to Fanny that a house was prepared,
and that she was on the spot to receive her. The answer which Fanny
returned to the letter of her friend, consisted almost wholly of an
enumeration of objections to the quitting her family, which she had
not thought of before, but which now appeared to her of considerable
weight.

The judgment which experience had taught Mary to form of the
mind of her friend, determined her in the advice she gave, at the
period to which I have brought down the story. Fanny was recommended to seek a softer climate, but she had no funds to defray the
expence of such an undertaking. At this time Mr Hugh Skeys of
Dublin,[17] but then resident in the kingdom of Portugal, paid his
addresses to her. The state of her health Mary considered as such as
scarcely to afford the shadow of a hope; it was not therefore a time at
which it was most obvious to think of marriage. She conceived however that nothing should be omitted, which might alleviate, if it could
not cure; and accordingly urged her speedy acceptance of the proposal.
Fanny accordingly made the voyage to Lisbon; and the marriage took
place on the twenty-fourth of February 1785.[c]

The change of climate and situation was productive of little benefit;
and the life of Fanny was only prolonged by a period of pregnancy,
which soon declared itself. Mary, in the mean time, was impressed
with the idea that her friend would die in this distant country; and,

c. Second edition adds: 'The advice of Mary in this instance, though dictated by the
sincerest anxiety for her friend's welfare, is scarcely entitled to our approbation.'

shocked with the recollection of her separation from the circle of her friends, determined to pass over to Lisbon to attend her. This resolution was treated by her acquaintance as in the utmost degree visionary; but she was not to be diverted from her point. She had not money to defray her expenses: she must quit for a long time the school, the very existence of which probably depended upon her exertions.[18]

No person was ever better formed for the business of education; if it be not a sort of absurdity to speak of a person as formed for an inferior object, who is in possession of talents, in the fullest degree adequate to something on a more important and comprehensive scale. Mary had a quickness of temper, not apt to take offence with inadvertencies, but which led her to imagine that she saw the mind of the person with whom she had any transaction, and to refer the principle of her approbation or displeasure to the cordiality or injustice of their sentiments. She was occasionally severe and imperious in her resentments; and, when she strongly disapproved was apt to express her censure in terms that gave a very humiliating sensation to the person against whom it was directed. Her displeasure however never assumed its severest form, but when it was barbed by disappointment. Where she expected little, she was not very rigid in her censure of error.

But, to whatever the defects of her temper might amount, they were never exercised upon her inferiors in station or age. She scorned to make use of an ungenerous advantage, or to wound the defenceless. To her servants there never was a mistress more considerate or more kind. With children she was the mirror of patience. Perhaps, in all her extensive experience upon the subject of education, she never betrayed one symptom of irascibility. Her heart was the seat of every benevolent feeling; and accordingly, in all her intercourse with children, it was kindness and sympathy alone that prompted her conduct. Sympathy, when it mounts to a certain height, inevitably begets affection in the person towards whom it is exercised; and I have heard her say, that she never was concerned in the education of one child, who was not personally attached to her, and earnestly concerned not to incur her displeasure. Another eminent advantage she possessed in the business of education, was that she was little troubled with scepticism and uncertainty. She saw, as it were by intuition, the path which her mind determined to pursue, and had a firm confidence in her own power to effect what she desired. Yet, with all this, she had scarcely a tincture of obstinacy. She carefully watched symptoms as they rose, and the success of her experiments; and governed herself accordingly. While I thus enumerate her more than maternal qualities, it is impossible not to feel a pang at the recollection of her orphan children![19]

Though her friends earnestly dissuaded her from the journey to Lisbon, she found among them a willingness to facilitate the execution of her project, when it was once fixed. Mrs Burgh in particular, supplied her with money, which however she always conceived came from Dr Price. This loan, I have reason to believe, was faithfully repaid.

Her residence in Lisbon was not long. She arrived but a short time before her friend was prematurely delivered, and the event was fatal to both mother and child. Frances Blood, hitherto the chosen object of Mary's attachment, died on the twenty-ninth of November 1785.

It is thus that she speaks of her in her *Letters from Norway*, written ten years after her decease. 'When a warm heart has received strong impressions, they are not to be effaced. Emotions become sentiments; and the imagination renders even transient sensations permanent, by fondly retracing them. I cannot, without a thrill of delight, recollect views I have seen, which are not to be forgotten, nor looks I have felt in every nerve, which I shall never more meet. The grave has closed over a dear friend, the friend of my youth; still she is present with me, and I hear her soft voice warbling as I stray over the heath.'[20]

Chapter Four
1785–1787

No doubt the voyage to Lisbon tended considerably to enlarge the understanding of Mary. She was admitted into the best company the English factory afforded. She made many profound observations on the character of the natives, and the baleful effect of superstition. The obsequies of Fanny, which it was necessary to perform by stealth and in darkness, tended to invigorate these observations in her mind.

She sailed upon her voyage home about the twentieth of December. On this occasion a circumstance occurred, that deserves to be recorded. While they were on their passage, they fell in with a French vessel, in great distress, and in daily expectation of foundering at sea, at the same time that it was almost destitute of provisions. The Frenchman hailed them, and intreated the English captain, in consideration of his melancholy situation, to take him and his crew on board. The Englishman represented in reply, that his stock of provisions was by no means adequate to such an additional number of mouths, and absolutely refused compliance. Mary, shocked at his apparent insensibility, took up the cause of the sufferers, and threatened the captain to have him called to a severe account, when he arrived in England. She finally prevailed, and had the satisfaction to reflect, that the persons in question possibly owed their lives to her interposition.[21]

When she arrived in England, she found that her school had suffered considerably in her absence. It can be little reproach to any one, to say that they were found incapable of supplying her place. She not only excelled in the management of the children, but had also the talent of being attentive and obliging to the parents, without degrading herself.

The period at which I am now arrived is important, as conducting to the first step of her literary career. Mr Hewlet had frequently mentioned literature to Mary as a certain source of pecuniary produce, and had urged her to make trial of the truth of his judgment. At this time she was desirous of assisting the father and mother of Fanny in an object they had in view, the transporting themselves to Ireland; and, as usual, what she desired in a pecuniary view, she was ready to take on herself to effect. For this purpose she wrote a duodecimo pamphlet of one hundred and sixty pages, entitled, *Thoughts on the Education of Daughters*.[22] Mr Hewlet obtained from the bookseller, Mr Johnson in St Paul's Church Yard,[23] ten guineas for the copyright of the manuscript, which she immediately applied to the object for the sake of which the pamphlet was written.

Every thing urged Mary to put an end to the affair of the school. She was dissatisfied with the different appearance it presented upon her return, from the state in which she left it. Experience impressed upon her a rooted aversion to that sort of cohabitation with her sisters, which the project of the school imposed. Cohabitation is a point of delicate experiment, and is, in a majority of instances, pregnant with ill-humour and unhappiness. The activity and ardent spirit of adventure which characterized Mary, were not felt in an equal degree by her sisters, so that a disproportionate share of every burthen attendant upon the situation, fell to her lot. On the other hand, they could scarcely perhaps be perfectly easy, in observing the superior degree of deference and courtship, which her merit extorted from almost every one that knew her. Her kindness for them was not diminished, but she resolved that the mode of its exertion in future should be different, tending to their benefit, without intrenching upon her own liberty.

Thus circumscribed, a proposal was made her, such as, regarding only the situations through which she had lately passed, is usually termed advantageous. This was, to accept the office of governess to the daughters of lord viscount Kingsborough, eldest son to the earl of Kingston of the kingdom of Ireland. The terms held out to her were such as she determined to accept, at the same time resolving to retain the situation only for a short time. Independence was the object after which she thirsted, as she was fixed to try whether it might not be found in literary occupation. She was desirous however first to accumulate a small sum of money, which should enable her to consider at leisure the different literary engagements that might offer, and provide in some degree for the eventual deficiency of her earliest attempts.

The situation in the family of lord Kingsborough, was offered to her through the medium of the rev. Mr Prior, at that time one of the under masters of Eton school. She spent some time at the house of this gentleman, immediately after her giving up the school at Newington Green. Here she had an opportunity of making an accurate observation upon the manners and conduct of that celebrated seminary, and the ideas she retained of it were by no means favourable. By all that she saw, she was confirmed in a very favourite opinion of her's, in behalf of day-schools, where, as she expressed it, 'children have the opportunity of conversing with children, without interfering with domestic affections, the foundation of virtue.' [24]

Though her residence in the family of lord Kingsborough continued scarcely more than twelve months, she left behind her, with them and their connections, a very advantageous impression. The governesses the young ladies had hitherto had, were only a species of upper servants, controlled in every thing by the mother; Mary insisted upon the unbounded exercise of her own discretion. When the young ladies heard of their governess coming from England, they heard in imagination of a new enemy, and declared their resolution to guard themselves accordingly. Mary however speedily succeeded in gaining their confidence, and the friendship that soon grew up between her and Margaret King, now countess Mount Cashel,[25] the eldest daughter, was in an uncommon degree cordial and affectionate. Mary always spoke of this young lady in terms of the truest applause, both in relation to the eminence of her intellectual powers, and the ingenuous amiableness of her disposition. Lady Kingsborough, from the best motives, had imposed upon her daughters a variety of prohibitions, both as to the books they should read, and in many other respects. These prohibitions had their usual effects; inordinate desire for the things forbidden, and clandestine indulgence. Mary immediately restored the children to their liberty, and undertook to govern them by their affections only. The consequence was, that their indulgences were moderate, and they were uneasy under any indulgence that had not the sanction of their governess. The salutary effects of

the new system of education were speedily visible; and lady Kingsborough soon felt no other uneasiness, than lest the children should
love their governess better than their mother.

Mary made many friends in Ireland, among the persons who visited
lord Kingsborough's house, for she always appeared there with the
air of an equal, and not of a dependent. I have heard her mention the
ludicrous distress of a woman of quality, whose name I have forgotten, that, in a large company, singled out Mary, and entered into a
long conversation with her. After the conversation was over, she
enquired whom she had been talking with, and found, to her utter
mortification and dismay, that it was Miss King's governess.

One of the persons among her Irish acquaintance, whom Mary was
accustomed to speak of with the highest respect, was Mr George
Ogle, member of parliament for the county of Wexford. She held his
talents in very high estimation; she was strongly prepossessed in
favour of the goodness of his heart; and she always spoke of him as the
most perfect gentleman she had ever known. She felt the regret of a
disappointed friend, at the part he has lately taken in the politics of
Ireland.[26]

Lord Kingsborough's family passed the summer of the year 1787
at Bristol Hot-Wells, and had formed the project of proceeding from
thence to the continent, a tour in which Mary purposed to accompany
them. The plan however was ultimately given up, and Mary in consequence closed her connection with them, earlier than she otherwise
had purposed to do.

At Bristol Hot-Wells she composed the little book which bears the
title of *Mary, a Fiction*.[27] A considerable part of this story consists,
with certain modifications, of the incidents of her own friendship
with Fanny. All the events that do not relate to that subject are
fictitious.

This little work, if Mary had never produced any thing else, would
serve, with persons of true taste and sensibility, to establish the
eminence of her genius. The story is nothing. He that looks into the
book only for incident, will probably lay it down with disgust. But
the feelings are of the truest and most exquisite class; every circumstance is adorned with that species of imagination, which enlists itself
under the banners of delicacy and sentiment. A work of sentiment, as

it is called, is too often another name for a work of affectation. He that should imagine that the sentiments of this book are affected, would indeed be entitled to our profoundest commiseration.[a]

---

a. .... 'would I believe, betray a total want of sensibility and taste'.

Chapter Five
1787–1790

Being now determined to enter upon her literary plan, Mary came immediately from Bristol to the metropolis. Her conduct under this circumstance was such as to do credit both to her own heart, and that of Mr Johnson, her publisher, between whom and herself there now commenced an intimate friendship. She had seen him upon occasion of publishing her *Thoughts on the Education of Daughters*, and she addressed two or three letters to him during her residence in Ireland. Upon her arrival in London in August 1787, she went immediately to his house, and frankly explained to him her purpose, at the same time requesting his advice and assistance as to its execution. After a short conversation, Mr Johnson invited her to make his house her home, till she should have suited herself with a fixed residence. She accordingly resided at this time two or three weeks under his roof. At the same period she paid a visit or two of similar duration to some friends, at no great distance from the metropolis.

At Michaelmas 1787, she entered upon a house in George street, on the Surrey side of Black Friar's Bridge, which Mr Johnson had provided for her during her excursion into the country.[a] The three years immediately ensuing, may be said, in the ordinary acceptation of the term, to have been the most active period of her life. She brought with her to this habitation, the novel of *Mary*, which had not yet been sent to the press, and the commencement of the sort of oriental tale, entitled, *The Cave of Fancy*,[28] which she thought proper afterwards to lay aside unfinished. I am told that at this period she appeared under great dejection of spirits, and filled with melancholy regret for the loss of her youthful friend. A period of two years had elapsed since the death of that friend; but it was possibly the composition of the fiction of *Mary*, that renewed her sorrows in their

a. This reference to Joseph Johnson's help with the house was deleted in the second edition.

original force. Soon after entering upon her new habitation, she produced a little work, entitled, *Original Stories from Real Life*,[29] intended for the use of children. At the commencement of her literary career, she is said to have conceived a vehement aversion to the being regarded, by her ordinary acquaintance, in the character of an author, and to have employed some precautions to prevent its occurrence.

The employment which the bookseller suggested to her, as the easiest and most certain source of pecuniary income, of course, was translation. With this view she improved herself in her French, with which she had previously but a slight acquaintance, and acquired the Italian and German languages. The greater part of her literary engagements at this time, were such as were presented to her by Mr Johnson. She new-modelled and abridged a work, translated from the Dutch, entitled, *Young Grandison*: she began a translation from the French, of a book, called, *The New Robinson*; but in this undertaking, she was, I believe, anticipated by another translator: and she compiled a series of extracts in verse and prose, upon the model of Dr Enfield's Speaker, which bears the title of *The Female Reader*;[30] but which, from a cause not worth mentioning, has hitherto been printed with a different name in the title-page.

About the middle of the year 1788, Mr Johnson instituted the *Analytical Review*,[31] in which Mary took a considerable share. She also translated Necker *On the Importance of Religious Opinions*; made an abridgment of Lavater's *Physiognomy*, from the French, which has never been published; and compressed Salzmann's *Elements of Morality*, a German production, into a publication in three volumes duodecimo.[32] The translation of Salzmann produced a correspondence between Mary and the author; and he afterwards repaid the obligation to her in kind, by a German translation of *The Rights of Woman*. Such were her principal literary occupations, from the autumn of 1787, to the autumn of 1790.

It perhaps deserves to be remarked that this sort of miscellaneous literary employment, seems, for the time at least, rather to damp and contract, than to enlarge and invigorate, the genius. The writer is accustomed to see his performances answer the mere mercantile purpose of the day, and confounded with those of persons to whom he is secretly conscious of a superiority. No neighbour mind serves as a mirror to reflect the generous confidence he felt within himself; and perhaps the man never yet existed, who could maintain his enthusiasm to its full vigour, in the midst of this kind of solitariness. He is touched with the torpedo of mediocrity. I believe that nothing which Mary produced during this period, is marked with those daring flights, which exhibit themselves in the little fiction she composed just before its commencement. Among effusions of a nobler cast, I find occasionally interspersed some of that homily-language, which, to speak from my own feelings, is calculated to damp the moral courage it was intended to awaken. This is probably to be assigned to the causes above described.[33]

I have already said that one of the purposes which Mary had conceived, a few years before, as necessary to give a relish to the otherwise insipid, or embittered, draught of human life, was usefulness. On this side, the period of her existence of which I am now treating, is more brilliant, than in a literary view. She determined to apply as great a part as possible of the produce of her present employments, to the assistance of her friends and of the distressed; and, for this purpose, laid down to herself rules of the most rigid economy. She began with endeavouring to promote the interest of her sisters. She conceived that there was no situation in which she could place them, at once so respectable and agreeable, as that of governesses in private families. She determined therefore in the first place, to endeavour to qualify them for such an undertaking. Her younger sister she sent to Paris, where she remained near two years. The elder she placed in a school near London, first as a parlour-boarder, and afterwards as a teacher. Her brother James, who had already been at sea, she first took into her house, and next sent to Woolwich for instruction, to qualify him for a respectable situation in the royal navy, where he was shortly after made a lieutenant. Charles, who was her favourite brother, had been articled to the eldest, an attorney in the Minories;[34] but not being satisfied with his situation she removed him and in some time after, having first placed him with a farmer for instruction, she fitted him out for America, where his speculations, founded upon the basis she had provided, are said to have been extremely prosperous. The reason so much of this parental sort of care fell upon her was, that her father had by this time considerably embarrassed his circumstances. His affairs having grown too complex for himself to disentangle, he had entrusted them to the management of a near relation; but Mary, not being satisfied with the conduct of the business took them into her own hands. The exertions she made, and the struggle into which she entered however, in this instance, were ultimately fruitless. To the day of her death her father was almost wholly supported by funds which she supplied to him. In addition to her exertions for her own family, she took a young girl of about seven years of age under her protection and care, the niece of Mrs John Hunter, and of the present Mrs Skeys, for whose mother, then lately dead, she had entertained a sincere friendship.

The period, from the end of the year 1787 to the end of the year 1790, though consumed in labours of little eclat, served still further to establish her in a friendly connection from which she derived many pleasures. Mr Johnson, the bookseller, contracted a great personal regard for her, which resembled in many respects that of a parent. As she frequented his house, she of course became acquainted with his guests. Among these may be mentioned as persons possessing her esteem, Mr Bonnycastle, the mathematician, the late Mr George Anderson, accountant to the board of control, Dr George Fordyce,[35] and Mr Fuseli, the celebrated painter. Between both of the two latter and herself, there existed sentiments of genuine affection and friendship.

Chapter Six

1790–1792

Hitherto the literary career of Mary, had for the most part, been silent; and had been productive of income to herself, without apparently leading to the wreath of fame. From this time she was destined to attract the notice of the public, and perhaps no female writer ever obtained so great a degree of celebrity throughout Europe.

It cannot be doubted that, while, for three years of literary employment, she 'held the noiseless tenor of her way,' [36] her mind was insensibly advancing towards a vigorous maturity. The uninterrupted habit of composition gave a freedom and firmness to the expression of her sentiments. The society she frequented, nourished her understanding, and enlarged her mind. The French revolution, while it gave a fundamental shock to the human intellect through every region of the globe, did not fail to produce a conspicuous effect in the progress of Mary's reflections. The prejudices of her early years suffered a vehement concussion. Her respect for establishments was undermined. At this period occurred a misunderstanding upon public grounds, with one of her early friends, whose attachment to musty creeds and exploded absurdities, had been increased, by the operation of those very circumstances, by which her mind had been rapidly advanced in the race of independence.

The event, immediately introductory to the rank which from this time she held in the lists of literature, was the publication of Burke's *Reflections on the Revolution in France*. [37] This book, after having been long promised to the world, finally made its appearance on the first of November 1790; and Mary, full of sentiments of liberty, and impressed with a warm interest in the struggle that was now going on, seized her pen in the full burst of indignation, an emotion of which she was strongly susceptible. She was in the habit of composing with rapidity, and her answer, which was the first of the numerous ones that appeared, obtained extraordinary notice. Marked as it is with the vehemence and impetuousness of its eloquence, it is certainly chargeable with a too contemptuous and intemperate treatment of the great man against whom its attack is directed. But this circumstance was not injurious to the success of the publication. Burke had been warmly loved by the most liberal and enlightened friends of freedom, and they were proportionably inflamed and disgusted by the fury of his assault, upon what they deemed to be its sacred cause.

Short as was the time in which Mary composed her *Answer to Burke's Reflections*,[38] there was one anecdote she told me concerning it, which seems worth recording in this place. It was sent to the press, as is the general practice when the early publication of a piece is deemed a matter of importance, before the composition was finished. When Mary had arrived at about the middle of her work, she was seized with a temporary fit of torpor and indolence, and began to repent of her undertaking. In this state of mind, she called, one evening, as she was in the practice of doing, upon her publisher, for the purpose of relieving herself by an hour or two's conversation. Here, the habitual ingenuousness of her nature, led her to describe what had just past in her thoughts. Mr Johnson immediately, in a kind and friendly way, intreated her not to put any constraint upon her inclination, and to give herself no uneasiness about the sheets already printed, which he would cheerfully throw aside, if it would contribute to her happiness. Mary had wanted stimulus. She had not expected to be encouraged, in what she well knew to be an un-reasonable access of idleness. Her friend's so readily falling in with her ill-humour, and seeming to expect that she would lay aside her undertaking, piqued her pride. She immediately went home; and proceeded to the end of her work, with no other interruptions but what were absolutely indispensible.[39]

It is probable that the applause which attended her *Answer to Burke*, elevated the tone of her mind. She had always felt much confidence in her own powers; but it cannot be doubted, that the actual perception of a similar feeling respecting us in a multitude of others, must increase the confidence, and stimulate the adventure of any human being. Mary accordingly proceeded, in a short time after, to the composition of her most celebrated production, the *Vindication of the Rights of Woman*.[40]

Never did any author enter into a cause, with a more ardent desire to be found, not a flourishing and empty declaimer, but an effectual champion. She considered herself as standing forth in defence of one half of the human species, labouring under a yoke which, through all the records of time, had degraded them from the station of rational beings, and almost sunk them to the level of the brutes. She saw indeed, that they were often attempted to be held in silken fetters, and bribed into the love of slavery; but the disguise and the treachery served only the more fully to confirm her opposition. She regarded her sex, in the language of Calista[41] as

In every state of life the slaves of man:

the rich as alternately under the despotism of a father, a brother and a husband; and the middling and the poorer classes shut out from the acquisition of bread with independence, when they are not shut out from the very means of an industrious subsistence. Such were the views she entertained of the subject; and such were the feelings with which she warmed her mind.

The work is certainly a very bold and original production. The strength and firmness with which the author repels the opinions of Rousseau, Dr Gregory, and Dr James Fordyce, respecting the condition of women,[42] cannot but make a strong impression upon every ingenuous reader. The public at large formed very different opinions respecting the character of the performance. Many of the sentiments are undoubtedly of a rather masculine description. The spirited and decisive way in which the author explodes the system of gallantry, and the species of homage with which the sex is usually treated, shocked the majority. Novelty produced a sentiment in their mind, which they mistook for a sense of injustice. The pretty, soft creatures that are so often to be found in the female sex, and that class of men who believe they could not exist without such pretty, soft creatures to resort to, were in arms against the author of so heretical and blasphemous a doctrine. There are also, it must be confessed, occasional passages of a stern and rugged feature, incompatible with the true stamina of the writer's character. But, if they did not belong to her fixed and permanent character, they belonged to her character *pro tempore*; and what she thought, she scorned to qualify.

Yet, along with this rigid, and somewhat amazonian temper, which characterized some parts of the book, it is impossible not to remark a luxuriance of imagination, and a trembling delicacy of sentiment, which would have done honour to a poet, bursting[a] with all the visions of an Armida and a Dido.[43]

The contradiction, to the public apprehension, was equally great, as to the person of the author, as it was when they considered the temper of the book. In the champion of her sex, who was described as endeavouring to invest them with all the rights of man, those whom curiosity prompted to seek the occasion of beholding her, expected to find a sturdy, muscular, raw-boned virago[b] and they were not a little surprised, when, instead of all this, they found a woman, lovely in her person, and in the best and most engaging sense, feminine in her manners.

The *Vindication of the Rights of Woman* is undoubtedly a very unequal performance, and eminently deficient in method and arrangement. When tried by the hoary and long-established laws of literary composition, it can scarcely maintain its claim to be placed in the first class of human productions. But when we consider the importance of its doctrines, and the eminence of genius it displays, it seems not very improbable that it will be read as long as the English language endures. The publication of this book forms an epocha in the subject to which it belongs; and Mary Wollstonecraft will perhaps here-after be found to have performed more substantial service for the cause of her sex, than all the other writers, male or female, that ever felt themselves animated in the behalf of oppressed and injured beauty.[c]

The censure of the liberal critic as to the defects of this performance, will be changed into astonishment, when I tell him, that a work of this inestimable moment, was begun, carried on, and finished in the state in which it now appears, in a period of no more than six weeks.[d]

It is necessary here that I should resume the subject of the

a. 'burning'.

b. . . . 'a rude, pedantic, dictatorial virago'.

c. . . . 'animated by the contemplation of their oppressed and injured state'.

d. Second edition adds: 'The remainder of the story I have to relate is less literary, than personal. For the rest of her life Mary was continually occupied by a train of circumstances, which roused all the prepossessions and passions of her mind.'

friendship that subsisted between Mary and Mr Fuseli,[44] which proved the source of the most memorable events in her subsequent history. He is a native of the republic of Switzerland, but has spent the principal part of his life in the island of Great-Britain. The eminence of his genius can scarcely be disputed; it has indeed received the testimony which is the least to be suspected, that of some of the most considerable of his contemporary artists. He has one of the most striking characteristics of genius, a daring, as well as persevering, spirit of adventure. The work in which he is at present engaged, a series of pictures for the illustration of Milton, upon a very large scale, and produced solely upon the incitement of his own mind, is a proof of this, if indeed his whole life had not sufficiently proved it.

Mr Fuseli is one of Mr Johnson's oldest friends, and was at this time in the habit of visiting him two or three times a week. Mary, one of whose strongest characteristics was the exquisite sensations of pleasure she felt from the associations of visible objects, had hitherto never been acquainted, or never intimately acquainted, with an eminent painter. The being thus introduced therefore to the society of Mr Fuseli, was a high gratification to her; while he found in Mary, a person perhaps more susceptible of the emotions painting is calculated to excite, than any other with whom he ever conversed. Painting, and subjects closely connected with painting, were their almost constant topics of conversation; and they found them inexhaustible. It cannot be doubted, but that this was a species of exercise very conducive to the improvement of Mary's mind.

Nothing human however is unmixed. If Mary derived improvement from Mr Fuseli, she may also be suspected of having caught the infection of some of his faults. In early life Mr Fuseli was ardently attached to literature; but the demands of his profession have prevented him from keeping up that extensive and indiscriminate acquaintance with it, that belles-lettres scholars frequently possess.[e] The favourites of his boyish years remain his only favourites. Homer is with Mr Fuseli the abstract and deposit of every human perfection.

e. Second edition adds: 'When I say this, it is by no means intended to imply, that his intercourse with the writers of established fame is not considerable, or that he is not profoundly skilled in their beauties. One consequence however of his avocations from literature is, that' . . .

Milton, Shakespeare, and Richardson, have also engaged much of his attention. The nearest rival of Homer, I believe, if Homer can have a rival, is Jean Jacques Rousseau. A young man embraces entire the opinions of a favourite writer, and Mr Fuseli has not had leisure to bring the opinions of his youth to a revision. Smitten with Rousseau's conception of the perfectness of the savage state, and the essential abortiveness of all civilization, Mr Fuseli looks at all our little attempts at improvement, with a spirit that borders perhaps too much upon contempt and indifference. One of his favourite positions is the divinity of genius. This is a power that comes complete at once from the hands of the Creator of all things, and the first essays of a man of real genius are such, in all their grand and most important features, as no subsequent assiduity can amend. Add to this, that Mr Fuseli is somewhat of a caustic turn of mind, with much wit, and a disposition to search, in every thing new or modern, for occasions of censure. I believe Mary came something more a cynic out of the school of Mr Fuseli, than she went into it.

But the principal circumstance that relates to the intercourse of Mary, and this celebrated artist, remains to be told. She saw Mr Fuseli frequently; he amused, delighted and instructed her. As a painter, it was impossible she should not wish to see his works, and consequently to frequent his house. She visited him; her visits were returned. Notwithstanding the inequality of their years, Mary was not of a temper to live upon terms of so much intimacy with a man of merit and genius, without loving him.[f] The delight she enjoyed in his society, she transferred by association to his person. What she experienced in this respect, was no doubt heightened, by the state of celibacy and restraint in which she had hitherto lived, and to which the rules of polished society condemn an unmarried woman. She conceived a personal and ardent affection for him. Mr Fuseli was a married man, and his wife the acquaintance of Mary. She readily perceived the restrictions which this circumstance seemed to impose upon her; but she made light of any difficulty that might arise out of them. Not that she was insensible to the value of domestic endearments between persons of an opposite sex, but that she scorned to

f. Godwin's revision of the paragraphs that follow for the second edition can be found in the Appendix, p. 274.

suppose, that she could feel a struggle, in conforming to the laws she should lay down to her conduct.

There cannot perhaps be a properer place than the present, to state her principles upon this subject, such at least as they were when I knew her best. She set a great value on a mutual affection between persons of an opposite sex. She regarded it as the principal solace of human life. It was her maxim, 'that the imagination should awaken the senses, and not the senses the imagination.' In other words, that whatever related to the gratification of the senses, ought to arise, in a human being of a pure mind, only as the consequence of an individual affection. She regarded the manners and habits of the majority of our sex in that respect, with strong disapprobation. She conceived that true virtue would prescribe the most entire celibacy, exclusively of affection, and the most perfect fidelity to that affection when it existed.[45] – There is no reason to doubt that, if Mr Fuseli had been disengaged at the period of their acquaintance, he would have been the man of her choice. As it was, she conceived it both practicable and eligible, to cultivate a distinguishing affection for him, and to foster it by the endearments of personal intercourse and a reciprocation of kindness, without departing in the smallest degree from the rules she prescribed to herself.[g]

In September 1791, she removed from the house she occupied in George-street, to a large and commodious apartment in Store-street, Bedford-square. She began to think that she had been too rigid, in the laws of frugality and self-denial with which she set out in her literary career; and now added to the neatness and cleanliness which she had always scrupulously observed, a certain degree of elegance, and those temperate indulgences in furniture and accommodations, from which a sound and uncorrupted taste never fails to derive pleasure.

It was in the month of November in the same year (1791), that the writer of this narrative was first in company with the person to whom it relates. He dined with her at a friend's, together with Mr Thomas Paine[46] and one or two other persons. The invitation was of his own seeking, his object being to see the author of *The Rights of Man*, with whom he had never before conversed.

The interview was not fortunate. Mary and myself parted, mutually

g. Godwin's revision for the second edition ends here.

displeased with each other. I had not read her *Rights of Woman*. I had barely looked into her *Answer to Burke*, and been displeased, as literary men are apt to be, with a few offenses against grammar and other minute points of composition. I had therefore little curiosity to see Mrs Wollstonecraft, and a very great curiosity to see Thomas Paine. Paine, in his general habits, is no great talker; and, though he threw in occasionally some shrewd and striking remarks, the conversation lay principally between me and Mary. I, of consequence, heard her, very frequently when I wished to hear Paine.

We touched on a considerable variety of topics, and particularly on the characters and habits of certain eminent men. Mary, as has already been observed, had acquired in a very blameable degree,[h] the practice of seeing every thing on the gloomy side, and bestowing censure with a plentiful hand, where circumstances were in any respect doubtful. I, on the contrary, had a strong propensity, to favourable construction, and particularly, where I found unequivocal marks of genius, strongly to incline to the supposition of generous and manly virtues. We ventilated in this way the characters of Voltaire and others, who have obtained from some individuals an ardent admiration, while the greater number have treated them with extreme moral severity. Mary was at last provoked to tell me, that praise, lavished in the way that I lavished it, could do no credit either to the commended or the commender. We discussed some questions on the subject of religion, in which her opinions approached much nearer to the received one, than mine. As the conversation proceeded, I became dissatisfied with the tone of my own share in it. We touched upon all topics, without treating forcibly and connectedly upon any. Meanwhile, I did her the justice, in giving an account of the conversation to a party in which I supped, though I was not sparing of my blame, to yield to her the praise of a person of active and independent thinking. On her side, she did me no part of what perhaps I considered as justice.

We met two or three times in the course of the following year, but made a very small degree of progress towards a cordial acquaintance.[47]

In the close of the year 1792, Mary went over to France, where she

h. 'in a very blameable degree' deleted in the second edition.

continued to reside for upwards of two years. One of her principal inducements to this step, related, I believe, to Mr Fuseli. She had, at first, considered it as reasonable and judicious, to cultivate what I may be permitted to call, a Platonic affection for him; but she did not, in the sequel, find all the satisfaction in this plan, which she had originally expected from it. It was in vain that she enjoyed much pleasure in his society, and that she enjoyed it frequently. Her ardent imagination was continually conjuring up pictures of the happiness she should have found, if fortune had favoured their more intimate union. She felt herself formed for domestic affection, and all those tender charities, which men of sensibility have constantly treated as the dearest band of human society. General conversation and society could not satisfy her. She felt herself alone, as it were, in the great mass of her species; and she repined when she reflected, that the best years of her life were spent in this comfortless solitude. These ideas made the cordial intercourse of Mr Fuseli, which had at first been one of her greatest pleasures, a source of perpetual torment to her. She conceived it necessary to snap the chain of this association in her mind; and, for that purpose, determined to seek a new climate, and mingle in different scenes.

It is singular, that during her residence in Store-street, which lasted more than twelve months, she produced nothing, except a few articles in the *Analytical Review*. Her literary meditations were chiefly employed upon the sequel to *The Rights of Woman*; but she has scarcely left behind her a single paper, that can, with any certainty, be assigned to have had this destination.

Chapter Seven

1792–1795

The original plan of Mary, respecting her residence in France, had no precise limits in the article of duration; the single purpose she had in view being that of an endeavour to heal her distempered mind. She did not proceed so far as even to discharge her lodging in London; and, to some friends who saw her immediately before her departure, she spoke merely of an absence of six weeks.

It is not to be wondered at, that her excursion did not originally seem to produce the effects she had expected from it. She was in a land of strangers; she had no acquaintance; she had even to acquire the power of receiving and communicating ideas with facility in the language of the country. Her first residence was in a spacious mansion to which she had been invited, but the master of which (monsieur Fillietaz)[48] was absent at the time of her arrival. At first therefore she found herself surrounded only with servants. The gloominess of her mind communicated its own colour to the objects she saw; and in this temper she began a series of *Letters on the Present Character of the French Nation*,[49] one of which she forwarded to her publisher, and which appears in the collection of her posthumous works. This performance she soon after discontinued; and it is, as she justly remarks, tinged with the saturnine temper which at that time pervaded her mind.

Mary carried with her introductions to several agreeable families in Paris. She renewed her acquaintance with Paine. There also subsisted a very sincere friendship between her and Helen Maria Williams,[50] author of a collection of poems of uncommon merit, who at that time resided in Paris. Another person, whom Mary always spoke of in terms of ardent commendation, both for the excellence of his disposition and the force of his genius, was a count Slabrendorf,[51] by birth, I believe, a Swede. It is almost unnecessary to mention, that she was personally acquainted with the majority of the leaders in the French revolution.[a]

But the house that, I believe, she principally frequented at this time, was that of Mr Thomas Christie, a person whose pursuits were mercantile, and who had written a volume on the French revolution. With Mrs Christie her acquaintance was more intimate than with her husband.[52]

It was about four months after her arrival at Paris in December 1792, that she entered into that species of connection for which her heart secretly panted, and which had the effect of diffusing an immediate tranquillity and cheerfulness over her manners.[b] The person with whom it was formed (for it would be an idle piece of delicacy to attempt to suppress a name, which is known to every one whom the reputation of Mary has reached), was Mr Gilbert Imlay,[53] native of the United States of North America.

The place at which she first saw Mr Imlay was at the house of Mr Christie; and it perhaps deserves to be noticed, that the emotions he then excited in her mind, were, I am told, those of dislike, and that, for some time, she shunned all occasions of meeting him. This sentiment however speedily gave place to one of greater kindness.

Previously to the partiality she conceived for him, she had determined upon a journey to Switzerland, induced chiefly by motives of economy. But she had some difficulty in procuring a passport; and it was probably the intercourse that now originated between her and Mr Imlay, that changed her purpose, and led her to prefer a lodging at Neuilly, a village three miles from Paris. Her habitation here was a solitary house in the midst of a garden, with no other inhabitants than herself and the gardener, an old man, who performed for her many of the offices of a domestic, and would sometimes contend for the honour of making her bed. The gardener had a great veneration for his guest, and would set before her, when alone, some grapes of a

a. Second edition adds: 'Her country, combined with her known political sentiments, recommended her; and the celebrity of her writings had prepared the way for her personal reception.'

b. Second edition reads: . . . 'she entered into that connection, from which the tranquillity and the sorrows of the immediately succeeding years of her life were solely derived'.

particularly fine sort, which she could not without the greatest difficulty obtain when she had any person with her as a visitor. Here it was that she conceived, and for the most part executed, her *Historical and Moral View of the French Revolution,** [54] into which, as she observes, are incorporated most of the observations she had collected for her *Letters*, and which was written with more sobriety and cheerfulness than the tone in which they had been commenced. In the evening she was accustomed to refresh herself by a walk in a neighbouring wood, from which her old host in vain endeavoured to dissuade her, by recounting divers horrible robberies and murders that had been committed there.

The commencement of the attachment Mary now formed, had neither confidant nor adviser. She always conceived it to be a gross breach of delicacy to have any confidant in a matter of this sacred nature, an affair of the heart. The origin of the connection was about the middle of April 1793, and it was carried on in a private manner for four months. At the expiration of that period a circumstance occurred that induced her to declare it. The French convention, exasperated at the conduct of the British government, particularly in the affair of Toulon,[55] formed a decree against the citizens of this country, by one article of which the English, resident in France, were ordered into prison till the period of a general peace. Mary had objected to a marriage with Mr Imlay, who, at the time their connection was formed, had no property whatever; because she would not involve him in certain family embarrassments to which she conceived herself exposed, or make him answerable for the pecuniary demands that existed against her. She however considered their engagement as of the most sacred nature; and they had mutually formed the plan of emigrating to America, as soon as they should have realized a sum, enabling them to do it in the mode they desired. The decree however that I have just mentioned, made it necessary, not that a marriage should actually take place, but that Mary should take the name of Imlay, which, from the nature of their connection,[c] she

---

* [*Godwin's footnote:*] No part of the proposed continuation of this work, has been found among the papers of the author.

c. Second edition adds: . . . 'formed, on her part at least, with no capricious or fickle design'.

conceived herself entitled to do, and obtain a certificate from the American ambassador, as the wife of a native of that country.

Their engagement being thus avowed, they thought proper to reside under the same roof, and for that purpose removed to Paris.

Mary was now arrived at the situation, which, for two or three preceding years, her reason had pointed out to her as affording the most substantial prospect of happiness.[56] She had been tossed and agitated by the waves of misfortune. Her childhood, as she often said, had known few of the endearments, which constitute the principal happiness of childhood. The temper of her father had early given to her mind a severe cast of thought, and substituted the inflexibility of resistance for the confidence of affection. The cheerfulness of her entrance upon womanhood, had been darkened, by an attendance upon the death-bed of her mother, and the still more afflicting calamity of her eldest sister. Her exertions to create a joint independence for her sisters and herself, had been attended, neither with the success, nor the pleasure, she had hoped from them. Her first youthful passion, her friendship for Fanny, had encountered many disappointments, and, in fine, a melancholy and premature catastrophe. Soon after these accumulated mortifications, she was engaged in a contest with a near relation, whom she regarded as unprincipled, respecting the wreck of her father's fortune. In this affair she suffered the double pain, which arises from moral indignation, and disappointed benevolence. Her exertions to assist almost every member of her family, were great and unremitted. Finally, when she indulged a romantic affection for Mr Fuseli, and fondly imagined that she should find in it the solace of her cares, she perceived too late, that, by continually impressing on her mind fruitless images of unreserved affection and domestic felicity, it only served to give new pungency to the sensibility that was destroying her.

Some persons may be inclined to observe, that the evils here enumerated, are not among the heaviest in the catalogue of human calamities. But evils take their rank more from the temper of the mind that suffers them, than from their abstract nature. Upon a man of a hard and insensible disposition, the shafts of misfortune often fall pointless and impotent. There are persons, by no means hard and insensible, who, from an elastic and sanguine turn of mind, are continually prompted to look on the fair side of things, and, having suffered one fall, immediately rise again, to pursue their course, with the same eagerness, the same hope, and the same gaiety, as before. On the other hand, we not unfrequently meet with persons, endowed with the most exquisite and delicious sensibility, whose minds seem almost of too fine a texture to encounter the vicissitudes of human affairs, to whom pleasure is transport, and disappointment is agony indescribable. This character is finely portrayed by the author of *The Sorrows of Werter*. Mary was in this respect a female Werter.

She brought then, in the present instance, a wounded and sick heart, to take refuge in the bosom of a chosen friend. Let it not however be imagined, that she brought a heart, querulous, and ruined in its taste for pleasure. No; her whole character seemed to change with a change of fortune. Her sorrows, the depression of her spirits, were forgotten, and she assumed all the simplicity and the vivacity of a youthful mind. She was like a serpent upon a rock, that casts its slough, and appears again with the brilliancy, the sleekness, and the elastic activity of its happiest age.[d] She was playful, full of confidence, kindness and sympathy. Her eyes assumed new lustre, and her cheeks new colour and smoothness. Her voice became chearful; her temper overflowing with universal kindness; and that smile of bewitching tenderness from day to day illuminated her countenance, which all who knew her will so well recollect, and which won, both heart and soul, the affection of almost every one that beheld it.

Mary now reposed herself upon a person, of whose honour and principles she had the most exalted idea. She nourished an individual affection, which she saw no necessity of subjecting to restraint; and a heart like hers was not formed to nourish affection by halves. Her conception of Mr Imlay's 'tenderness and worth had twisted him closely round her heart;' and she 'indulged the thought, that she had thrown out some tendrils, to cling to the elm by which she wished to be supported.' This was 'talking a new language to her;' but 'conscious that she was not a parasite-plant,' she was willing to encourage and

d. This sentence, with the sexual snake imagery, was deleted in the second edition.

foster the luxuriances of affection.[e] Her confidence was entire; her love was unbounded. Now, for the first time in her life, she gave a loose to all the sensibilities of her nature.[f]

Soon after the time I am now speaking of, her attachment to Mr Imlay gained a new link, by finding reason to suppose herself with child.

Their establishment at Paris, was however broken up almost as soon as formed, by the circumstance of Mr Imlay's entering into business, urged, as he said, by the prospect of a family, and this being a favourable crisis in French affairs for commercial speculations. The pursuits in which he was engaged, led him in the month of September to Havre de Grace, then called Havre Marat, probably to superintend the shipping of goods, in which he was jointly engaged with some other person or persons.[58] Mary remained in the capital.

The solitude in which she was now left, proved an unexpected trial. Domestic affections constituted the object upon which her heart was fixed; and she early felt, with an inward grief, that Mr Imlay 'did not attach those tender emotions round the idea of home, which, every time they recurred, dimmed her eyes with moisture.' She had expected his return from week to week, and from month to month; but a succession of business still continued to detain him at Havre. At

e. These phrases, describing her love for Imlay, were deleted in the second edition.[57]

f. Second edition adds: 'It might be considered as a trite remark, if I were to observe here, that the highest pleasures of human life are nearly connected with its bitterest sorrows, and that the being who restlessly aspires to superior gratifications, has some reason to fear, lest his refinement should be a precursor to anguish and repentance. Influenced by this anticipation, there are persons who resolutely circumscribe themselves within the sphere of a rigid and miserable separation from others, that they may be independent of their injustice or folly. But this is a sordid policy. The mistake of Mary in this instance is easy of detection. She did not give full play to her judgment in this most important choice of life. She was too much under the influence of the melancholy and disappointment which had driven her from her native land; and, gratified with the first gleam of promised relief, she ventured not to examine with too curious a research into the soundness of her expectation. The least that can be said of the connection that she now formed, is, that it was a very unequal one. In years the parties were a match for each other; in every other point they were ill fitted for so entire an intimacy.'

the same time the sanguinary character which the government of France began every day to assume, contributed to banish tranquillity from the first months of her pregnancy. Before she left Neuilly, she happened one day to enter Paris on foot (I believe, by the *Place de Louis Quinze*), when an execution, attended with some peculiar aggravations, had just taken place, and the blood of the guillotine appeared fresh upon the pavement. The emotions of her soul burst forth in indignant exclamations, while a prudent bystander warned her of her danger, and intreated her to hasten and hide her discontents. She described to me, more than once, the anguish she felt at hearing of the death of Brissot, Vergniaud, and the twenty deputies,[59] as one of the most intolerable sensations she had ever experienced.

Finding the return of Mr Imlay continually postponed, she determined, in January 1794, to join him at Havre. One motive that influenced her, though, I believe, by no means the principal, was the growing cruelties of Robespierre, and the desire she felt to be in any other place, rather than the devoted[60] city; in the midst of which they were perpetrated.

From January to September, Mr Imlay and Mary lived together, with great harmony, at Havre, where the child, with which she was pregnant, was born, on the fourteenth of May, and named Frances,[61] in remembrance of the dear friend of her youth, whose image could never be erased from her memory.

In September, Mr Imlay took his departure from Havre for the port of London. As this step was said to be necessary in the way of business, he endeavoured to prevail upon Mary to quit Havre, and once more take up her abode at Paris. Robespierre was now no more;[62] and, of consequence, the only objection she had to residing in the capital, was removed. Mr Imlay was already in London, before she undertook her journey, and it proved the most fatiguing journey she ever made; the carriage, in which she travelled, being overturned no less than four times between Havre and Paris.

This absence, like that of the preceding year in which Mr Imlay had removed to Havre, was represented as an absence that was to have a short duration. In two months he was once again to join her in Paris. It proved however the prelude to an eternal separation. The agonies of such a separation, or rather desertion, great as Mary would have found them upon every supposition, were vastly increased, by the lingering method in which it was effected, and the ambiguity that, for a long time, hung upon it. This circumstance produced the effect, of holding her mind, by force, as it were, to the most painful of all subjects, and not suffering her to derive the just advantage from the energy and elasticity of her character.

The procrastination of which I am speaking was however productive of one advantage. It put off the evil day. She did not suspect the calamities that awaited her, till the close of the year. She gained an additional three months of comparative happiness. But she purchased it at a very dear rate. Perhaps no human creature ever suffered greater misery, than dyed the whole year 1795, in the life of this incomparable woman. It was wasted in that sort of despair, to the sense of which the mind is continually awakened, by a glimmering of fondly cherished, expiring hope.

Why did she thus obstinately cling to an ill-starred unhappy passion?[g][63] Because it is of the very essence of affection, to seek to perpetuate itself. He does not love, who can resign this cherished sentiment, without suffering some of the sharpest struggles that our nature is capable of enduring. Add to this, Mary had fixed her heart upon this chosen friend; and one of the last impressions a worthy mind can submit to receive, is that of the worthlessness of the person upon whom it has fixed all its esteem. Mary had struggled to entertain a favourable opinion of human nature; she had unweariedly fought for a kindred mind, in whose integrity and fidelity to take up her rest.[h] Mr Imlay undertook to prove, in his letters written immediately after their complete separation, that his conduct towards her was reconcilable to the strictest rectitude; but undoubtedly Mary was of a different opinion. Whatever the reader may decide in this respect, there is one sentiment that, I believe, he will unhesitatingly admit: that of pity for the mistake of the man, who, being in possession of

g. . . . 'a passion, at once ill-assorted, and unpromising'.

h. Second edition adds: 'Wounded affection, wounded pride, all those principles which hold most absolute empire in the purest and loftiest minds, urged her to still further experiments to recover her influence, and to a still more poignant desperation, long after reason would have directed her to desist, and resolutely call off her mind from thoughts of so hopeless and fatal a description.'

such a friendship and attachment as those of Mary, could hold them
at a trivial price, and, 'like the base Indian, throw a pearl away, richer
than all his tribe.' *64

* [*Godwin's footnote:*] A person, from whose society at this time Mary derived particular
gratification,i 'was Archibald Hamilton Rowan,65 who had lately become a fugitive
from Ireland, in consequence of a political prosecution, and in whom she found those
qualities which were always eminently engaging to her, great integrity of disposition,
and great kindness of heart'.

i. In the second edition Godwin altered the ambiguous phrase 'particular gratification'.

Chapter Eight

1795–1796

In April 1795, Mary returned once more to London, being requested to do so by Mr Imlay, who even sent a servant to Paris to wait upon her in the journey, before she could complete the necessary arrangements for her departure. But, notwithstanding these favourable appearances, she came to England with a heavy heart, not daring, after all the uncertainties and anguish she had endured, to trust to the suggestions of hope.

The gloomy forebodings of her mind, were but too faithfully verified. Mr Imlay had already formed another connection; as it is said, with a young actress from a strolling company of players. His attentions therefore to Mary were formal and constrained, and she probably had but little of his society. This alteration could not escape her penetrating glance. He ascribed it to pressure of business, and some pecuniary embarrassments which, at that time, occurred to him; it was of little consequence to Mary what was the cause. She saw, but too well, though she strove not to see, that his affections were lost to her for ever.

It is impossible to imagine a period of greater pain and mortification than Mary passed, for about seven weeks, from the sixteenth of April to the sixth of June, in a furnished house that Mr Imlay had provided for her. She had come over to England, a country for which she, at this time, expressed 'a repugnance, that almost amounted to horror,' in search of happiness. She feared that that happiness had altogether escaped her; but she was encouraged by the eagerness and impatience which Mr Imlay at length seemed to manifest for her arrival. When she saw him, all her fears were confirmed. What a picture was she capable of forming to herself, of the overflowing kindness of a meeting, after an interval of so much anguish and apprehension! A thousand images of this sort were present to her burning imagination. It is in vain, on such occasions, for reserve and reproach to endeavour to curb in the emotions of an affectionate heart. But the hopes she nourished were speedily blasted. Her reception by Mr Imlay was cold and embarrassed. Discussions ('explanations' they were called) followed; cruel explanations, that only added to the anguish of a heart already overwhelmed in grief! They had small pretensions indeed to explicitness; but they sufficiently told, that the case admitted not of remedy.

Mary was incapable of sustaining her equanimity in this pressing emergency. 'Love, dear, delusive love!' as she expressed herself to a friend some time afterwards, 'rigorous reason had forced her to resign; and now her rational prospects were blasted, just as she had learned to be contented with rational enjoyments.' Thus situated, life became an intolerable burthen. While she was absent from Mr Imlay, she could talk of purposes of separation and independence. But, now that they were in the same house, she could not withhold herself from endeavours to revive their mutual cordiality; and unsuccessful endeavours continually added fuel to the fire that destroyed her. She formed a desperate purpose to die.

This part of the story of Mary is involved in considerable obscurity. I only know, that Mr Imlay became acquainted with her purpose, at a moment when he was uncertain whether or not it were already executed, and that his feelings were roused by the intelligence. It was perhaps owing to his activity and representations, that her life, was, at this time, saved. She determined to continue to exist. Actuated by this purpose, she took a resolution, worthy both of the strength and affectionateness of her mind. Mr Imlay was involved in a question of considerable difficulty, respecting a mercantile adventure in Norway.[66] It seemed to require the presence of some very judicious agent, to conduct the business to its desired termination. Mary determined to make the voyage, and take the business into her own hands. Such a voyage seemed the most desireable thing to recruit her health, and, if possible, her spirits, in the present crisis. It was also gratifying to her feelings, to be employed in promoting the interest of a man, from whom she had experienced such severe unkindness, but to whom she ardently desired to be reconciled. The moment of desperation I have mentioned, occurred in the close of May, and, in about a week after, she set out upon this new expedition.[67]

The narrative of this voyage is before the world, and perhaps a book of travels that so irresistably seizes on the heart, never, in any other instance, found its way from the press. The occasional harshness and ruggedness of character, that diversify her *Vindication of the Rights of Woman*, here totally disappear. If ever there was a book calculated to make a man in love with its author, this appears to me to be the book. She speaks of her sorrows, in a way that fills us with melancholy, and dissolves us in tenderness, at the same time that she displays a genius which commands all our admiration. Affliction had tempered her heart to a softness almost more than human; and the gentleness of her spirit seems precisely to accord with all the romance of unbounded attachment.

Thus softened and improved, thus fraught with imagination and sensibility, with all, and more than all, 'that youthful poets fancy, when they love,' she returned to England, and, if he had so pleased, to the arms of her lover.[a] Her return was hastened by the ambiguity, to her apprehension, of Mr Imlay's conduct. He had promised to meet her upon her return from Norway, probably at Hamburg; and they were then to pass some time in Switzerland. The style however of his letters to her during her tour, was not such as to inspire confidence; and she wrote to him very urgently, to explain himself, relative to the footing upon which they were hereafter to stand to each other. In his answer, which reached her at Hamburg, he treated her questions as 'extraordinary and unnecessary,' and desired her to be at the pains to decide for herself.[68] Feeling herself unable to accept this as an explanation, she instantly determined to sail for London by the very first opportunity, that she might thus bring to a termination the suspense that preyed upon her soul.

It was not long after her arrival in London in the commencement of October, that she attained the certainty she sought. Mr Imlay procured her a lodging. But the neglect she experienced from him after she entered it, flashed conviction upon her, in spite of his asseverations. She made further inquiries, and at length was informed by a servant, of the real state of the case. Under the immediate shock

a. Most of this passage about her feelings, from 'Affliction had tempered her heart . . .' to '. . . the arms of her lover', was deleted in the second edition.

which the painful certainty gave her, her first impression was to repair to him at the ready-furnished house he had provided for his new mistress.[b] What was the particular nature of their conference I am unable to relate. It is sufficient to say that the wretchedness of the night which succeeded this fatal discovery, impressed her with the feeling, that she would sooner suffer a thousand deaths, than pass another of equal misery.

The agony of her mind determined her; and that determination gave her a sort of desperate serenity. She resolved to plunge herself in the Thames; and, not being satisfied with any spot nearer to London, she took a boat, and rowed to Putney. Her first thought had led her to Battersea-bridge, but she found it too public.[c] It was night when she arrived at Putney, and by that time it had begun to rain with great violence. The rain suggested to her the idea of walking up and down the bridge, till her clothes were thoroughly drenched and heavy with the wet, which she did for half an hour without meeting a human being. She then leaped from the top of the bridge, but still seemed to find a difficulty in sinking, which she endeavoured to counteract by pressing her clothes closely round her. After some time she became insensible; but she always spoke of the pain she underwent as such, that, though she could afterwards have determined upon almost any other species of voluntary death, it would have been impossible for her to resolve upon encountering the same sensations again. I am doubtful, whether this is to be ascribed to the mere nature of suffocation, or was not rather owing to the preternatural action of a desperate spirit.[d] [69]

b. Second edition adds: 'The characteristic of her mind upon all trying occasions, was energy; but it was a concentrated energy, active in resolution, and not the unresisting slave of feeling; disdaining to waste itself in the empty war of words; and never hurried into any thing incompatible with the elevation of her character.'

c. Second edition adds: 'and accordingly proceeded further up the river'.

d. Second edition adds: 'How strange is the condition of our nature! The whole scene of human life may at last be pronounced a delusion! Speculation for ever deceives us, and is the appropriate office of castle-builders; but the active concerns of life cheat us still more! Mary was in the first instance mistaken in the object of her attachment, imputing to him qualities which, in the trial, proved to be imaginary. By insensible degrees she proceeded to stake her life upon the consequences of her error: and, for the disappointment of this choice, for a consideration so foreign to the true end of her

After having been for a considerable time insensible, she was re-covered by the exertions of those by whom the body was found. She had sought, with cool and deliberate firmness, to put a period to her existence, and yet she lived to have every prospect of a long possession of enjoyment and happiness. It is perhaps not an unfrequent case with suicides, that we find reason to suppose, if they had survived their gloomy purpose, that they would, at a subsequent period, have been considerably happy. It arises indeed, in some measure, out of the very nature of a spirit of self-destruction; which implies a degree of anguish, that the constitution of the human mind will not suffer to remain long undiminished. This is a serious reflection. Probably no man would destroy himself from an impatience of present pain, if he felt a moral certainty that there were years of enjoyment still in reserve for him. It is perhaps a futile attempt, to think of reasoning with a man in that state of mind which precedes suicide. Moral reasoning is nothing but the awakening of certain feelings; and the feeling by which he is actuated, is too strong to leave us much chance of impressing him with other feelings, that should have force enough to counter-balance it. But, if the prospect of future tran-quillity and pleasure cannot be expected to have much weight with a man under an immediate purpose of suicide, it is so much the more to be wished, that men would impress their minds, in their sober moments, with a conception, which, being rendered habitual, seems to promise to act as a successful antidote in a paroxysm of desperation.

The present situation of Mary, of necessity produced some further intercourse between her and Mr Imlay. He sent a physician to her; and Mrs Christie, at his desire, prevailed on her to remove to her house in Finsbury-square. In the mean time Mr Imlay assured her that his present was merely a casual sensual connection; and, of course, fostered in her mind the idea that it would be once more in

---

powers and cultivation, she was willing to consign those powers and that cultivation, pregnant as they were with pleasure to herself and gratification to others, formed to adorn society, and give a relish the most delicate and unrivalled to domestic life, as well as, through the medium of the press, to delight, instruct, and reform mankind – she was willing, I say, to consign all these to premature destruction! How often is the sagacity of our moral judgment reserved for the hour of meditation, and how little does it sometimes bestead us in the time of our greatest need!'

her choice to live with him. With whatever intention the idea was suggested, it was certainly calculated to increase the agitation of her mind. In one respect however it produced an effect unlike that which might most obviously have been looked for. It roused within her the characteristic energy of mind, which she seemed partially to have forgotten. She saw the necessity of bringing the affair to a point, and not suffering months and years to roll on in uncertainty and suspence. This idea inspired her with an extraordinary resolution. The language she employed, was, in effect, as follows: 'If we are ever to live together again, it must be now. We meet now, or we part for ever. You say, You cannot abruptly break off the connection you have formed. It is unworthy of my courage and character, to wait the uncertain issue of that connection. I am determined to come to a decision. I consent then, for the present, to live with you, and the woman to whom you have associated yourself. I think it important that you should learn habitually to feel for your child the affection of a father. But, if you reject this proposal, here we end. You are now free. We will correspond no more. We will have no intercourse of any kind. I will be to you as a person that is dead.'[70]

The proposal she made, extraordinary and injudicious as it was, was at first accepted; and Mr Imlay took her accordingly, to look at a house he was upon the point of hiring, that she might judge whether it was calculated to please her. Upon second thoughts however he retracted his concession.

In the following month, Mr Imlay, and the woman with whom he was at present connected, went to Paris, where they remained three months. Mary had, previously to this, fixed herself in a lodging in Finsbury-place, where, for some time, she saw scarcely any one but Mrs Christie, for the sake of whose neighbourhood she had chosen this situation; 'existing,' as she expressed it, 'in a living tomb, and her life but an exercise of fortitude, continually on the stretch.'

Thus circumstanced, it was unavoidable for her thoughts to brood upon a passion, which all that she had suffered had not yet been able to extinguish. Accordingly, as soon as Mr Imlay returned to England, she could not restrain herself from making another effort, and desiring to see him once more. 'During his absence, affection had led her to make numberless excuses for his conduct,' and she probably wished to believe that his present connection was, as he represented it, purely of a casual nature. To this application, she observes, that 'he returned no other answer, except declaring, with unjustifiable passion, that he would not see her.'

This answer, though, at the moment, highly irritating to Mary, was not the ultimate end of the affair. Mr Christie was connected in business with Mr Imlay, at the same time that the house of Mr Christie was the only one at which Mary habitually visited. The consequence of this was, that, when Mr Imlay had been already more than a fortnight in town, Mary called at Mr Christie's one evening, at a time when Mr Imlay was in the parlour. The room was full of company. Mrs Christie heard Mary's voice in the passage, and hastened to her, to intreat her not to make her appearance. Mary however was not to be controlled. She thought, as she afterwards told me, that it was not consistent with conscious rectitude, that she should shrink, as if abashed, from the presence of one by whom she deemed herself injured. Her child was with her. She entered; and, in a firm manner, immediately led up the child, now near two years of age, to the knees of its father.[e] He retired with Mary into another apartment, and promised to dine with her at her lodging, I believe, the next day.

In the interview which took place in consequence of this appointment, he expressed himself to her in friendly terms, and in a manner calculated to sooth her despair. Though he could conduct himself, when absent from her, in a way which she censured as unfeeling; this species of sternness constantly expired when he came into her presence. Mary was prepared at this moment to catch at every phantom of happiness; and the gentleness of his carriage, was to her as a sunbeam, awakening the hope of returning day. For an instant she gave herself up to delusive visions; and, even after the period of delirium expired, she still dwelt, with an aching eye, upon the air-built and unsubstantial prospect of a reconciliation.

At his particular request, she retained the name of Imlay, which, a short time before, he had seemed to dispute with her. 'It was not,' as

e. Second edition adds: 'While she sought relief for the anguish of her mind, the mother was still uppermost in her gestures and manner, and the appeal her action appeared to make, or rather the sentence it inforced, would, one would have thought, have proved irresistible.'

she expresses herself in a letter to a friend, 'for the world that she did so – not in the least – but she was unwilling to cut the Gordian knot, or tear herself away in appearance, when she could not in reality.'

The day after this interview, she set out upon a visit to the country,[f] where she spent nearly the whole of the month of March. It was, I believe, while she was upon this visit, that some epistolary communication with Mr Imlay, induced her resolutely to expel from her mind, all remaining doubt as to the issue of the affair.

Mary was now aware that every demand of forbearance towards him, of duty to her child, and even of indulgence to her own deep-rooted predilection, was discharged. She determined to rouse herself, and cast off for ever an attachment, which to her had been a spring of inexhaustible bitterness. Her present residence among the scenes of nature, was favourable to this purpose. She was at the house of an old and intimate friend, a lady of the name of Cotton, whose partiality for her was strong and sincere. Mrs Cotton's nearest neighbour was Sir William East, baronet; and, from the joint effect of the kindness of her friend, and the hospitable and distinguishing attentions of this respectable family, she derived considerable benefit.[g] She had been amused and interested in her journey to Norway; but with this difference, that, at that time, her mind perpetually returned with trembling anxiety to conjectures respecting Mr Imlay's future conduct, whereas now, with a lofty and undaunted spirit, she threw aside every thought that recurred to him, while she felt herself called upon to make one more effort for life and happiness.

Once after this, to my knowledge, she saw Mr Imlay; probably, not long after her return to town. They met by accident upon the New Road;[71] he alighted from his horse, and walked with her for some time; and the rencounter passed, as she assured me, without producing in her any oppressive emotion.

Be it observed, by the way, and I may be supposed best to have known the real state of the case, she never spoke of Mr Imlay with acrimony, and was displeased when any person, in her hearing, expressed contempt of him.[72] She was characterized by a strong sense

f. 'Berkshire'.
g. These two sentences, describing Mrs Cotton and Sir William East's family, were deleted in the second edition.

of indignation; but her emotions of this sort,[h] were short-lived, and in no long time subsided into a dignified sereneness and equanimity.

The question of her connection with Mr Imlay, as we have seen, was not completely dismissed, till March 1796. But it is worthy to be observed, that she did not, like ordinary persons under extreme anguish of mind, suffer her understanding, in the mean time, to sink into littleness and debility. The most inapprehensive reader may conceive what was the mental torture she endured, when he considers, that she was twice, with an interval of four months, from the end of May to the beginning of October, prompted by it to purposes of suicide. Yet in this period she wrote her *Letters from Norway*.[73] Shortly after its expiration she prepared them for the press, and they were published in the close of that year. In January 1796, she finished the sketch of a comedy, which turns, in the serious scenes, upon the incidents of her own story. It was offered to both the winter-managers, and remained among her papers at the period of her decease; but it appeared to me to be in so crude and imperfect a state, that I judged it most respectful to her memory to commit it to the flames.[74] To understand this extraordinary degree of activity, we must recollect however the entire solitude, in which most of her hours at that time were consumed.

h. Second edition adds: 'however great might be the provocation that roused them,'.

Chapter Nine
1796–1797

I am now led, by the progress of the story, to the last branch of her history, the connection between Mary and myself. And this I shall relate with the same simplicity that has pervaded every other part of my narrative. If there ever were any motives of prudence or delicacy, that could impose a qualification upon the story, they are now over. They could have no relation but to factitious rules of decorum. There are no circumstances of her life, that, in the judgment of honour and reason, could brand her with disgrace.[a] Never did there exist a human being, that needed, with less fear, expose all their actions, and call upon the universe to judge them. An event of the most deplorable sort, has awfully imposed silence upon the gabble of frivolity.

We renewed our acquaintance in January 1796, but with no particular effect, except so far as sympathy in her anguish, added in my mind to the respect I had always entertained for her talents. It was in the close of that month that I read her *Letters from Norway*; and the impression that book produced upon me has been already related.

It was on the fourteenth of April that I first saw her after her excursion into Berkshire. On that day she called upon me in Somers Town, she having, since her return, taken a lodging in Cumming-street, Pentonville, at no great distance from the place of my habitation. From that time our intimacy increased, by regular, but almost imperceptible degrees.[b]

a. Second edition adds: 'She had errors; but her errors, which were not those of a sordid mind, were connected and interwoven with the qualities most characteristic of her disposition and genius.'
b. This sentence deleted, and the following passage added in the second edition: 'Her visit, it seems, is to be deemed a deviation from etiquette; but she had through life trampled on those rules which are built on the assumption of the imbecility of her sex; and had trusted to the clearness of her spirit for the direction of her conduct, and to

The partiality we conceived for each other, was in that mode, which I have always regarded as the purest and most refined style of love. It grew with equal advances in the mind of each. It would have been impossible for the most minute observer to have said who was before, and who was after. One sex did not take the priority which long-established custom has awarded it, nor the other overstep that delicacy which is so severely imposed. I am not conscious that either party can assume to have been the agent or the patient, the toil-spreader or the prey, in the affair. When, in the course of things, the disclosure came, there was nothing, in a manner, for either party to disclose to the other.

In July 1796 I made an excursion into the county of Norfolk,[75] which occupied nearly the whole of that month. During this period Mary removed, from Cumming-street, Pentonville, to Judd-place West, which may be considered as the extremity of Somers Town. In the former situation, she had occupied a furnished lodging. She had meditated a tour to Italy or Switzerland, and knew not how soon she should set out with that view. Now however she felt herself reconciled to a longer abode in England, probably without exactly knowing why this change had taken place in her mind. She had a quantity of furniture locked up at a broker's ever since her residence in Store-street, and she now found it adviseable to bring it into use. This circumstance occasioned her present removal.

The temporary separation attendant on my little journey, had its effect on the mind of both parties. It gave a space for the maturing of inclination. I believe that, during this interval, each furnished to the other the principal topic of solitary and daily contemplation. Absence bestows a refined and aerial delicacy upon affection, which it with difficulty acquires in any other way. It seems to resemble the communication of spirits, without the medium, or the impediment, of this earthly frame.

When we met again, we met with new pleasure, and, I may add,

---

the integrity of her views for the vindication of her character. Nor was she deceived in her trust. If, in the latter part of her life, she departed from the morality of vulgar minds too decidedly to be forgiven by its abettors, be it remembered that, till this offense was given, calumny itself had not dared to utter an insinuation against her.'

with a more decisive preference for each other. It was however three weeks longer, before the sentiment which trembled upon the tongue, burst from the lips of either. There was, as I have already said, no period of throes and resolute explanation attendant on the tale. It was friendship melting into love. Previously to our mutual declaration, each felt half-assured, yet each felt a certain trembling anxiety to have assurance complete.[c]

Mary rested her head upon the shoulder of her lover,[d] hoping to find a heart with which she might safely treasure her world of affection; fearing to commit a mistake, yet, in spite of her melancholy experience, fraught with that generous confidence, which, in a great soul, is never extinguished. I had never loved till now; or, at least, had never nourished a passion to the same growth, or met with an object so consummately worthy.

We did not marry.[76] It is difficult to recommend any thing to indiscriminate adoption, contrary to the established rules and prejudices of mankind; but certainly nothing can be so ridiculous upon the face of it, or so contrary to the genuine march of sentiment, as to require the overflowing of the soul to wait upon a ceremony, and that at which, wherever delicacy and imagination exist, is of all things most sacredly private, to blow a trumpet before it, and to record the moment when it has arrived at its climax.[e]

There were however other reasons why we did not immediately marry.[f] Mary felt an entire conviction of the propriety of her conduct. It would be absurd to suppose that, with a heart withered by desertion, she was not right to give way to the emotions of kindness which our

c. Second edition adds: 'The sort of connection of which I am here speaking, between parties of whom the intercourse of mind, and not sordid and casual gratification, is the object proposed, is certainly the most important choice in the departments of private life.'

d. This phrase deleted in the second edition.

e. This passage rewritten in the second edition is as follows: 'We did not immediately marry. Ideas which I am now willing to denominate prejudices, made me by no means eager to conform to a ceremony as an individual, which, coupled with the conditions our laws annex to it, I should undoubtedly, as a citizen, be desirous to abolish. Fuller examination however has since taught me to rank this among those cases, where an accurate morality will direct us to comply with customs and institutions, which, if we had had a voice in their introduction, it would have been incumbent on us to negative.'

f. 'The motives of Mary were not precisely those which influenced my judgment.'

intimacy produced, and to seek for that support in friendship and affection, which could alone give pleasure to her heart, and peace to her meditations. It was only about six months since she had resolutely banished every thought of Mr Imlay; but it was at least eighteen that he ought to have been banished, and would have been banished, had it not been for her scrupulous pertinacity in determining to leave no measure untried to regain him. Add to this, that the laws of etiquette ordinarily laid down in these cases, are essentially absurd, and that the sentiments of the heart cannot submit to be directed by the rule and square.[g] But Mary had an extreme aversion to be made the topic of vulgar discussion; and, if there be any weakness in this, the dreadful trials through which she had recently passed, may well plead in its excuse. She felt that she had been too much, and too rudely spoken of, in the former instance; and she could not resolve to do any thing that should immediately revive that painful topic.

For myself, it is certain that I had for many years regarded marriage with so well-grounded an apprehension, that, notwithstanding the partiality for Mary that had taken possession of my soul, I should have felt it very difficult, at least in the present stage of our intercourse, to have resolved on such a measure. Thus, partly from similar, and partly from different motives, we felt alike in this, as we did perhaps in every other circumstance that related to our intercourse.[h]

I have nothing further that I find it necessary to record, till the commencement of April 1797. We then judged it proper to declare our marriage, which had taken place a little before. The principal motive for complying with this ceremony, was the circumstance of Mary being in a state of pregnancy. She was unwilling, and perhaps with reason, to incur that exclusion from the society of many valuable and excellent individuals, which custom awards in cases of this sort. I should have felt an extreme repugnance to the having caused her such an inconvenience. And, after the experiment of seven months of as intimate an intercourse as our respective modes of living would admit, there was certainly less hazard to either, in the subjecting ourselves to those consequences which the laws of England annex to the relations

g. These two sentences, from 'It was only about six months since . . .' were deleted in the second edition.

h. This entire paragraph was deleted in the second edition.

of husband and wife. On the sixth of April we entered into possession of a house, which had been taken by us in concert.[77]

In this place I have a very curious circumstance to notice, which I am happy to have occasion to mention, as it tends to expose certain regulations of polished society, of which the absurdity vies with the odiousness. Mary had long possessed the advantage of an acquaintance with many persons of genius, and with others whom the effects of an intercourse with elegant society, combined with a certain portion of information and good sense, sufficed to render amusing companions. She had lately extended the circle of her acquaintance in this respect; and her mind, trembling between the opposite impressions of past anguish and renovating tranquillity, found ease in this species of recreation. Wherever Mary appeared, admiration attended upon her. She had always displayed talents for conversation; but maturity of understanding, her travels, her long residence in France, the discipline of affliction, and the smiling, newborn peace which awaked a corresponding smile in her animated countenance, inexpressibly increased them. The way in which the story of Mr Imlay was treated in these polite circles, was probably the result of the partiality she excited. These elegant personages were divided between their cautious adherence to forms, and the desire to seek their own gratification. Mary made no secret of the nature of her connection with Mr Imlay; and in one instance, I well know, she put herself to the trouble of explaining it to a person totally indifferent to her, because he never failed to publish every thing he knew, and, she was sure, would repeat her explanation to his numerous acquaintance. She was of too proud and generous a spirit to stoop to hypocrisy. These persons however, in spite of all that could be said, persisted in shutting their eyes, and pretending they took her for a married woman.

Observe the consequence of this! While she was, and constantly professed to be, an unmarried mother; she was fit society for the squeamish and the formal. The moment she acknowledged herself a wife, and that by a marriage perhaps unexceptionable, the case was altered. Mary and myself, ignorant as we were of these elevated refinements, supposed that our marriage would place her upon a surer footing in the calendar of polished society, than ever. But it forced these people to see the truth, and to confess their belief of what they had carefully been told; and this they could not forgive. Be it remarked, that the date of our marriage had nothing to do with this, that question being never once mentioned during this period. Mary indeed had, till now, retained the name of Imlay which had first been assumed from necessity in France; but its being retained thus long, was purely from the awkwardness that attends the introduction of a change, and not from an apprehension of consequences of this sort. Her scrupulous explicitness as to the nature of her situation, surely sufficed to make the name she bore perfectly immaterial.

It is impossible to relate the particulars of such a story, but in the language of contempt and ridicule. A serious reflection however upon the whole, ought to awaken emotions of a different sort. Mary retained the most numerous portion of her acquaintance, and the majority of those whom she principally valued. It was only the supporters and the subjects of the unprincipled manners of a court, that she lost. This however is immaterial. The tendency of the proceeding, strictly considered, and uniformly acted upon, would have been to proscribe her from all valuable society. And who was the person proscribed? The firmest champion, and, as I strongly suspect, the greatest ornament her sex ever had to boast! A woman, with sentiments as pure, as refined, and as delicate, as ever inhabited a human heart! It is fit that such persons should stand by, that we may have room enough for the dull and insolent dictators, the gamblers, and demireps of polished society.

Two of the persons, the loss of whose acquaintance Mary principally regretted upon this occasion, were Mrs Inchbald and Mrs Siddons.[78] Their acquaintance, it is perhaps fair to observe, is to be ranked among her recent acquisitions. Mrs Siddons, I am sure, regretted the necessity, which she conceived to be imposed on her by the peculiarity of her situation, to conform to the rules I have described. She is endowed with that rich and generous sensibility, which should best enable its possessor completely to feel the merits of her deceased friend. She very truly observes, in a letter now before me, that the *Travels in Norway* were read by no one, who was in possession of 'more reciprocity of feeling, or more deeply impressed with admiration of the writer's extraordinary powers.'

Mary felt a transitory pang, when the conviction reached her of so unexpected a circumstance, that was rather exquisite. But she disdained to sink under the injustice (as this ultimately was) of the supercilious and the foolish, and presently shook off the impression of the first surprize. That once subsided, I well knew that the event was thought of, with no emotions, but those of superiority to the injustice she sustained; and was not of force enough to diminish a happiness, which seemed hourly to become more vigorous and firm.

I think I may venture to say, that no two persons ever found in each other's society, a satisfaction more pure and refined. What it was in itself, can now only be known, in its full extent, to the survivor. But, I believe, the serenity of her countenance, the increasing sweetness of her manners, and that consciousness of enjoyment that seemed ambitious that every one she saw should be happy as well as herself, were matters of general observation to all her acquaintance. She had always possessed, in an unparalleled degree, the art of communicating happiness, and she was now in the constant and unlimited exercise of it. She seemed to have attained that situation, which her disposition and character imperiously demanded, but which she had never before attained; and her understanding and her heart felt the benefit of it.

While we lived as near neighbours only, and before our last removal, her mind had attained considerable tranquillity, and was visited but seldom with those emotions of anguish, which had been but too familiar to her. But the improvement in this respect, which accrued upon our removal and establishment, was extremely obvious. She was a worshipper of domestic life. She loved to observe the growth of affection between me and her daughter, then three years of age, as well as my anxiety respecting the child not yet born. Pregnancy itself, unequal as the decree of nature seems to be in this respect, is the source of a thousand endearments. No one knew better than Mary how to extract sentiments of exquisite delight, from trifles, which a suspicious and formal wisdom would scarcely deign to remark. A little ride into the country with myself and the child, has sometimes produced a sort of opening of the heart, a general expression of confidence and affectionate soul, a sort of infantile, yet dignified endearment, which those who have felt may understand, but which I should in vain attempt to portray.[79]

In addition to our domestic pleasures, I was fortunate enough to introduce her to some of my acquaintance of both sexes, to whom she attached herself with all the ardour of approbation and friendship.

Ours was not an idle happiness, a paradise of selfish and transitory pleasures. It is perhaps scarcely necessary to mention, that, influenced by the ideas I had long entertained upon the subject of cohabitation, I engaged an apartment, about twenty doors from our house in the Polygon, Somers Town, which I designed for the purpose of my study and literary occupations. Trifles however will be interesting to some readers, when they relate to the last period of the life of such a person as Mary. I will add therefore, that we were both of us of opinion, that it was possible for two persons to be too uniformly in each other's society. Influenced by that opinion, it was my practice to repair to the apartment I have mentioned as soon as I rose, and frequently not to make my appearance in the Polygon, till the hour of dinner. We agreed in condemning the notion, prevalent in many situations in life, that a man and his wife cannot visit in mixed society, but in company with each other; and we rather sought occasions of deviating from, than of complying with, this rule. By these means, though, for the most part, we spent the latter half of each day in one another's society, yet we were in no danger of satiety. We seemed to combine, in a considerable degree, the novelty and lively sensation of a visit, with the more delicious and heart-felt pleasures of domestic life.

Whatever may be thought, in other respects, of the plan we laid down to ourselves, we probably derived a real advantage from it, as to the constancy and uninterruptedness of our literary pursuits. Mary had a variety of projects of this sort, for the exercise of her talents, and the benefit of society; and, if she had lived, I believe the world would have had very little reason to complain of any remission of her industry. One of her projects, which has been already mentioned, was of a series of *Letters on the Management of Infants*. Though she had been for some time digesting her views on this subject with a view to the press, I have found comparatively nothing that she had committed to paper respecting it. Another project, of longer standing, was of a series of books for the instruction of children. A fragment she left in execution of this project, is inserted in her *Posthumous Works*.[80]

But the principal work, in which she was engaged for more than twelve months before her decease, was a novel, entitled, *The Wrongs of Woman*.[81] I shall not stop here to explain the nature of the work, as so much of it as was already written, is now given to the public. I shall only observe that, impressed, as she could not fail to be, with the consciousness of her talents, she was desirous, in this instance, that they should effect what they were capable of effecting. She was sensible how arduous a task it is to produce a truly excellent novel; and she roused her faculties to grapple with it. All her other works were produced with a rapidity, that did not give her powers time fully to expand. But this was written slowly and with mature considerations. She began it in several forms, which she successively rejected, after they were considerably advanced. She wrote many parts of the work again and again, and, when she had finished what she intended for the first part, she felt herself more urgently stimulated to revise and improve what she had written, than to proceed, with constancy of application, in the parts that were to follow.

Chapter Ten

I am now led, by the course of my narrative, to the last fatal scene of her life. She was taken in labour on Wednesday, the thirtieth of August. She had been somewhat indisposed on the preceding Friday, the consequence, I believe, of a sudden alarm. But from that time she was in perfect health. She was so far from being under any apprehension as to the difficulties of child-birth, as frequently to ridicule the fashion of ladies in England, who keep their chamber for one full month after delivery. For herself, she proposed coming down to dinner on the day immediately following. She had already had some experience on the subject in the case of Fanny; and I cheerfully submitted in every point to her judgment and her wisdom. She hired no nurse. Influenced by ideas of decorum, which certainly ought to have no place, at least in cases of danger, she determined to have a woman to attend her in the capacity of midwife. She was sensible that the proper business of a midwife, in the instance of a natural labour, is to sit by and wait for the operations of nature, which seldom, in these affairs, demand the interposition of art.

At five o'clock in the morning of the day of delivery, she felt what she conceived to be some notices of the approaching labour. Mrs Blenkinsop, matron and midwife to the Westminster Lying-in Hospital, who had seen Mary several times previous to her delivery, was soon after sent for, and arrived about nine. During the whole day Mary was perfectly cheerful. Her pains came on slowly; and, in the morning, she wrote several notes, three addressed to me, who had gone, as usual, to my apartments, for the purpose of study. About two o'clock in the afternoon, she went up to her chamber, – never more to descend.

The child was born at twenty minutes after eleven at night. Mary had requested that I would not come into the chamber till all was over, and signified her intention of then performing the interesting office of presenting the new-born child to its father. I was sitting in a parlour; and it was not till after two o'clock on Thursday morning, that I received the alarming intelligence, that the placenta was not yet removed, and that the midwife dared not proceed any further, and gave her opinion for calling in a male practitioner. I accordingly went for Dr Poignand, physician and man-midwife to the same hospital, who arrived between three and four hours after the birth of the child. He immediately proceeded to the extraction of the placenta, which he brought away in pieces, till he was satisfied that the whole was removed. In that point however it afterwards appeared that he was mistaken.

The period from the birth of the child till about eight o'clock the next morning, was a period full of peril and alarm. The loss of blood was considerable, and produced an almost uninterrupted series of fainting fits. I went to the chamber soon after four in the morning, and found her in this state. She told me some time on Thursday, 'that she should have died the preceding night, but that she was determined not to leave me.' She added, with one of those smiles which so eminently illuminated her countenance, 'that I should not be like Porson,'[82] alluding to the circumstance of that great man having lost his wife, after being only a few months married. Speaking of what she had already passed through, she declared, 'that she had never known what bodily pain was before.'

On Thursday morning Dr Poignand repeated his visit. Mary had just before expressed some inclination to see Dr George Fordyce,[83] a man probably of more science than any other medical professor in England, and between whom and herself there had long subsisted a mutual friendship. I mentioned this to Dr Poignand, but he rather discountenanced the idea, observing that he saw no necessity for it, and that he supposed Dr Fordyce was not particularly conversant with obstetrical cases; but that I would do as I pleased. After Dr Poignand was gone, I determined to send for Dr Fordyce. He accordingly saw the patient about three o'clock on Thursday afternoon. He however perceived no particular cause of alarm; and, on that or the next day, quoted, as I am told, Mary's case, in a mixed company, as a corroboration of a favourite idea of his, of the propriety of employing females in the capacity of midwives. Mary 'had had a woman, and was doing extremely well.'

What had passed however in the night between Wednesday and Thursday, had so far alarmed me, that I did not quit the house, and scarcely the chamber, during the following day. But my alarms wore off, as time advanced. Appearances were more favourable, than the exhausted state of the patient would almost have permitted me to expect. Friday morning therefore I devoted to a business of some urgency, which called me to different parts of the town, and which, before dinner, I happily completed. On my return, and during the evening, I received the most pleasurable sensations from the promising state of the patient. I was now perfectly satisfied that every thing was safe, and that, if she did not take cold, or suffer from any external accident, her speedy recovery was certain.

Saturday was a day less auspicious than Friday, but not absolutely alarming.

Sunday, the third of September, I now regard as the day, that finally decided on the fate of the object dearest to my heart that the universe contained. Encouraged by what I considered as the progress of her recovery, I accompanied a friend in the morning in several calls, one of them as far as Kensington, and did not return till dinner-time. On my return I found a degree of anxiety in every face, and was told that she had had a sort of shivering fit, and had expressed some anxiety at the length of my absence. My sister and a friend of hers, had been engaged to dine below stairs, but a message was sent to put them off, and Mary ordered that the cloth should not be laid, as usual, in the room immediately under her on the first floor, but in the ground-floor parlour. I felt a pang at having been so long and so unseasonably absent, and determined that I would not repeat the fault.

In the evening she had a second shivering fit, the symptoms of which were in the highest degree alarming. Every muscle of the body trembled, the teeth chattered, and the bed shook under her. This continued probably for five minutes. She told me, after it was over, that it had been a struggle between life and death, and that she had been more than once, in the course of it, at the point of expiring. I now apprehend these to have been the symptoms of a decided mortification, occasioned by the part of the placenta that remained in the womb. At the time however I was far from considering it in that light. When I went for Dr Poignand, between two and three o'clock on the morning of Thursday, despair was in my heart. The fact of the adhesion of the placenta was stated to me; and, ignorant as I was of obstetrical science, I felt as if the death of Mary was in a manner decided. But hope had re-visited my bosom; and her cheerings were so delightful, that I hugged her obstinately to my heart. I was only mortified at what appeared to me a new delay in the recovery I so earnestly longed for. I immediately sent for Dr Fordyce, who had been with her in the morning, as well as on the three preceding days. Dr Poignand had also called this morning, but declined paying any further visits, as we had thought proper to call in Dr Fordyce.

The progress of the disease was now uninterrupted. On Tuesday I found it necessary again to call in Dr Fordyce in the afternoon, who brought with him Dr Clarke of New Burlington-street, under the idea that some operation might be necessary. I have already said, that I pertinaciously persisted in viewing the fair side of things; and therefore the interval between Sunday and Tuesday evening, did not pass without some mixture of cheerfulness. On Monday, Dr Fordyce forbad the child's having the breast, and we therefore procured puppies to draw off the milk. This occasioned some pleasantry of Mary with me and the other attendants. Nothing could exceed the equanimity, the patience and affectionateness of the poor sufferer. I intreated her to recover; I dwelt with trembling fondness on every favourable circumstance; and, as far as it was possible in so dreadful a situation, she, by her smiles and kind speeches, rewarded my affection.

Wednesday was to me the day of greatest torture in the melancholy series. It was now decided that the only chance of supporting her through what she had to suffer, was by supplying her rather freely with wine. This task was devolved upon me. I began about four o'clock in the afternoon. But for me, totally ignorant of the nature of diseases and of the human frame, thus to play with a life that now seemed all that was dear to me in the universe, was too dreadful a task. I knew neither what was too much, nor what was too little. Having begun, I felt compelled, under every disadvantage, to go on. This lasted for three hours. Towards the end of that time, I happened foolishly to ask the servant who came out of the room, 'What she thought of her mistress?' she replied, 'that, in her judgment, she was going as fast as possible.' There are moments, when any creature that lives, has power to drive one into madness. I seemed to know the absurdity of this reply; but that was of no consequence. It added to the measure of my distraction. A little after seven I intreated a friend to go for Mr Carlisle and bring him instantly wherever he was to be found. He had voluntarily called on the patient on the preceding Saturday, and two or three times since. He had seen her that morning, and had been earnest in recommending the wine-diet. That day he dined four miles out of town, on the side of the metropolis, which was furthest from us. Notwithstanding this, my friend returned with him after three-quarters of an hour's absence. No one who knows my friend, will wonder either at his eagerness or success, when I name Mr Basil Montagu.[84] The sight of Mr Carlisle thus unexpectedly, gave me a stronger alleviating sensation, that I thought it possible to experience.

Mr Carlisle left us no more from Wednesday evening, to the hour of her death. It was impossible to exceed his kindness and affectionate attention. It excited in every spectator a sentiment like adoration. His conduct was uniformly tender and anxious, ever upon the watch, observing every symptom, and eager to improve every favourable appearance. If skill or attention could have saved her, Mary would still live.

In addition to Mr Carlisle's constant presence, she had Dr Fordyce and Dr Clarke every day. She had for nurses, or rather for friends, watching every occasion to serve her, Mrs Fenwick, author of an excellent novel, entitled *Secrecy*, another very kind and judicious lady, and a favourite female servant. I was scarcely ever out of the room. Four friends, Mr Fenwick, Mr Basil Montagu, Mr Marshal, and Mr Dyson, sat up nearly the whole of the last week of her existence in the house, to be dispatched, on any errand, to any part of the metropolis, at a moment's warning.[85]

Mr Carlisle being in the chamber, I retired to bed for a few hours on Wednesday night. Towards morning he came into my room with an account that the patient was surprisingly better. I went instantly into the chamber. But I now sought to suppress every idea of hope. The greatest anguish I have any conception of, consists in that crushing of a new-born hope which I had already two or three times experienced. If Mary recovered, it was well, and I should see it time enough. But it was too mighty a thought to bear being trifled with, and turned out and admitted in this abrupt way.

I had reason to rejoice in the firmness of my gloomy thoughts, when, about ten o'clock on Thursday evening, Mr Carlisle told us to prepare ourselves, for we had reason to expect the fatal event every moment. To my thinking, she did not appear to be in that state of total exhaustion, which I supposed to precede death; but it is probable that death does not always take place by that gradual process I had pictured to myself; a sudden pang may accelerate his arrival. She did not die on Thursday night.

Till now it does not appear that she had any serious thoughts of dying; but on Friday and Saturday, the two last days of her life, she occasionally spoke as if she expected it. This was however only at intervals; the thought did not seem to dwell upon her mind. Mr Carlisle rejoiced in this. He observed, and there is great force in the suggestion, that there is no more pitiable object, than a sick man, that knows he is dying. The thought must be expected to destroy his courage, to co-operate with the disease, and to counteract every favourable effort of nature.

On these two days her faculties were in too decayed a state, to be able to follow any train of ideas with force or any accuracy of connection. Her religion, as I have already shown, was not calculated to be the torment of a sick bed; and, in fact, during her whole illness, not one word of a religious cast fell from her lips.[86]

She was affectionate and compliant to the last. I observed on Friday and Saturday nights, that, whenever her attendants recommended to her to sleep, she discovered her willingness to yield, by breathing, perhaps for the space of a minute, in the manner of a person that sleeps, though the effort, from the state of her disorder, usually proved ineffectual.

She was not tormented by useless contradiction. One night the servant, from an error in judgment teazed her with idle expostulations, but she complained of it grievously, and it was corrected. 'Pray, pray, do not let her reason with me,' was her expression. Death itself is scarcely so dreadful to the enfeebled frame, as the monotonous importunity of nurses everlastingly repeated.

Seeing that every hope was extinct, I was very desirous of obtaining from her any directions, that she might wish to have followed after her decease. Accordingly, on Saturday morning, I talked to her for a good while of the two children. In conformity to Mr Carlisle's maxim of not impressing the idea of death, I was obliged to manage my expressions. I therefore affected to proceed wholly upon the ground of her having been very ill, and that it would be some time before she could expect to be well; wishing her to tell me any thing that she would choose to have done respecting the children, as they would now be principally under my care. After having repeated this idea to her in a great variety of forms, she at length said, with a significant tone of voice, 'I know what you are thinking of,' but added, that she had nothing to communicate to me upon the subject.

The shivering fits had ceased entirely for the two last days. Mr Carlisle observed that her continuance was almost miraculous, and he was on the watch for favourable appearances, believing it highly improper to give up all hope, and remarking, that perhaps one in a million, of persons in her state might possibly recover. I conceive that not one in a million, unites so good a constitution of body and of mind.

These were the amusements of persons in the very gulph of despair. At six o'clock on Sunday morning, September the tenth, Mr Carlisle called me from my bed to which I had retired at one, in conformity to my request, that I might not be left to receive all at once the intelligence that she was no more. She expired at twenty minutes before eight.

. . . .

Her remains were deposited, on the fifteenth of September, at ten o'clock in the morning, in the church-yard of the parish church of St Pancras, Middlesex.[87] A few of the persons she most esteemed, attended the ceremony; and a plain monument is now erecting on the spot, by some of her friends, with the following inscription:

MARY WOLLSTONECRAFT GODWIN,
Author of
A VINDICATION
OF THE RIGHTS OF WOMAN:
Born 27 April, 1759:
Died 10 September, 1797.

. . . .

The loss of the world in this admirable woman, I leave to other men to collect; my own I well know, nor can it be improper to describe it. I do not here allude to the personal pleasures I enjoyed in her conversation: these increased every day, in proportion as we knew each other better, and as our mutual confidence increased. They can be measured only by the treasures of her mind, and the virtues of her heart. But this is a subject for meditation, not for words. What I purposed alluding to, was the improvement that I have for ever lost.[a]

We had cultivated our powers (if I may venture to use this sort of language) in different directions; I chiefly an attempt at logical and metaphysical distinction, she a taste for the picturesque. One of the leading passions of my mind has been an anxious desire not to be deceived. This has led me to view the topics of my reflection on all sides; and to examine and re-examine without end, the questions that interest me.

But it was not merely (to judge at least from all the reports of my memory in this respect) the difference of propensities, that made the difference in our intellectual habits. I have been stimulated, as long as I can remember, by an ambition for intellectual distinction; but, as long as I can remember, I have been discouraged, when I have endeavoured to cast the sum of my intellectual value, by finding that I did not possess, in the degree of some other men, an intuitive perception of intellectual beauty. I have perhaps a strong and lively sense of the pleasures of the imagination; but I have seldom been right in assigning to them their proportionate value, but by dint of persevering examination, and the change and correction of my first opinions.

What I wanted in this respect, Mary possessed, in a degree superior to any other person I ever knew. The strength of her mind lay in intuition. She was often right, by this means only, in matters of mere speculation. Her religion, her philosophy, (in both of which the errors were comparatively few, and the strain dignified and generous) were, as I have already said, the pure result of feeling and taste. She adopted one opinion, and rejected another, spontaneously, by a sort of tact, and the force of a cultivated imagination; and yet, though

a. Godwin's revision, for the second edition, of the summary which follows can be found in the Appendix.

perhaps, in the strict sense of the term, she reasoned little, it is surprising what a degree of soundness is to be found in her determinations. But, if this quality was of use to her in topics that seem the proper province of reasoning, it was much more so in matters directly appealing to the intellectual taste. In a robust and unwavering judgment of this sort, there is a kind of witchcraft; when it decides justly, it produces a responsive vibration in every ingenuous mind. In this sense, my oscillation and scepticism were fixed by her boldness. When a true opinion emanated in this way from another mind, the conviction produced in my own assumed a similar character, instantaneous and firm. This species of intellect probably differs from the other, chiefly in the relation of earlier and later. What the one perceives instantaneously (circumstances having produced in it, either a premature attention to objects of this sort, or a greater boldness of decision) the other receives only by degrees. What it wants, seems to be nothing more than a minute attention to first impressions, and a just appreciation of them; habits that are never so effectually generated, as by the daily recurrence of a striking example.

This light was lent to me for a very short period, and is now extinguished for ever!

While I have described the improvement I was in the act of receiving, I believe I have put down the leading traits of her intellectual character.[88]

THE END

Appendix

Two Passages rewritten for the Second Edition

1. From Chapter Six, concerning
Henry Fuseli (see p. 234)

The delight she enjoyed in his society, she transferred by association to his person. To understand this, we have only to recollect how dear to persons of sensibility is the exercise of the affections. A sound morality requires that 'nothing human should be regarded by us with indifference;' but it is impossible that we should not feel the strongest interest for those persons, whom we know most intimately, and whose welfare and sympathies are united to our own. True wisdom will recommend to us individual attachments; for with them our minds are more thoroughly maintained in activity and life than they can be under the privation of them, and it is better that man should be a living being, than a stock or a stone. True virtue will sanction this recommendation, since it is the object of virtue to produce happiness, and since the man who lives in the midst of domestic relations, will have many opportunities of conferring pleasure, minute in the detail, yet not trivial in the amount, without interfering with the purposes of general benevolence. Nay, by kindling his sensibility, and harmonizing his soul, they may be expected, if he is endowed with a liberal and manly spirit, to render him more prompt in the service of strangers and of the public.

But, in the catalogue of domestic charities, there are none so capable of affording strong and permanent delight, as that of two persons of opposite sexes who have conceived a preference for each other. Human beings differ so much in their tempers and views, that, except in cases of a tender attachment, cohabitation brings with it small prospect of harmony and happiness. The connection between parents and children, between grown persons and young, is of too unequal a nature; and is bounded and restrained by a sense of responsibility on the one side, and the inattention and heedlessness particularly incident to the other. The charm of domestic life consists in a mutual desire to study each other's gratification; and this can scarcely subsist in sufficient force, but in this particular connection.

Mary had now lived for upwards of thirty years in a state of celibacy and seclusion. As her sensibilities were exquisitely acute, she had felt this sort of banishment from social charities, so frequent in a state of high civilization and refinement, more painfully than persons in general are likely to feel it. Or rather, as I believe, she suffered occasional accesses of uneasiness, torpor, and vacuity, without having clearly traced the sources and remedy of the evil. She was like what we are told of those lofty and aspiring geniuses, who, being formed for busy scenes and daring projects, find the activity of their temper, when debarred its proper field, corroding and preying upon itself. The sentiments which Mr Fuseli excited in her mind, taught her the secret, to which she was so long in a manner a stranger.

Let it not however be imagined, that this was any other than the dictate of a most refined sentiment, and the simple deduction of morality and reason. Never was there a woman on the face of the earth more alien to that mire and grossness, in which the sensual part of our species are delighted to wallow. Superior at the same time to the idleness of romance, and the pretense of an ideal philosophy, no one knew more perfectly how to assign to the enjoyments of affection their respective rank, or to maintain in virgin and unsullied purity the chasteness of her mind.

It happened in the present case that Mr Fuseli was already married; and, in visiting at his house, his wife became the acquaintance of Mary. Mary did not disguise from herself how desirable it would have been, that the man in whom she discovered qualities calling forth all the strength of her attachment, should have been equally free with herself. But she chearfully submitted to the empire of circumstances. She conceived it practicable to cultivate a distinguishing affection, and to foster it by the endearments of personal intercourse and reciprocation of kindness, without departing from the consideration due to his previous engagements. She scorned to suppose, that she could feel a struggle, in conforming to the laws she should lay down to her conduct.

2. From Chapter 10, summarizing Wollstonecraft's
 'intellectual character' (see p. 272)

A circumstance by which the two sexes are particularly distinguished from each other, is, that the one is accustomed more to the exercise of its reasoning powers, and the other of its feelings. Women have a frame of body more delicate and susceptible of impression than men, and, in proportion as they receive a less intellectual education, are more unreservedly under the empire of feeling. Feeling is liable to become a source of erroneous decisions, because a mind not accustomed to logical analysis, cannot be expected accurately to discriminate between the simple dictates of an ingenuous mind, and the factitious sentiments of a partial education. Habits of deduction enable us to correct this defect. But habits of deduction may generate habits of sophistry; and scepticism and discussion, while they undermine our prejudices, have sometimes a tendency to weaken or distort our feelings. Hence we may infer one of the advantages accruing from the association of persons of an opposite sex: they may be expected to counteract the principal mistake into which either is in danger to fall.

Mary and myself perhaps each carried farther than to its common extent the characteristic of the sexes to which we belonged. I have been stimulated, as long as I can remember, by the love of intellectual distinction; but, as long as I can remember, I have been discouraged, when casting the sum of my intellectual value, by finding that I did not possess, in the degree of some other persons, an intuitive sense of the pleasures of the imagination. Perhaps I feel them as vividly as most men; but it is often rather by an attentive consideration, than an instantaneous survey. They have been liable to fail of their effect in the first experiment; and my scepticism has often led me anxiously to call in the approved decisions of taste, as a guide to my judgment, or a countenance to my enthusiasm. One of the leading passions of my mind has been an anxious desire not to be deceived. This has led me to view the topics of my reflection on all sides, and to examine and re-examine without end the questions that interest me. Endless disquisition however is not always the parent of certainty.

What I wanted in this respect, Mary possessed in a degree superior to any other person I ever knew. Her feelings had a character of peculiar strength and decision; and the discovery of them, whether in matters of taste or of moral virtue, she found herself unable to control. She had viewed the objects of nature with a lively sense and an ardent admiration, and had developed their beauties. Her education had been fortunately free from the prejudices of system and bigotry, and her sensitive and generous spirit was left to the spontaneous exercise of its own decisions. The warmth of her heart defended her from artificial rules of judgment; and it is therefore surprising what a degree of soundness pervaded her sentiments. In the strict sense of the term, she had reasoned comparatively little; and she was therefore little subject to diffidence and scepticism. Yet a mind more candid in perceiving and retracting error, when it was pointed out to her, perhaps never existed. This arose naturally out of the directness of her sentiments, and her fearless and unstudied veracity.

A companion like this, excites and animates the mind. From such an one we imbibe, what perhaps I principally wanted, the habit of minutely attending to first impressions, and justly appreciating them. Her taste awakened mine; her sensibility determined me to a careful development of my feelings. She delighted to open her heart to the beauties of nature; and her propensity in this respect led me to a more intimate contemplation of them. My scepticism in judging, yielded to the coincidence of another's judgment; and especially when the judgment of that other was such, that the more I made experiment of it, the more was I convinced of its rectitude.

The improvement I had reason to promise myself, was however yet in its commencement, when a fatal event, hostile to the moral interests of mankind, ravished from me the light of my steps, and left to me nothing but the consciousness of what I had possessed, and must now possess no more!

While I have described the improvement I was in the act of receiving, I believe I have put down the leading traits of her intellectual character from which it flowed.

NOTES TO WOLLSTONECRAFT'S
A SHORT RESIDENCE IN SWEDEN

ADVERTISEMENT

1. Wollstonecraft emphasizes the autobiographical nature of her travel book from the outset. Though taking the form of a series of letters (addressed to Gilbert Imlay), the original manuscript – which has not survived – was probably composed as a journal carried with her throughout the journey, and later intended to be shown to Imlay. She discusses the importance of such journal-keeping while travelling in Letter 3; and in one of her actual letters to Imlay, dated Tønsberg, 18 July 1795, she mentions that she has begun the book 'which will, I hope, discharge, all my obligations of a pecuniary kind'. Otherwise there is little overlap between these brief private letters and the sustained writing of *A Short Residence*, with the exception of a paragraph from her letter of 20 June 1795, which reappears in Letter 15, 'how am I altered by disappointment'. If the book did begin life as a journal, 'designed for publication', yet it remains spontaneous and 'unrestrained' as Wollstonecraft says. She seems to have made little attempt to edit or revise it for the press, and she always composed at high speed, as Godwin notes. Her quotations are unchecked; missing information is lamented, but not supplied; and something like the first favourable impression of Crown Prince Frederik (in Letter 7) is allowed to stand, though it is largely contradicted later on (Letter 18). Above all, Wollstonecraft makes no attempt to suppress those outpourings of grief and loneliness which must have filled her travel notes. This emphasis on personal sincerity, rather than literary polish, is of course what gives the book its life: 'a new passage in the history of my heart' (Letter 9).

LETTER ONE

2. This was probably the lighthouse on the Nording Reef, which identifies Wollstonecraft's landing point as somewhere in the bay of Möllosund, some thirty miles up the coast from Gothenburg in Sweden.

3. Compare *Memoirs*, Chapter 4, p. 220 and note 21.

4. The French maid, whom she had first employed in Paris. Marguerite obviously worshipped Mary Wollstonecraft, and was deeply attached to

her baby, Fanny Imlay, then one year old, who was also travelling with them.

5. Throughout, Wollstonecraft makes skilful literary use of the novelty of a woman travelling on her own, though her physical courage makes it appear almost normal. The 'other evil' was rape.

6. The theme of her search for a 'golden age', that ideal state of society much discussed by eighteenth-century *philosophes*, is developed in Letters 9 and 14.

7. The District Pilot Officer of Möllosund.

8. *Midsummer Night's Dream*, II, i. The flowers were wild pansies or heartsease (*Viola tricolor*), which Oberon squeezed into Titania's eyes so that she fell in love with the ass-headed Bottom. A piece of Wollstonecraft mockery. Note also the Bergmanesque 'wild strawberries' that follow.

9. During Wollstonecraft's period in Paris, 1792–5, when she was appalled by the execution of the king, the guillotining of her friends the Girondists, and the various excesses of the Terror. See *Memoirs*, Chapter 7. Her reflections on France run throughout the book, especially Letter 23.

10. Compare Godwin's analysis of her melancholy in *Memoirs*, Chapter 6, p. 237, and Chapter 7, pp. 241–2.

LETTER TWO

11. The First War of the Allied Coalition (England, Austria, Prussia) against revolutionary France, 1792–7. The Scandinavian ports had neutral status and did a brisk trade in raw materials with France, though from 1793 it had to run the British naval blockade. Wollstonecraft does not mention, here or at any point, her own interest in this trade through Imlay. See Introduction, section 4.

12. *Ecclesiastes*, i, 4.

13. When governess to the Kingsborough family in 1787. See *Memoirs*, Chapter 4.

14. The now famous Scandinavian smorgasbord.

15. The first of many landscape descriptions in the 'sublime' manner, here full of Shakespearian echoes from *Macbeth* and *The Tempest*, as well as accurate, naturalistic observations of cow bells and mown grass. On Wollstonecraft's 'transitional' literary style, see Introduction, sections 5–6.

LETTER THREE

16. Wollstonecraft's hatred of drinking stems from the behaviour of her drunken father. Compare Letter 20 and see *Memoirs*, Chapter 1, pp. 205–6

17. The first of many acute and angry observations on the oppressed state of women throughout the book which show that Wollstonecraft's passionate commitment to feminism had not altered.

18. Gustavus III of Sweden had been assassinated by Jacobin sympathizers in 1792. The Swedish kings waged continual wars throughout the eighteenth century against Russia, which had to be financed by crippling taxes. There was a state monopoly of alcohol, and coffee – being a luxury import – was banned by the 'sumptuary laws'.

19. Charles XII ruled Sweden 1697–1718. The 'Lion of the North', he was a legendary soldier who slept and ate with his soldiers on campaign. He was killed by an unlucky bullet at the siege of Frederikhald (Halden). See Letter 5.

20. Thomas Cooper, *Some Information Respecting America* (1794), published by Joseph Johnson. Cooper (1759–1840), born in London, lawyer and scientific writer, was in Paris in the early days of the Revolution, and re-commended Imlay to Brissot. (See *Memoirs*, Chapter 7.) He emigrated to America with Priestley, and ended his days as president of South Carolina College.

21. *A Short Residence* was probably first written as just such a journal. See note 1 above.

22. This charming little essay on the contrasted merits of sun and shade reflects the declining influence of the formal eighteenth-century garden in landscape design (based on French models), and the growing interest in the indigenous English cottage garden, variously planted with 'shrubs and flowers' (together with herbs and vegetables). The combination of the two ideals, Classical and Romantic, can today be seen in a public garden like Sissinghurst in Kent. Wollstonecraft sadly never owned a garden, but she was delighted by them, and was glad to visit the English garden of a Nor-wegian merchant outside Christiania. See Letter 13.

LETTER FOUR

23. Wollstonecraft's views on child-care were progressive: she disapproved of swaddling clothes and wet nurses (who could pass on venereal infections).

24. A version of one of Wollstonecraft's favourite mottos, which appears for example in *The Rights of Woman*, Chapter 2:

> *If weak women go astray*
> *The stars are more in fault than they.*

It seems to be an ironic echo of Cassius' speech in *Julius Caesar*, I, ii:

> *The fault, dear Brutus, is not in our stars,*
> *But in ourselves, that we are underlings.*

25. These and other frank criticisms of the ladies of Gothenburg caused great offence, according to the French travel-writer de la Tocnaye. See Introduc-tion, section 6.

26. These phrases seem to echo lines from William Blake's *Songs of Innocence*

(1794), notably – as Carol Poston has pointed out – 'The Divine Image'. Blake (1757–1827), the great visionary poet and artist, was an intimate of Joseph Johnson's circle. He illustrated two of Wollstonecraft's early books; see *Memiors*, note 29. He was an admirer of Fuseli, and a friend of Tom Paine's, whom he once saved from arrest.

LETTER FIVE

27. A disguised reference to Wollstonecraft's interviews with two judges on the Ellefsen case, A. J. Unger and C. Nordberg, who lived at Strömstad. See Introduction, section 4.

28. Little Fanny and the maid Marguerite remained behind at the Backman family house in Gothenburg throughout Wollstonecraft's journey into Norway. Elias Backman, Imlay's Swedish agent, accompanied her as far as Strömstad.

29. The forerunner of the Scandinavian duvet – a large cotton sheet in the form of a bag, filled with duck down – now widely used throughout Europe.

30. A remark perhaps inspired by the 'Seventh Walk' of Rousseau's *Les Rêveries du promeneur solitaire* (1782), one of Wollstonecraft's favourite books, which shaped the confessional nature of *A Short Residence*. The Swedish botanist was Carl von Linné (1707–78), whose Linnaean system of binomial nomenclature by genera and species was universally adopted.

31. A tripartite peace was signed; Sweden retained her frontiers and Danish influence in Scandinavia began slowly to wane, despite the efforts of A. P. Bernstorff. See Letter 21.

32. This romantic tale of the beautiful lady innkeeper of Kvistram obviously appealed to the novelist in Wollstonecraft, who was always fascinated by an example of women exercising their power over men. Compare the story of Queen Matilda, Letter 18.

33. Wollstonecraft was much taken by the idea of sun-worship, which she regarded as the most primitive form of all religions. She uses it here to attack the biblical idea of a warm, fruitful Eden (a 'spontaneous Paradise' of the south) from which mankind was expelled; and instead suggests a more Darwinian notion of mankind slowly evolving in a long trek from a cold and inhospitable north. Shelley brilliantly exploits a similar idea in the creation passage from *Prometheus Unbound*, II, iv:

> . . . *and the unseasonable seasons drove*
> *With alternating shafts of frost and fire,*
> *Their shelterless, pale tribes to mountain caves* . . .

34. She is thinking of Johnson's views as described by Boswell in his *Journal of a Tour to the Hebrides* (1785). Wollstonecraft had met and admired Johnson;

see *Memoirs*, Chapter 3, p. 216.

35. The anecdote goes that Swift, on climbing into the pulpit of a country church near Dublin, found no one in his congregation except his faithful clerk Roger. Undaunted, he launched into his sermon with the ringing words, 'Dearly beloved Roger, the Scripture moveth you and me . . .' Lord Orrery, *Remarks* (1751).

36. Wollstonecraft often picks out the prettiest girl from her companions; compare Letters 8 and 22. Perhaps they reminded her of Fanny Blood; see *Memoirs*, Chapter 2.

37. This emphasis on the 'spirit of inquiry' is characteristic of Wollstonecraft as an educationalist, and one glimpses the model 'paper globe' that no doubt stood in the schoolroom at Newington Green. The idea that people do not have fixed 'national characters', but develop as society progresses, is pursued throughout the book. Compare Letter 19, and the author's Appendix.

38. See Letter 3, note 19.

39. Edward Young (1683–1765), playwright and leading exponent of the 'graveyard school' of poetry. Disappointed in worldly ambitions, he retired to Welwyn where he was rector until his death. His famous blank-verse poem in nine books, *Night Thoughts on Life, Death and Immortality*, was published between 1742 and 1745, and began the vogue for melancholy, reflective, semi-autobiographical poetry which attracted Wollstonecraft. Book 3 contains his invocation to the moon. (Another of Young's admirers was Robespierre, whose interest in graveyards was somewhat different.) Southey particularly liked the 'sublime' moonlit passage which follows.

40. This description later inspired the author of *The Wanderer* (1816). See Introduction, section 6.

LETTER SIX

41. The Kattegat is the strip of sea lying between the southern Swedish coast and Denmark, where Wollstonecraft first landed. Here she is crossing the narrows of the Skagerrak, between Sweden and Norway, now known as Oslofjord.

42. Benjamin Franklin (1706–90), American statesman, writer and inventor, US Ambassador to France. Much admired in British radical circles, and friend of Tom Paine and Joseph Priestley. His *Autobiography* was first published in France, then in England (1793); the idea of a traveller carrying an information-sheet about himself, to gratify public curiosity, is a character-istic piece of homespun humour. In fact the Norwegians treated Wolls-tonecraft with overwhelming kindness, and obviously admired her pluck.

43. A light, two-wheeled carriage, whose single horse was changed at each 'post' station. The scene that follows here – the unspoken communication between Wollstonecraft and the gentleman with the 'significant' smile – is

strongly reminiscent of one of Sterne's wordless flirtations in *A Sentimental Journey*.

44. Judge Wulfsberg, mayor of Tønsberg, and one of the commissioners on the Ellefsen case. See note 27, and Introduction, section 4.

45. William Cowper, *The Retirement* (1782). Cowper (1731–1800), like Edward Young a melancholy, pre-Romantic poet, greatly appealed to Wollstonecraft. He suffered from religious guilt and suicidal depressions. His best-known works are the *Olney Hymns* (1779) and *The Task* (1785). Coleridge's 'conversation poems' have many Cowperesque echoes, and his quiet, thoughtful voice helped to shape Romantic autobiography.

46. An eighteenth-century novelty instrument, consisting of a set of tuned strings stretched over a box-shaped sounding board. Not played by hand, but placed on a windowsill to catch the strokes of the wind (Aeolus). It became a symbol of Nature's influence on the human heart or imagination, and appears frequently in the poetry of Coleridge and Shelley.

47. Fanny Blood, who died in Portugal in 1785. Godwin quotes this passage at the end of Chapter 3 of the *Memoirs*.

LETTER SEVEN

48. Norway remained part of Denmark from the Union of 1389 to the Peace of 1815. It was then re-established as a constitutional monarchy with a parliament – the Storting – on the British model. However, sovereign power was transferred to Sweden, and Norway did not become fully independent until 1905. Yet the Norwegians, because of their geography and their natural self-reliance, always showed remarkable independence, and retained a strong sympathy with the English and Americans. Wollstonecraft greatly appreciated these qualities.

49. The Norwegian capital was called Christiania from 1624 until 1925; it then reverted to the old Nordic name of Oslo.

50. The Danish Crown Prince, the future Frederik VI. He was the son of Queen Matilda, whose tragic story is discussed by Wollstonecraft in Letter 18. The expedition of 1788 was the war against Sweden which ended in the battle of Kvistram, mentioned in Letter 5 and note 31. Frederik assumed the powers of regent during his father's idiocy, 1784–1808. Wollstonecraft's favourable impression of Frederik was later changed, see note 1.

51. The Danish capital, and executive centre of the Union until 1815. See note 48.

52. Irish exports were also required to pass through English ports at this time, where excise duty was levied. Wollstonecraft, being half-Irish herself (on her mother's side), sympathized with this sense of 'colonial exploitation',

and drew other parallels with the Norwegian 'subordination' to Denmark (compare Letter 13). However, she evidently thought the Norwegians were much more enterprising.

53. For all her bitter experiences during the Terror, Wollstonecraft never seems to have lost her fundamental faith in the long-term, positive effects of the French Revolution, especially with regard to the philosophy of the in-alienable 'rights' of men and women; see notes 9 and 158. In this respect she was like Hazlitt and Shelly, rather than Wordsworth.

54. That is, Crown Prince Frederik.

55. A. P. Bernstorff, see Letter 21 and Introduction, section 3.

56. The university was established at Christiania (Oslo) in 1811, when the population was still less than 12,000.

57. This amusing account of Wollstonecraft's irreverent visit to St George's Chapel in 1780 suggests not only her humorous appreciation of Gothick 'gloom' and 'venerable rust', but also a less than pious attitude to the Anglican Church. Godwin would have liked it. However the passage that follows, on the horrors of embalming, shows her more serious reflections on mortality. Wollstonecraft's religious feelings contain both these aspects, and Godwin was surely right to call attention to their complexity; *Memoirs*, Chapter 3, pp. 215–16, and note 14.

LETTER EIGHT

58. This passage of the 'sublime', which drew the criticism of de la Tocnaye, is discussed in Introduction, section 6.

59. From *A Sentimental Journey*. A passage of arch and lachrimose flirtation, in which the traveller, Yorick, surrenders his tear-soaked handkerchief to the sorrowing Maria. Maria offers to wash it and dry in her generous bosom. Yorick, seeing the possibilities of this kindly service, murmurs gratefully, 'And is your heart still so warm, Maria?' It is interesting that Mary Wolls-tonecraft should have recalled this incident: could she have been teasing Imlay?

60. Mineral spa water, taken for health.

61. The fashion for sea-bathing, like that for hill-walking, was really started by the Romantic generation (and given its royal blessing by the Prince Regent at Brighton). Coleridge bathed in Malta, Shelley bathed in Italy (mostly rivers), Byron bathed in Greece.

62. Jellyfish. Passage discussed in Introduction, section 5.

63. In 1785, to nurse Fanny Blood; *Memoirs*, Chapter 3.

64. Compare Letter 5 and note 36.

65. A transparently autobiographic passage, addressed to Imlay, but also

gradually building up the reader's image of him as a cruel, faithless and 'demonic' lover who haunts Wollstonecraft's imagination. The implied comparison with the runaway father is not entirely just: at least Imlay consistently offered to support little Fanny until Wollstonecraft married Godwin. See Introduction, section 5, for this 'demon-lover' theme.

66. A reference to the Inca dynasty in Peru, who claimed direct descent from the Sun God. The 'pair' were probably the Inca King and his daughter Orazia, who appear in Dryden's play *The Indian Queen* (1663) and Purcell's stage spectacle of the same name (1695).

67. Prometheus, the Titan who rebelled against Jupiter, and was chained to a rock for stealing fire and giving it to mankind. Promethean fire becomes an important symbol of the 'divine spark' (and hence the imagination) in the poetry of Shelley and Byron; and also in Mary Shelley's *Frankenstein, or the Modern Prometheus* (1818). Wollstonecraft turns the myth to humorous account as well, in Letter 16.

LETTER NINE

68. In *Romeo and Juliet*.

69. A hint of Adam Smith, *The Wealth of Nations* (1776).

70. In the French Revolutionary calendar, each month was divided into three weeks of ten days. Thus the tenth day, or *decadi*, became the official day of rest and relaxation, which was cheerfully celebrated. By contrast the British Sunday was renowned for its gloomy inactivity – no theatres, no sports, no dancing, no pubs – long into the nineteenth century. Dr Johnson said it was appropriate to go for a walk on a Sunday, but not to throw stones at dogs – 'relaxation, but not levity'. The French poet Théophile Gautier said it was inadvisable to cross any bridge on an English Sunday, because the general gloom would almost certainly inspire you to throw yourself off it.

71. The idea of mankind's innocent happiness in a primitive 'state of nature' is propounded notably in Rousseau's *Discours sur l'origine de l'inégalité* (1755), though subsequently abandoned in *Émile* (1762). Wollstonecraft consistently attacks it in *The Rights of Woman*, as it denies the possibilities of social progress. Nevertheless, she still sought for a Golden Age in some ideal state of future society. See Letter I, note 6, and *Memoirs*, Chapter 6 and note 42.

LETTER TEN

72. Dryden, *The Flower and the Leaf* (1700). An allegory, adapted from Chaucer, which contrasts the flower of ephemeral delights with the laurel leaf of labour rewarded. Gazing up at the towering beech trees, with their shimmering sunlit foliage, Wollstonecraft seems momentarily to prefer the former.

73. Trial by jury, on the British model, was established in Norway with the new constitution of 1815.

74. Carol Poston cannot identify this quotation, nor can I. It sounds like early-eighteenth-century verse, with a touch of garden moralizing, somewhere between Dryden and Akenside.

75. In Vancouver Island, Western Canada.

76. A type of thickly glazed domestic pottery. This whole interior, snug and gleaming amidst the remote wilderness of Portør, shows Wollstonecraft using the word 'romantic' in its transitional sense.

LETTER ELEVEN

77. Fifteen Norwegian rixdollars was about £3 in eighteenth-century British currency according to Wollstonecraft's 'Supplementary Note'. This was, for comparison, approximately the cost of a copy of *Political Justice*.

78. This debate on population and resources was to be taken up by Godwin's rival, Thomas Malthus, in *An Essay on the Principle of Population as it Affects the Future Improvements of Society* (1798). Malthus visited Scandinavia in 1799.

79. The fall of the Bastille, a state prison in the south-east of Paris, on 14 July 1789, marked the beginning of the Revolution. This passage is discussed in the Introduction, section 5.

80. Wollstonecraft seems to be attacking the whole culture of the 'gentleman's smoking-room', as well as its smell. Her 'inuendo' appears to mean she had no such feelings of disgust towards Imlay.

81. This ideal of the writer's life – divided between an apartment in town, and a rambling house in the country – has remained a permanent dream of British intellectuals. In fact it reflects the old eighteenth-century lifestyle of the European aristocracy, from Paris to St Petersburg.

82. This marks the final stage of Wollstonecraft's attempt to settle the Ellefsen case, in his home port of Risør. See Introduction, section 4.

83. Poland was successively partitioned between Austria, Prussia and Russia in 1772, 1793 and 1796. The nationalist leader, General Kosciusko, who tried to re-unite his country, became a hero in France and England. Coleridge published a sonnet to him in 1794.

84. Prospero's island in *The Tempest*.

LETTER TWELVE

85. *Macbeth*, V, iii. The phrase, 'thick-coming fancies' is used to describe Lady Macbeth's hallucinations.

86. Compare Godwin's description of domestic happiness with Mary Wollstonecraft in *Memoirs*, Chapter 9, p. 262, and note 79.

87. Sparkish, in William Wycherley's *The Country Wife*, III, ii (1675). The play was a daring satire on sexual hypocrisy; Garrick produced a bowdlerized version in 1766.

LETTER THIRTEEN

88. Bernhard Anker, FRS, one of Norway's leading merchants and an anglophile. Described in Introduction, section 5.

89. The Jacobin leader, who was responsible for the death of many of Wollstonecraft's friends among the Girondists, was himself executed during the coup of Thermidor, July 1794. Compare Letter 7 and note 53. British radicals generally believed that he had betrayed the Revolution through extremism; see Coleridge and Southey, *The Fall of Robespierre* (1794).

90. For a discussion of this revealing autobiographical passage, see Introduction, section 6.

91. Alum is extracted from rocks by smelting them with coal, and then washing with hot water. The red stain left behind is made by iron salts; characteristically Wollstonecraft saw it as an image of exploitation, as if the maternal earth was bleeding from man's assaults. Alum, used in the printing, dyeing and tanning processes, was one of the minerals shipped by Imlay into France.

92. William Coxe, *Voyages and Travels into Poland, Russia, Sweden and Denmark* (1784). His description of the 'eternal snows' appears on the carriage ride from Skydjord to Christiania.

93. The British were blockading Scandinavian and Baltic ports to prevent supplies of naval materials, arms and other vital supplies reaching France. But there were various ways of circumventing the blockade, as Imlay knew.

94. Wollstonecraft was greatly interested in prison reform, perhaps as a result of her experiences in Paris. Compare Letter 19; and see *Memoirs*, Chapter 7.

95. It belonged to Peder Anker, the son of Bernhard Anker. See notes 88 and 22, and Introduction, section 5.

LETTER FOURTEEN

96. Dr Richard Price (1723–91). See *Memoirs*, Chapter 3 and notes 12 and 13.

97. See Letter 9 and note 71.

98. Milton, *L'Allegro*:

> Come, and trip it as you go,
> On the light fantastic toe;
> And in thy right hand lead with thee,
> The mountain-nymph, sweet Liberty.

Milton was regarded by all the Romantics, but especially Wordsworth, Blake and Shelley, as primarily the Republican poet of Liberty and as belonging soundly to 'the Devil's party'. This whole passage is discussed in Introduction, section 3.

99. The 'allodial right', as Wollstonecraft lucidly explains, was the traditional right of the heir of a tenant farmer in Norway to inherit the estate, on payment of certain state dues. The difficulty was that while guaranteeing the yeoman status of these small farmers, the allodial right hindered larger, progressive farmers – using English methods – from buying up smallholdings and developing them with proper capital investment. Norwegian farming was thus backward and unproductive, and the population suffered. For once it was a case of 'rights' being opposed to 'progress'. The probable answer was a system of state subsidy.

LETTER FIFTEEN

100. Not 'missed', but 'crossed'.

101. This paragraph is adapted from Wollstonecraft's private letter to Gilbert Imlay, written from Hull, 20 June 1795. See note 1.

102. This remarkable descriptive passage is discussed in the Introduction, section 5.

103. For the possible influence of Wollstonecraft's description of this waterfall outside Frederikstad on Coleridge's 'Kubla Khan' see Introduction, section 6. Compare also Letter 17, describing Trollhättan.

104. The British have a perennial interest in monsters of the deep. The fabled Norwegian 'Kraken' was first described in Pontoppidan's *History of Norway* (1752), and later appears in Tennyson's poem 'The Kraken'. Coleridge and Keats discussed the Kraken on Hampstead Heath in 1819. See also Kipling's story, 'A Matter of Fact'. The Loch Ness Monster has attracted similar devotion. Casting the net a little wider, there is Melville's *Moby Dick* and Steven Spielberg's *Jaws* – a puritan symbol of the suppressed Id, no doubt. It is characteristic that Wollstonecraft (with a wink) required 'ocular demonstration'.

LETTER SIXTEEN

105. After this lively chapter of perils and discomforts, touched in with Wollstonecraft's brisk humour, there is a distinct darkening in the tone of the rest of her travels. Wollstonecraft seems to have learned, perhaps from a letter awaiting her at Gothenburg, that Imlay would not after all meet her at Hamburg as originally planned. She was exhausted, and increasingly desperate.

LETTER SEVENTEEN

106. The Trollhättan canal was eventually completed in 1800, connecting the large inland lake of Vänern with the port of Gothenburg and the Kattegat. It stretched some fifty miles, a remarkable feat of engineering.

107. See Letter 15, and note 103. Detailed observations of the appearance of waterfalls and rivers are a constant topic in Coleridge's *Notebooks* between 1798 and 1804; and the extended trope, or image-complex, of the 'river of life' appears frequently in the poetry of Wordsworth and Shelley. The latter's *Alastor* (1815) may also have been partly shaped by Wollstonecraft's experiences.

108. Wollstonecraft admired the liberality of the Swedish divorce laws, but also saw them as an inherent criticism of the married state. Compare her discussion of unofficial engagements and premarital sexual relations in Letter 19.

LETTER EIGHTEEN

109. One of the earliest references to the recreation of camping under canvas, which like sea-bathing, was part of the Romantic back-to-Nature movement as it became popular. De Quincey gives an amusing account of 'bivouacing' (probably a Swiss-German military term) in Wales, in his *Confessions of an English Opium Eater* (1821).

110. The Great Fire of Copenhagen in June 1795 destroyed nearly a thousand buildings in the centre of the city, including the City Hall and the church of St Nicholas. Wollstonecraft had entered a disaster area, but her own misery and depression soon made her 'weary of observing the ravages'.

111. In the architectural sense, a circular terrace of town houses.

112. This critical account of Crown Prince Frederik contradicts the favourable impression made in Letter 7. See note 1.

113. See note 130.

114. Queen Caroline Matilda (1751–75). Wollstonecraft was fascinated by her tragic story. The sister of King George III of England, she was married, aged fifteen, to the highly unstable Christian VII, who succeeded to the Danish throne in 1766, aged seventeen. His cruel excesses were brought under control by Struensee, the royal physician, who probably treated him with drugs. Matilda and Struensee, now in effective control of the state, initiated a liberal, reforming regime which made many enemies at the Danish Court. They also became lovers, and Christian VII was forced to recognize Matilda's baby daughter Louise, who was probably not his child. Finally, the Dowager Queen and the young Prince Frederik plotted their downfall. Struensee was arrested and beheaded, while Queen Matilda escaped from her

ımprisonment aboard a British warship. She died at Celle, in Hanover, aged twenty-four. Frederik remained Prince Regent until the death of mad King Christian in 1808.

115. 'Gallantry' in the sense of 'amorous intrigue'; and 'attachment' meaning a specifically sexual relationship. But these eighteenth-century terms are curiously ambiguous (as Godwin discovered in the first edition of the *Memoirs*), and it is not quite clear whether Wollstonecraft really thought Matilda and Struensee were lovers or not. Perhaps she intended that.

116. *King Lear*, II, i.

LETTER NINETEEN

117. This paragraph on the psychology of the criminal is very close to the theme of Mary Shelley's *Frankenstein*; see particularly Percy Shelley's Preface to his wife's novel (reprinted in Penguin Classics). Compare also note 94.

118. William Pitt the Younger (1759–1806). British Prime Minister from 1783 to 1801, the sworn enemy of Revolutionary France, and subsequently, of Napoleon. After 1792 he adopted repressive wartime policies, and was responsible for the Treason Trials of 1794 and the measures that provoked the United Irishmen's Rebellion of 1798. His Secret Service was renowned both at home and abroad. Wordsworth and Coleridge were visited by one of his 'emissaries', the famous 'Spy Nozy', in the Quantocks, Somerset, in 1797, as recounted in Coleridge's *Biographia Literaria* (1817).

119. *The Tempest*, IV, i.

120. 'Empiricism', here used in its popular eighteenth-century medical sense, meaning 'quackery' or unscientific practice. It was only later in the nineteenth century that Empiricism gained its philosophical meaning, almost exactly the opposite: the process of direct scientific observation, or precise experiment, and the conclusions drawn therefrom.

121. Compare this passage on the sexual freedom of young Scandinavians with Letter 17 and note 108. It is discussed in the Introduction, section 5.

122. This is Wollstonecraft's view, as an educationalist, of the value of travel. Compare Letter 5 and note 37. It is discussed in the Introduction, section 5.

LETTER TWENTY

123. On Wollstonecraft's severe disapproval of drinking, see Letter 3 and note 16.

124. The Royal Theatre, opened in 1748.

125. Molière's *Le Médecin malgré lui* (1666), a prose comedy, in which the crafty woodcutter Sganarelle poses as a learned doctor. It debunks professional

mumbo-jumbo with exquisite effect. When Sganarelle makes the elementary error of confusing the respective positions of the heart and the liver in Lucinda's body (he reverses them), he extricates himself by airily remarking: '*Oui, cela était autrefois ainsi, mais nous avons changé tout cela.*'

126. Rosenborg Castle was built as a summer palace for Christian IV, and subsequently became a royal museum. Wollstonecraft describes similar sensations when she wandered through the deserted palace at Fontainebleau, in 1793, in her *Historical and Moral View of the French Revolution* (1794).

127. The Royal Library was founded by Frederik III in the seventeenth century, and was used to house the priceless collection of early Icelandic manuscripts collected by Arni Magnússon, which are the chief source for Norse folklore and mythology.

128. Pope, *An Essay on Man*, II.

129. The Grande Galerie de la Louvre was opened as a public museum in August 1793, at the height of the Terror. Its collection of confiscated paintings made it the finest art gallery in Europe, and at the Peace of Amiens (1802) many English people – including Turner and the young Hazlitt – eagerly flocked to view its treasures.

LETTER TWENTY-ONE

130. Andreas Peter Bernstorff (1735–97). Danish Foreign Minister and great Scandinavian statesman who pursued a policy of liberal reform at home, and armed neutrality abroad. He remained in office from 1784 until his death. He refused to join any of the anti-French coalitions, and in 1794 concluded a treaty of neutrality with Sweden. His death was marked by national mourning, and without his stabilizing influence Denmark's dominating position in Scandinavia began to decline.

131. Jacques Necker (1732–1804), Swiss banker, liberal author and French Finance Minister, dismissed in July 1789 immediately before the fall of the Bastille. His wife's *salon* in Paris was frequented by Buffon, Diderot, Grimm and Talleyrand. Wollstonecraft knew his work, and had translated his book, *On the Importance of Religious Opinions* for Joseph Johnson; see *Memoirs*, Chapter 5. His daughter, Madame de Staël, was a key figure in European Romanticism, and wrote the famous study *De l'Allemagne* (1810).

132. Johann-Kasper Lavater (1741–1801), a Swiss Protestant pastor who invented the pseudo-science of physiognomy, the analysis of character from facial features. Wollstonecraft translated his book on the subject, and was not impressed. He was a Christian mystic and died peacefully, believing he was a reincarnation of the Apostle St John.

133. *Hamlet*, I, ii. Misquoted.

134. The French Revolutionary armies were advancing into southern Germany under Generals Jourdan and Moreau. They were temporarily repulsed by the Austrians at the battle of Würzburg (1795).

135. Wollstonecraft was making the crossing from Denmark to mainland Germany via the island of Fyn. The first strait is known as the Great Belt, the second as the Little Belt.

136. Count Ugolino was imprisoned in a tower at Pisa, and starved to death with his children, whom he ate. The story is told in Dante's *Inferno*, Canto XXXIII; and also in Chaucer's 'The Monk's Tale'. Shelley translated it from Dante while living at Pisa in 1821. Wollstonecraft seems to be indulging in black humour.

137. *Hamlet*, III, i. Again misquoted. These misquotations in fact suggest that Wollstonecraft knew the play so well that it had become almost 'proverbial' to her, and she simply quoted from memory. The great vogue for *Hamlet*, and identifying oneself with the Prince, is a Romantic phenomenon, well expressed in the Shakespearian lectures of Coleridge (1811–12) and Hazlitt (1817).

138. *Paradise Lost*, I. Milton describes in two wonderful lines how the devils, 'Dilated or condensed, bright or obscure,/Can execute their aery purposes.'

139. This watchword of Wollstonecraft's echoes down through literary history. In *Nightmare Abbey* (1817), Peacock ironically described how the young Shelley – in the person of Scythrop Glowry – 'now became troubled with the passion for reforming the world'.

140. Compare Letter 8 and note 64.

141. A barely disguised reference to Imlay's betrayal of Mary Wollstonecraft in April 1795, when she found he was living with another woman and tried to commit suicide. (See *Memoirs*, Chapter 8.) The increasingly confessional nature of such passages, as the book draws to a close, is discussed in the Introduction, section 5.

142. Dryden, *Alexander's Feast*.

143. An order of military merit, instituted by Louis XIV in 1693, and discontinued by the Convention in 1792. The situation in Hamburg, full of French emigrés who had fled the Revolution, was similar to that in Paris after 1917, full of White Russians.

144. That is, a 100 per cent return on financial investments.

145. This bitter outburst against Imlay is discussed in the Introduction, section 5.

146. Lafayette (1757–1834), revolutionary soldier and French politician who fought in the American War of Independence, and was commander of the Garde Nationale in Paris during the early days of the Revolution. Charged with treason, he fled to Austria and was imprisoned at Olmütz. Madame Lafayette joined him there and obtained his release ('*enlargement*') in 1797. Lafayette again commanded the Garde Nationale during the heady days of the July Revolution of 1830. A French squadron was named after him in the Spanish Civil War, 1936. (The expression 'two pair of stairs', by the way, merely means 'on the second floor' – a storey usually reserved for servants or children.)

147. Madame de Genlis (1746–1830), playwright, novelist and feminist writer. She fled from Paris in 1793 and returned in 1802. Her *Mémoires inédits* of the Revolution were a *succès de scandale* when published in 1825. Her husband, le comte de Genlis, was the first of the Girondists to be guillotined in 1793. Wollstonecraft had probably met them both in Paris at Helen Maria Williams's house. See *Memoirs*, Chapter 7.

148. That is, either the manager of a restaurant; or, the manager of a shop that supplies cooked food to the customer's own house. Thus the duke was not necessarily reduced to wearing an apron.

149. That is, a public eating-house.

150. A series of letters published in the *Pennsylvania Chronicle* in 1767, attacking English colonialism, by John Dickinson (1732–1808). He was a friend of Imlay's, and his critical views were obviously quoted by Wollstonecraft to demonstrate Imlay's surrender to the commercial spirit.

151. Hermes, the patron deity of thieves and tricksters, as well as messengers.

LETTER TWENTY-FOUR

152. *Macbeth*, IV, i. The witches.

153. Friedrich Gottlieb Klopstock (1724–1803), German poet and key figure in the revival of German literature. He wrote patriotic and religious odes; an epic, *Der Messias* (The Messiah) inspired by *Paradise Lost*; and lyrics to 'Cidli', his wife. Coleridge and Wordsworth met him when they visited Hamburg in autumn 1798.

154. The river-scapes around Hamburg which Wollstonecraft describes with such feeling were frequently painted by the German Romantic artist, Caspar David Friedrich. Indeed his 'Woman at the Window', looking out on the shipping of the Elbe, could almost be Mary Wollstonecraft herself.

155. *Paradise Lost*, i.

156. Quotation unidentified.

157. It is clear from Wollstonecraft's private letter to Imlay, dated Hamburg 27 September 1795, that her precipitate departure was prompted by his refusal to join her in Germany. She planned to earn some money with her travel book in London, and then go back to France with Fanny, refusing all further financial support from him. But it is obvious that she is suicidally depressed: 'I leaned on a spear, that has pierced me to the heart.'

APPENDIX

158. This crucial sentence strongly suggests that all Wollstonecraft's travels and experience of the world had now convinced her that revolutionary change – 'unnatural fermentation' – was less effective than progressive reform – 'gradual fruit' – in making permanent social progress towards that Golden Age she had so long dreamed of. She also seems to replace the French Jacobin doctrine of international revolution with a concept of individual, national self-development, 'the growth of each particular soil' (as she had seen in Norway). This philosophy is close to that of her friends the Girondists, and points for example towards the British movement for parliamentary reform, which started to bear fruit in 1832. None the less, this short passage cannot be taken as any general change in her belief in the immense benefits of the French Revolution and the philosophy of the 'rights of man and woman', which Wollstonecraft supported to the end of her days.

SUPPLEMENTARY NOTES

159. Wollstonecraft is pointing out the contrast in size between the small, professional, 'standing' army of some 6,000 troops and the large, citizen army of part-time militia, of some 25,000. Fear of standing armies grew steadily in England during the Napoleonic Wars: by 1812 there were more troops stationed in the north of England against the Luddites than Wellington commanded in the Spanish Peninsula. Her observant eye does not miss the Norwegian skis, either. Given half a chance she would probably have tried those, too.

NOTES TO GODWIN'S MEMOIRS

PREFACE

1. A quiet remark, like many of Godwin's most important ones. It reveals his instinctive interest in the psychology of personality and in the biographic process itself. In 1803 he published the first *Life* of Chaucer.

CHAPTER ONE

2. Godwin was reputed to underestimate 'domestic affections', and their influence. This seems wrong. He wrote on the death of his mother in 1809: 'While my mother lived, I always felt to a certain degree as if I had somebody who was my superior, and who exercised a mysterious protection over me. I belonged to something – I hung to something – there is nothing that has so much reverence and religion in it as affection to parents. The knot is now severed, and I am, for the first time, at more than fifty years of age, alone.' Letter to Mary Jane Clairmont, 21 August 1809.

3. Anthony Carlisle (1768–1840), famous London physician and surgeon, later knighted. He was much liked in literary circles, and in 1810–12 attempted to cure Coleridge of his opium addiction. No luck.

4. For a moment we glimpse in that wild and ruined garden the symbol of a lost childhood which will become such a powerful theme in later Romantic writing: Wordsworth's *Prelude* or Chateaubriand's *Mémoires d'outre-tombe*.

5. From this teenage period in Yorkshire Wollstonecraft fondly retained many local expressions which she used in later letters; she could also put on a 'downright' Yorkshire accent.

6. Unfortunately little is known of this charming and eccentric English clergyman and his wife, who surely deserve a role in one of Jane Austen's novels. The poet Alexander Pope (1688–1744) was also crippled.

7. A good example of Godwin's further reflections on biographical writing for the second edition: the idea of the inward growth and modification of the mind is central to his interpretation of the subject, rather than a mere outward record of events and facts. Wordsworth subtitled *The Prelude*: 'The Growth of a Poet's Mind'.

CHAPTER TWO

8. A reference to Goethe's novel *The Sorrows of Young Werther* (1774), a touchstone of the new Romantic sensibility. Werther's fateful first meeting with Lotte is described in Book One, letter of June 16th. In despair of fulfilling his love for her, he eventually commits suicide. Godwin pursues this comparison between Werther and Wollstonecraft in Chapter 7, in terms of their passionate natures and sufferings. Perhaps it can best be summed up by Werther's exclamation in Book Two: 'Yes, I am a wanderer on this earth – a pilgrim. Are you anything more than that?'

9. Josiah Wedgwood (1730–95), the famous manufacturer of Staffordshire pottery who employed Flaxman as his designer. His sons Tom and Josiah were notable patrons of Coleridge, Wordsworth and Humphry Davy.

10. Elizabeth Wollstonecraft suffered from extreme postnatal depression and great unhappiness as Bishop's wife. Wollstonecraft encouraged a separation, finally spiriting her away in a coach. Godwin may not have known the full story here: see Introduction, section 8.

CHAPTER THREE

11. Here, and in the passage that follows, Godwin shows his willingness to offer a crucial criticism of Wollstonecraft's behaviour – that she made herself a victim of others' demands. It is a shrewd psychological insight, which lends both conviction and sympathy to his portrait, mixing light and shade. It is this kind of authority that reminds one of Johnson's *Life of Richard Savage*. It will be noted that, in the second edition, far from retracting his views, Godwin makes them more explicit.

12. An eighteenth-century building still stands on the probable site of Wollstonecraft's school, in the south-east corner of the square of Newington Green, London, N1. The Unitarian chapel where Dr Price used to preach (see next note) is diagonally across the road on the eastern side.

13. Dr Richard Price (1723–91), dissenting minister, mathematician, philosopher and democrat. A man of great influence in British radical circles, he preached in favour of both the American and French Revolutions, and advocated parliamentary reform. His sermon at the Old Jewry in 1789 celebrating the centenary of the Bloodless Revolution of 1688 provoked Edmund Burke's *Reflections on the Revolution in France*, and thus indirectly Wollstonecraft's *Rights of Woman*. See note 37.

14. Godwin the atheist cannot resist mocking the idea of public worship. But otherwise this seems a fair statement of Wollstonecraft's religious beliefs, relying on an imaginative response to human experience and nature, rather than on doctrine. See below, note 86. Compare her remarks on Christianity in

A Short Residence, Letter 7 and note 57; on the Creator, Letter 8; on death
and immortality, Letter 15; and on piety, Letter 19.

15. James Burgh, *Political Disquisitions* (1780), a work of liberal political
theory, in the same vein as Richard Price's *Observations on the Nature of Civil
Liberty*. Burgh and Price were friends, and Wardle thinks both books influenced Wollstonecraft's early political thinking.

16. Sadly there is no record of this historic meeting in Boswell, or in any
later biography of Dr Johnson. Although he disapproved of women preachers,
the Great Cham had a surprising soft spot for bluestockings; for example,
Elizabeth Carter, the translator of Epictetus.

17. Hugh Skeys, a young Irish businessman, became a close friend of
Wollstonecraft's after Fanny's death, and was one of Godwin's chief bio-
graphical sources. Tomalin perceptively observes that perhaps 'they had more
in common in their relationship with Fanny than they could acknowledge'.

18. Wollstonecraft's stubborn determination to go to Lisbon is a vivid
example of her headstrong nature and her restless urge to travel. Godwin
makes no secret of the fact that her passion for her friend meant abandoning
her duty to her school.

19. This moving account of Wollstonecraft's gifts as a teacher gains weight
from the immense importance which Godwin attached to education generally
in *Political Justice*. For both of them it was the foundation of all long-term
social progress; and in *A Short Residence* it is the real purpose of travel: see
Letter 19, p. 173 – 'the completion of a liberal education'.

20. *A Short Residence*, Letter 6, pp. 99–100.

CHAPTER FOUR

21. Wollstonecraft had a way with British sea-captains. Compare *A Short
Residence*, Letter I, p. 64.

22. Published 1786.

23. Joseph Johnson (1738–1809), brilliant radical publisher, born in Everton
near Liverpool; he came to London in 1752. In rooms above his shop at 72 St
Paul's Churchyard he entertained many writer friends, among them William
Cowper, Joseph Priestley, Erasmus Darwin, Maria Edgeworth, William Blake,
Tom Paine and William Wordsworth. In 1798 he was imprisoned for six
months for selling a pamphlet by Gilbert Wakefield. His professional support
of Mary Wollstonecraft and steady enduring friendship – she called him a
brother and a father to her – were vital, as Godwin brings out in Chapter 5.
He never married and his private life is something of a mystery.

24. Wollstonecraft's strictures on Eton, that 'celebrated seminary', are based

less on its class privileges, than on the emotional deprivations of the public-school boarder, cut off from home and family. However, Eton also produced Shelley.

25. Margaret King eventually divorced Lord Mountcashell, and became involved in the United Irishmen's rebellion. She left Ireland under the name of Mason, and finally settled in Pisa with her lover, the agronomist George William Tighe, known as 'Tatty'. Here the wheel came full circle, and she befriended the young Mary Shelley and Claire Clairmont when they lived in Pisa between 1818 and 1821 with Shelley. Mary learned a lot about her mother from 'Mrs Mason', who still worshipped the name of Wollstonecraft. The governess's effect on the pupil was evidently life-long.

26. George Ogle (1742–1814). Irish statesman with conservative views which obviously surprised Wollstonecraft. He became an Irish Privy Councillor in 1783, and Governor of Wexford in 1796. Author of many popular poems and songs, including 'On the Banks of the Banna'.

27. Published 1788.

CHAPTER FIVE

28. Published in the *Posthumous Works*, 1798. Extracts are printed in Durant's edition of the *Memoirs*, 1927. They show Wollstonecraft experimenting with the high-flown, pre-Romantic language of 'sensibility'.

29. Published 1788, and illustrated by William Blake.

30. Published 1789, as the work of 'Mr Creswick, Teacher of Elocution'.

31. Co-founded with Thomas Christie, this was really Joseph Johnson's 'house magazine', publishing radical essays, book reviews, extracts, obituaries, and literary gossip. It provided Wollstonecraft with her main source of regular income. On one occasion she anonymously reviewed her own book, a translation of Necker (see next note), for the *Analytical*. The review was cool but favourable.

32. Of these translated authors, Jacques Necker and Johan-Kaspar Lavater are described in *A Short Residence*, Letter 21 and notes. Despite its forbidding title, the *Moralisches Elementarbuch* (Leipzig, 1785–7) by Christian Gotthilf Salzmann was actually a collection of 'moral tales for young folk'. Salzmann became a fan of Wollstonecraft's, and translated into German not only the *Rights of Woman*, but also Godwin's *Memoirs* (1799). Wollstonecraft's translations were not entirely hackwork, since they were also a process of self-education, requiring her to read widely in current European literature; and learn French, German and some Italian.

33. Another Johnsonian touch: Godwin well understood the pressures of regular reviewing, translating and editing, which subtly undermine the long-term,

sustained effort required to write an original work. It is often forgotten how many other Romantic writers had to struggle to survive through literary journalism – Coleridge, Hazlitt, De Quincey. It is an interesting sociological fact that nearly all the poets had some form of private income.

34. A street in the commercial district of the City of London.

35. Among these friends of Joseph Johnson, it may be noted that Dr George Fordyce was one of the physicians who attended Wollstonecraft in her last illness. Not to be confused with James Fordyce, the author, mentioned in Chapter 6 and note 42.

CHAPTER SIX

36. Thomas Gray, 'Elegy in a Country Churchyard'.

37. Edmund Burke (1729–97), advocate, writer and politician, had previously been associated with liberal causes: reform of the British parliament, independence for the American colonists, emancipation of Ireland and destruction of the slave trade. His eloquent attack on the principles of the French Revolution and the philosophy of 'the rights of man' published in 1790, caused dismay in liberal circles and was considered a betrayal by Paine, Godwin, Wollstonecraft and other radicals. See also Chapter 3, note 3. As a young man in his twenties, Burke wrote the famous *Philosophical Enquiry into the Sublime and the Beautiful* (1757), a key text for the early Romantics, which analysed the sensations of religious awe evoked by the vastness and wildness of Nature. This powerfully influenced the landscape descriptions and meditations in *A Short Residence*; see Introduction, section 6. Altogether Burke was a vital intellectual stimulus for Wollstonecraft, and her attitude to him was more complex than perhaps Godwin suggests.

38. Published anonymously, December 1790. Second edition, with her name, 1791.

39. The anecdote shows not only Joseph Johnson's shrewdness as a publisher, but also Godwin's subtle understanding of the Wollstonecraft temperament. The feeling that she was being patronized (however kindly), immediately put her on her mettle.

40. Published early in 1792.

41. Calista was the suffering heroine of Nicholas Rowe's play *The Fair Penitent* (1703), a role made famous by the tragic actress, Mrs Siddons. (See Chapter 9, note 78.) 'Rowe is the best of the tragic playwrights of the whole century, which is to make no extravagant claim,' *Oxford History of English Literature*, vol. 7 (1959), p. 245. One of the characters is the famous villain, 'the gay Lothario.'

42. Jean-Jacques Rousseau (1712–78), author of *Julie* (1761); *Emile* (1762, a

treatise on education); *Confessions* (1781, 1788); and *Les Rêveries du promeneur solitaire* (1782, a collection of reminiscences which influenced *A Short Residence*). Dr John Gregory (1724–73), author of *A Father's Legacy to his Daughters* (1774). Dr James Fordyce (1720–96), a Scots presbyterian minister, author of *Sermons to Young Women* (1765) and *The Character and Conduct of the Female Sex* (1776). In brief, one can say that Wollstonecraft vigorously attacked Rousseau's sentimental version of the Romantic woman, and the views of Gregory and Fordyce on their biological and social inferiority. See especially *The Rights of Woman*, Chapters 2 and 3, 'The Prevailing Opinion of a Sexual Character Discussed'.

43. Dido Queen of Carthage, one of the 'valiant women' of classical mythology, and the queen whom Aeneas loves and abandons in Virgil's *Aeneid*. Their confrontation in the Underworld in Book 6 is one of the most heartbreaking episodes in all classical literature. Armida is the heroine of Tasso's *Jerusalem Delivered*: a beautiful enchantress who saves the city by luring the Christian knights into a Garden of Indolence.

44. Henry Fuseli (1741–1825), energetic and eccentric Swiss painter, originally a pastor in Zürich. In 1763 he came to London and wrote articles and translations for Joseph Johnson. He made his name with his celebrated painting 'The Nightmare', and weird illustrations of Milton and Shakespeare. He was much admired by William Blake. Domineering, bisexual, and obsessed with his own genius, his entanglement with Wollstonecraft remains something of a puzzle, and Godwin always seems uneasy about it (which may account for some of his re-writing in the second edition). Fuseli's erotic drawings usually concern men held in bondage by beautiful women with small, insect-like and evidently brainless heads. He married one of his former models, Sophie Rawlins, in 1786.

45. This view of sexual relations argues that personal fidelity, the private emotional contract 'of affections', is far more important than marriage, a mere public and legal contract. It does not advocate promiscuity, and indeed Wollstonecraft's whole life demonstrates the tenacity of her affections in this respect. (Nevertheless her behaviour towards Fuseli remains ambiguous, and Godwin struggled to redefine it in his second edition.) It is found frequently in the writings of Godwin, Wollstonecraft and later Shelley, and became the basis for the nineteenth-century idea of the 'free union'. See *Political Justice*, Book 8, Chapter 8, Appendix, 'Of Cooperation, Cohabitation and Marriage'; Shelley's Note 9, 'Even Love is Sold', to *Queen Mab* (1812); and *A Short Residence*, Letter 17 (of divorce), Letter 19 (of engagements), and note 121.

46. Thomas Paine (1737–1809), radical British writer, polemicist and master of the plain style. An enthusiast of the American and French Revolutions, he

argued their case in a series of popular works: *Common Sense* (1776), *The Rights of Man* (1791, 1792), and *The Age of Reason* (1793, an attack on Christianity). He was a friend of Benjamin Franklin's and a member of the French Convention. Arrested by the Committee of Public Safety, he was eventually released, and emigrated to America in 1802, a largely broken man. He died at his farm in New Rochelle, after years of neglect and ill-health. He remains however one of the heroic father-figures of Western democracy.

47. This remarkably laconic account of the first momentous meeting between Godwin and Wollstonecraft is discussed in the Introduction, section 1.

CHAPTER SEVEN

48. Monsieur Fillietaz was the French husband of one of Wollstonecraft's erstwhile pupils at the Newington Green school, who had a house in the rue Meslay, near the Temple where Louis XVI was imprisoned in Paris. From the window of this house Wollstonecraft watched the King going to his trial, as she vividly described in a private letter to Johnson, dated 26 December 1792.

49. Only one letter of the series was published, dated 15 February 1793.

50. Helen Maria Williams (1762–1827), poet, francophile and journal writer. She was a friend of Manon Roland, the Girondists, and Tom Paine, and was imprisoned in the Luxembourg for a short spell, where Wollstonecraft visited her. She survived the Revolution to write her *Souvenirs* (1827). The young Wordsworth's first published poem was dedicated to her.

51. Christophe Georg Gustav, Count von Schlabrendorf (1750–1824), liberal, traveller and writer. He was the son of the Prime Minister of Silesia. Imprisoned by the Committee of Public Safety, he was also visited by Wollstonecraft, and later wrote some interesting notes in his copy of a *A Short Residence*, praising her character and half-suggesting he had fallen in love with her. In 1806 he published *Napoleon and the French People under his Empire*.

52. Thomas Christie (1761–96), Scottish author and businessman, co-founder with Joseph Johnson of the *Analytical*, and commercial partner of Gilbert Imlay's. He died on a business venture in Surinam. His wife Rebecca became an intimate friend of Wollstonecraft's, and sheltered her in their house at Finsbury Place after her return from Scandinavia.

53. Gilbert Imlay (1754–1828), soldier, author, businessman and adventurer. Born in New Jersey, he served as an officer during the American Revolution, and travelled in Kentucky. He then came to Europe and published two books, *A Topographical Description of the Western Territory of America* (1792) and a wildly sentimental novel, *The Emigrants* (1793), which celebrated the pioneer

life. Thereafter he shuttled between London and Paris, engaged in business and love-affairs. His scheme to start a revolution in Louisiana, taken up by the French politician Brissot (see note 59), collapsed with the fall of the Girondists; and his import–export business with the Swede Elias Backman was made bankrupt by the Ellefsen affair (see Introduction, section 4). He is last definitely heard of in Paris in 1797–8, living with an actress; but there is a tombstone dedicated to him at St Brelade's, Jersey, Channel Islands, which mentions his interest in the 'social advances of the day'. His feelings towards Mary Wollstonecraft must always be a matter of dispute, and the disappearance of all his letters to her makes his character and attitudes difficult to assess. That he was faithless in matters of the heart is evident; but that she persisted in making herself his victim, is equally clear, as Godwin shows. He seems to have been a raffish, likeable, but feckless and rather childlike personality, who was continually getting himself out of his depth in all the important matters of life. There is just a hint that, towards the end, after regarding him as her demon lover, Wollstonecraft began to see him as a rather comic figure. Perhaps this is right. (See note 74.)

54. Only one volume was published, in 1794, covering the period up to the execution of Louis XVI.

55. The British navy began to mount offensive operations in the Mediterranean, summer 1793. On the night of 9–10 October 1793, the French responded by arresting some 400 British citizens in Paris – including Tom Paine and Helen Maria Williams – and incarcerating them in the Luxembourg Palace which had been converted into a prison. Imlay saved Wollstonecraft by registering her as his wife at the US embassy, so that she became an American citizen. She was thus able to make her prison visits, as America was still regarded as a friendly power.

56. The account that follows gives Godwin's central analysis of Wollstonecraft's character, and contains the romantic comparison with Goethe's Werther. It remained virtually unaltered in the second edition.

57. Godwin was here quoting from Wollstonecraft's love letters to Imlay, which he had already published in the Posthumous Works (1798).

58. Here begins the story of Peder Ellefsen and the treasure ship. See Introduction, section 4.

59. Jean-Pierre Brissot (1754–93), travel-writer, journalist and politician, leader of the Girondists who opposed the extremism of Robespierre and the Montagnards. He was the author of New Travels in the United States of America (1792), which Wollstonecraft reviewed for the Analytical; and architect of the scheme to subvert Spanish colonial rule in Louisiana, which Imlay presented to the Foreign Ministry in 1793. Pierre-Victurien Vergniaud

(1753–93), one of the Girondists' most powerful speakers in the Convention. Other members of the group included Pétion and Roland. They were all guillotined in October 1793.

60. In the sense of 'doomed'; Wollstonecraft uses the same word to describe France, in her private letters of 1794.

61. Fanny Imlay (1794–1816). A small, tragic figure, destined to live only in the footnotes of the Wollstonecraft-Godwin-Shelley story. She inherited her mother's melancholic temperament, with none of her counterbalancing energy. Her father, Imlay, made no attempt to look after her, or continue her allowance, once Wollstonecraft had married Godwin. Loved by Godwin, but neglected by her stepmother Mrs Clairmont (the second Mrs Godwin), she grew up in the shadow of her younger and cleverer sister, Mary. She neither wrote nor married, but there is some evidence that she fell in love with Shelley, at the time he eloped with Mary to France in 1814. Two years later she carried out the threat made by her mother so long before, and committed suicide in an upper room, at the Mackworth Arms, Swansea, while the Shelleys were living at Bath. Shelley's poem, 'Her voice did quiver as we parted', is traditionally taken as addressed to Fanny, her only epitaph. See also note 80.

62. Robespierre was guillotined, with Saint-Just, after the *coup d'état* of Thermidor, in July 1794, and the Terror came to an end in Paris.

63. The frank way Godwin poses this question about Wollstonecraft's behaviour, and the perception with which he answers it (further sharpened in the second edition), again suggests a moral weight comparable to Dr Johnson. His finest piece of psychology is to see that Imlay wounded not only her affections, but also her intellectual pride. She could not believe she had been mistaken in her lover; she was prepared to try to reform him at almost any price to herself – even her own life.

64. *Othello*, V, ii. Godwin's condemnation of Imlay is evident, but movingly held in check. He becomes more explicit in additions made to Chapter 8 in the second edition.

65. Archibald Hamilton Rowan (1751–1834), Irish politician, dandy and revolutionary adventurer. Born in County Down, educated at Cambridge, he inherited a fortune from his grandfather and became involved with the United Irishmen. Imprisoned in Dublin gaol for distributing a seditious pamphlet, he escaped to France – where he met Wollstonecraft and charmed her (a rare thing) – and then moved to America (where he printed *A Short Residence*); he then went back to Germany and finally received a pardon and returned to Ireland in 1803. Throughout these vicissitudes, he was patiently awaited by his beloved wife Sarah, and their ten children, at Killyleagh

Castle, County Down. Years later, Shelley and Harriet met him when they came to Dublin in 1811 to distribute a new generation of seditious pamphlets: they thought him a charming old rogue.

CHAPTER EIGHT

66. The Ellefsen affair: see Introduction, section 4.

67. Godwin wishes to make clear that the Scandinavian journey was, apart from anything else, an extraordinary feat of personal courage, undertaken between two attempts at suicide. The melancholy of her book is thus an expression of genuine feeling for 'her sorrows', not a literary pose.

68. Could Godwin have actually seen these letters from Imlay to Wollstonecraft? If so, they are unknown to all subsequent biographers. Perhaps Wollstonecraft had only spoken of them to him.

69. Amid the swift biographic narrative of this vivid passage, describing Wollstonecraft's attempt to drown herself, this remark appears as an almost mystic reflection. Godwin explores the idea of spiritual despair more fully in the second edition; but one may still wonder what the atheist philosopher meant by 'preternatural'.

70. Godwin is here making a kind of précis of Wollstonecraft's last letters to Imlay, as published in the *Posthumous Works*. It is notable that he makes no attempt to suppress her suggestion that she come and live with Imlay and his mistress, as a last resort. A generation later, influenced by the same disregard for matrimonial form, young Shelley would similarly invite his wife Harriet to come and live with his new mistress, Mary Godwin, in Switzerland in 1814.

71. Now part of the Euston Road, running from Somers Town (King's Cross) to Marylebone. On the north side, towards Hampstead, it was still bordered by fields and vegetable allotments.

72. This striking observation is one of Godwin's triumphs of objectivity as a biographer. How easy it would have been to express his own evident contempt for – and perhaps jealousy of – Imlay, through some bitter remark attributed to Wollstonecraft.

73. Published January 1796, though Godwin suggests earlier.

74. The idea that Wollstonecraft was writing a 'comedy', partly about her affair with Imlay, is biographically intriguing and perhaps suggests something of her final attitude towards him. Godwin's motives in burning it – rather than simply leaving it in her unpublished papers – are puzzling. Perhaps he lacked her sense of humour.

75. Godwin seems to have been doing some emotional stocktaking on this visit out of town: he was reconciled with his old political friend John Thelwall (with whom he had quarrelled), and went to see the father of Amelia Alderson (whom he had courted); he also probably saw his old mother, Ann Godwin, who lived at Guestwick, near Norwich.

76. The abrupt changes which Godwin made in the second edition, to this eloquent defence of two lovers living together in an unmarried state, are discussed in the Introduction, section 7. He also deleted an entire paragraph, a little further on, frankly describing his own 'apprehension' of marriage. It is easy to charge him (as his enemies did) with hypocrisy; less easy to appreciate the extreme sensitivity of the issue in English society at that time. However, a close reading of the rather tortuous defence of his 'prejudices' in the second edition, will show that he still felt that the conventional institution of marriage was something to be 'negatived'. Moreover, he made no attempt in either edition to disguise the fact that he and Mary Wollstonecraft had lived together 'an experiment of seven months' in a free union, and were supremely happy.

77. No. 29 Polygon Buildings, Chalton Street, Somers Town. Godwin explains later that he also took a working apartment near by, at No. 17 Evesham Buildings.

78. Elizabeth Inchbald (1753–1821), actress and novelist, renowned in youth for her beauty, and in middle age for her prim respectability. She was the author of *A Simple Story* (1791) and *Nature and Art* (1796). Charles Kemble had once been her lover, and Godwin her suitor. She was evidently jealous of Wollstonecraft. Sarah Siddons (1755–1831) was the greatest tragic actress of her age, the daughter of Roger Kemble. She was renowned for her roles as Jane Shore and Calista in Nicholas Rowe's plays; as Belvidera in Otway's *Venice Preserved*; and as Lady Macbeth. She introduced a new, brooding and inward interpretation of the tragic heroine, and critics from Dr Johnson to Hazlitt praised her for her solemn power. Gainsborough painted her portrait (National Portrait Gallery) and Reynolds depicted her as 'The Tragic Muse' (Dulwich Art Gallery). She was an intelligent and generous woman, who much admired Wollstonecraft's work, especially *A Short Residence*; so that her decision to close her doors socially on the marriage gives some indication of the pressures under which the couple lived (and under which Godwin wrote this chapter of the *Memoirs*).

79. Compare this emotionally revealing passage of Godwin's, with Wollstonecraft on the same subject of 'domestic happiness' in *A Short Residence*, Letter 12, p. 136, and note 86.

80. Fourteen 'Lessons for Children', which Godwin suggests in an editorial note in the *Posthumous Works* were probably 'written in a period of desperation in the month of October 1795'; that is, at the same time as *A Short Residence* was being prepared for the press. They give a rare and touching picture of Mary Wollstonecraft as a mother; and of little Fanny Imlay.

81. Published, unfinished, in the *Posthumous Works*, 1798.

CHAPTER TEN

82. Richard Porson (1759–1808), Regius Professor of Greek at Cambridge, classical scholar and – after his wife's death – an exquisite drunkard. He edited the plays of Euripides, contributed to the *Gentleman's Magazine* and was affectionately remembered for his witticisms and eccentricities. When Coleridge won the University Medal for his Greek Sapphic Ode on the Slave Trade in 1792, Professor Porson expressed his praise of the undergraduate's genius by offering to show 134 examples of bad Greek in the poem.

83. This is her old friend George Fordyce the doctor, not James Fordyce the tiresome author. See Chapter 5, note 35. Dr Fordyce or Dr Carlisle probably provided Godwin with the gynaecological information which makes this final chapter so harrowing.

84. Basil Montagu (1770–1851), barrister, legal author and in his youth a radical friend of Wordsworth, Coleridge, Godwin and their circle. He published works on bankruptcy, copyright and the death penalty, and a mock-heroic poem *Railroad Eclogues* (1846). He was renowned both for his generosity and his indiscretion, being the cause of the rupture between Coleridge and Wordsworth in 1812. He was also probably responsible for the cruel story in the Milnes–Gaskell manuscript, quoted by Durant, which purports to show Godwin correcting Wollstonecraft's religious sentiments on her deathbed. 'Basil Montagu brought Dr A. Carlisle who prescribed a soothing draught. – "I feel in Heaven," said Mrs Godwin to her husband who entered the room. "I suppose, my dear, that that is a form of saying you are less in pain."' (Durant, p. 324.)

85. The quiet, factual quality of the narrative should not hide the truth that Godwin was beside himself with anxiety and frustration at not being able to help his beloved wife. He had called, in succession, four different doctors – Poignand, Fordyce, Clarke and Carlisle; he had a relay of three different nurses to attend her (Elizabeth Fenwick, incidentally, was a feminist novelist); and several friends on constant standby to run errands. Most revealing of all perhaps, the gentle and stoic Godwin had almost completely lost his temper with his favourite servant, during that little exchange outside the sickroom.

86. Godwin was bitterly criticized for not suggesting at least the form of

some Christian sentiment at Wollstonecraft's deathbed. But given what he had already said about her religious beliefs in Chapter 3, and his scrupulosity as a biographer in recording elsewhere her views when he did not agree with them, I find this evidence of Wollstonecraft's absence of religious concerns as she lay dying both convincing and strangely moving. (James Boswell's account of the philosopher David Hume's death as 'a good atheist' in 1776, was already well known.) It may be objected that the point of the Montagu anecdote was that Godwin would not *allow* Mary Wollstonecraft to express Christian sentiments. But this seems to misunderstand utterly the depth of mutual trust between husband and wife.

87. Old St Pancras Church still stands on St Pancras Way, Somers Town, next to the public garden adjoining St Pancras Hospital. Wollstonecraft's tomb was sacred to the entire Godwin family, and it was there, in 1814, that Shelley took Mary Godwin on the memorable afternoon when they declared their love for each other. The tomb itself was broken up to make way for the railway in 1866; the young architect supervising the destruction was Thomas Hardy. He later wrote a poem about it, 'The Levelled Churchyard'.

88. This concluding summary, and its revision, is discussed in the Introduction, section 8.

SELECT BIBLIOGRAPHY

For readers wishing to find out more about Mary Wollstonecraft and William Godwin, I can warmly recommend the following general works: *The Life and Death of Mary Wollstonecraft*, by Claire Tomalin, Weidenfeld & Nicolson, 1974, and Penguin Books, 1977, 1985; and *A Fantasy of Reason: The Life and Thought of William Godwin*, by Don Locke, Routledge, 1980. Their ideological writings can best be studied in *Vindication of the Rights of Woman*, edited by Miriam Brody Kramnick, Penguin Books, 1982; and *Enquiry Concerning Political Justice*, edited by Isaac Kramnick, Penguin Books, 1976. Both these editions have excellent introductions. The letters are less easy to obtain, but can be found in *Collected Letters of Mary Wollstonecraft*, edited by Ralph M. Wardle, Cornell University Press, 1979; and *Godwin and Mary: Letters of William Godwin and Mary Wollstonecraft*, edited by Ralph M. Wardle, University of Kansas Press and Constable, 1967. There is still no complete edition of Godwin's letters, or his diary.

For readers requiring more specialist studies, editions and sources, those listed below will prove stimulating and suggest further lines of inquiry:

Charles Kegan Paul, *William Godwin: His Friends and Contemporaries*, 1876.

H. N. Brailsford, *Shelley, Godwin and their Circle*, 1913.

Carl B. Cone, *English Jacobins*, 1968.

Peter Marshall, *William Godwin*, 1984.

Margaret Tims, *Mary Wollstonecraft: a Social Pioneer*, 1976.

William Clark Durant, *Memoirs of Mary Wollstonecraft Written by William Godwin*, 1927. (This is both a variorum edition and a biographic study.)

Ralph M. Wardle, *Mary Wollstonecraft: A Critical Biography*, 1951.

—— 'Mary Wollstonecraft, *Analytical* Reviewer', in *PMLA*, No. 62, Dec. 1947.

*

Per Nyström, *Mary Wollstonecraft's Scandinavian Journey*, Acts of the Royal Society of Arts and Sciences of Gothenburg, Humaniora No. 17, 1980. (British Library General Catalogue Ac. 1063 (5a).)

Mitzi Myers, 'Mary Wollstonecraft's *Letters Written . . . in Sweden*: Toward Romantic Autobiography', in *Studies in Eighteenth Century Culture*, vol. 18, edited by Roseann Runte, 1979.

Mary Wollstonecraft, *Letters Written . . . in Sweden*, ed. Carol H. Poston, 1976.

George B. Parks, 'The Turn to the Romantic in the Travel Literature of the Eighteenth Century', in *Modern Languages Quarterly*, 25, 1964.

Finally, no bibliography of this kind should close without a reminder of that finest of Romantic life-studies, which forms a background to this whole period, William Hazlitt's *Spirit of the Age*, 1825.

FOR THE BEST IN PAPERBACKS, LOOK FOR THE 🐧

THE LIBRARY OF EVERY CIVILIZED PERSON

THE LIBRARY OF EVERY CIVILIZED PERSON

THE LIBRARY OF EVERY CIVILIZED PERSON

Benjamin Disraeli	**Sybil**
George Eliot	**Adam Bede**
	Daniel Deronda
	Felix Holt
	Middlemarch
	The Mill on the Floss
	Romola
	Scenes of Clerical Life
	Silas Marner
Elizabeth Gaskell	**Cranford and Cousin Phillis**
	The Life of Charlotte Brontë
	Mary Barton
	North and South
	Wives and Daughters
Edward Gibbon	**The Decline and Fall of the Roman Empire**
George Gissing	**New Grub Street**
Edmund Gosse	**Father and Son**
Richard Jefferies	**Landscape with Figures**
Thomas Macaulay	**The History of England**
Henry Mayhew	**Selections from London Labour and The London Poor**
John Stuart Mill	**On Liberty**
William Morris	**News from Nowhere and Selected Writings and Designs**
Walter Pater	**Marius the Epicurean**
John Ruskin	**'Unto This Last' and Other Writings**
Sir Walter Scott	**Ivanhoe**
Robert Louis Stevenson	**Dr Jekyll and Mr Hyde**
William Makepeace Thackeray	**The History of Henry Esmond**
	Vanity Fair
Anthony Trollope	**Barchester Towers**
	Framley Parsonage
	Phineas Finn
	The Warden
Mrs Humphrey Ward	**Helbeck of Bannisdale**
Mary Wollstonecraft	**Vindication of the Rights of Women**

THE LIBRARY OF EVERY CIVILIZED PERSON

Arnold Bennett	**The Old Wives' Tale**
Joseph Conrad	**Heart of Darkness**
	Nostromo
	The Secret Agent
	The Shadow-Line
	Under Western Eyes
E. M. Forster	**Howard's End**
	A Passage to India
	A Room With a View
	Where Angels Fear to Tread
Thomas Hardy	**The Distracted Preacher and Other Tales**
	Far From the Madding Crowd
	Jude the Obscure
	The Mayor of Casterbridge
	The Return of the Native
	Tess of the d'Urbervilles
	The Trumpet Major
	Under the Greenwood Tree
	The Woodlanders
Henry James	**The Aspern Papers** and **The Turn of the Screw**
	The Bostonians
	Daisy Miller
	The Europeans
	The Golden Bowl
	An International Episode and Other Stories
	Portrait of a Lady
	Roderick Hudson
	Washington Square
	What Maisie Knew
	The Wings of the Dove
D. H. Lawrence	**The Complete Short Novels**
	The Plumed Serpent
	The Rainbow
	Selected Short Stories
	Sons and Lovers
	The White Peacock
	Women in Love

THE LIBRARY OF EVERY CIVILIZED PERSON

Horatio Alger, Jr.	**Ragged Dick** and **Struggling Upward**
Phineas T. Barnum	**Struggles and Triumphs**
Ambrose Bierce	**The Enlarged Devil's Dictionary**
Kate Chopin	**The Awakening and Selected Stories**
Stephen Crane	**The Red Badge of Courage**
Richard Henry Dana, Jr.	**Two Years Before the Mast**
Frederick Douglass	**Narrative of the Life of Frederick Douglass, An American Slave**
Theodore Dreiser	**Sister Carrie**
Ralph Waldo Emerson	**Selected Essays**
Joel Chandler Harris	**Uncle Remus**
Nathaniel Hawthorne	**Blithedale Romance**
	The House of the Seven Gables
	The Scarlet Letter and Selected Tales
William Dean Howells	**The Rise of Silas Lapham**
Alice James	**The Diary of Alice James**
William James	**Varieties of Religious Experience**
Jack London	**The Call of the Wild and Other Stories**
	Martin Eden
Herman Melville	**Billy Budd, Sailor and Other Stories**
	Moby-Dick
	Redburn
	Typee
Frank Norris	**McTeague**
Thomas Paine	**Common Sense**
Edgar Allan Poe	**The Narrative of Arthur Gordon Pym of Nantucket**
	The Other Poe
	The Science Fiction of Edgar Allan Poe
	Selected Writings
Harriet Beecher Stowe	**Uncle Tom's Cabin**
Henry David Thoreau	**Walden** and **Civil Disobedience**
Mark Twain	**The Adventures of Huckleberry Finn**
	A Connecticut Yankee at King Arthur's Court
	Life on the Mississippi
	Pudd'nhead Wilson
	Roughing It
Edith Wharton	**The House of Mirth**

PENGUIN CLASSICS

THE LIBRARY OF EVERY CIVILIZED PERSON

Netochka Nezvanova   Fyodor Dostoyevsky

Dostoyevsky's first book tells the story of 'Nameless Nobody' and introduces many of the themes and issues which will dominate his great masterpieces.

Selections from the Carmina Burana   A verse translation by David Parlett

The famous songs from the *Carmina Burana* (made into an oratorio by Carl Orff) tell of lecherous monks and corrupt clerics, drinkers and gamblers, and the fleeting pleasures of youth.

Fear and Trembling   Søren Kierkegaard

A profound meditation on the nature of faith and submission to God's will which examines with startling originality the story of Abraham and Isaac.

Selected Prose   Charles Lamb

Lamb's famous essays (under the strange pseudonym of Elia) on anything and everything have long been celebrated for their apparently innocent charm; this major new edition allows readers to discover the darker and more interesting aspects of Lamb.

The Picture of Dorian Gray   Oscar Wilde

Wilde's superb and macabre novella, one of his supreme works, is reprinted here with a masterly Introduction and valuable Notes by Peter Ackroyd.

A Treatise of Human Nature   David Hume

A universally acknowledged masterpiece by 'the greatest of all British Philosophers' – A. J. Ayer

THE LIBRARY OF EVERY CIVILIZED PERSON

Honoré de Balzac	**Cousin Bette**
	Eugénie Grandet
	Lost Illusions
	Old Goriot
	Ursule Mirouet
Benjamin Constant	**Adolphe**
Corneille	**The Cid / Cinna / The Theatrical Illusion**
Alphonse Daudet	**Letters from My Windmill**
René Descartes	**Discourse on Method and Other Writings**
Denis Diderot	**Jacques the Fatalist**
Gustave Flaubert	**Madame Bovary**
	Sentimental Education
	Three Tales
Jean de la Fontaine	**Selected Fables**
Jean Froissart	**The Chronicles**
Théophile Gautier	**Mademoiselle de Maupin**
Edmond and Jules de Goncourt	**Germinie Lacerteux**
J.-K. Huysmans	**Against Nature**
Guy de Maupassant	**Selected Short Stories**
Molière	**The Misanthrope / The Sicilian / Tartuffe / A Doctor in Spite of Himself / The Imaginary Invalid**
Michel de Montaigne	**Essays**
Marguerite de Navarre	**The Heptameron**
Marie de France	**Lais**
Blaise Pascal	**Pensées**
Rabelais	**The Histories of Gargantua and Pantagruel**
Racine	**Iphigenia / Phaedra / Athaliah**
Arthur Rimbaud	**Collected Poems**
Jean-Jacques Rousseau	**The Confessions**
	Reveries of a Solitary Walker
Madame de Sevigné	**Selected Letters**
Voltaire	**Candide**
	Philosophical Dictionary
Émile Zola	**La Bête Humaine**
	Nana
	Thérèse Raquin